Language and Neolibera Governmentality

Against a background of the ongoing crisis of global capitalism and the fracturing of the neoliberal project, this book provides a detailed account of the ways in which language is profoundly imbricated in the neoliberalising of the fabric of social life.

With chapters from a cast list of international scholars covering topics such as the commodification of education and language, unemployment, and the governmentality of the self, and discussion chapters from Monica Heller and Jackie Urla bringing the various strands together, the book ultimately helps us to understand how language is part of political economy and the everyday making and remaking of society and individuals. It provides both a theoretical framework and a significant methodological "tool-box" to critically detect, understand, and resist the impact of neoliberalism on everyday social spheres, particularly in relation to language.

Presenting richly empirical studies that expand our understanding of how neoliberalism as a regime of truth and as a practice of governance performs within the terrain of language, this book is an essential resource for researchers and graduate students in English language, sociolinguistics, applied linguistics, linguistic anthropology, and related areas.

Luisa Martín Rojo is Professor in Linguistics at the Universidad Autónoma in Madrid.

Alfonso Del Percio is Lecturer in Applied Linguistics at UCL Institute of Education in London.

Language, Society and Political Economy
Series editor: David Block, *Institució Catalana de Recerca i Estudis Avançats, Universitat de Lleida*

This series aims to publish broadly accessible monographs which directly address how theoretical frameworks in political economy can directly inform the critical analysis and discussion of language in society issues. Contributions to the series include extensive theoretical background, dealing with an aspect or area of political economy, before moving to an application of this theoretical discussion to a particular language in society issue. The series takes up the challenge of interdisciplinarity, linking scholarship in the social sciences in general (and political economy in particular) with the kinds of issues which language in society researchers have traditionally focused on. The series also aims to publish books by authors whose ideas fall outside the mainstream of language in society scholarship and by authors in parts of the world which have traditionally been underrepresented in relevant international journals and book series.

Titles in the series:

Language and Neoliberalism
Marnie Holborow

The Discourses of Capitalism
Everyday Economists and the Production of Common Sense
Christian W. Chun

Language and Neoliberal Governmentality
Edited by Luisa Martín Rojo and Alfonso Del Percio

For more information on any of these and other titles, or to order, please go to www.routledge.com/Language-Society-and-Political-Economy/book-series/LSPE

Additional resources for Language and Communication are available on the Routledge Language and Communication Portal: www.routledgetextbooks.com/textbooks/languageandcommunication/

Language and Neoliberal Governmentality

Edited by Luisa Martín Rojo
and Alfonso Del Percio

Routledge
Taylor & Francis Group

LONDON AND NEW YORK

First published 2020
by Routledge
2 Park Square, Milton Park, Abingdon, Oxon OX14 4RN

and by Routledge
52 Vanderbilt Avenue, New York, NY 10017

Routledge is an imprint of the Taylor & Francis Group, an informa business

British Library Cataloguing-in-Publication Data
A catalogue record for this book is available from the British Library

Library of Congress Cataloging-in-Publication Data
A catalog record has been requested for this book

ISBN: 978-1-138-57519-6 (hbk)
ISBN: 978-1-138-57522-6 (pbk)
ISBN: 978-0-429-28671-1 (ebk)

Typeset in Sabon
by Newgen Publishing UK

Contents

PART II
Language and the neoliberal subject 111

Contributors

Eva Codó is Associate Professor of English at Universitat Autònoma de Barcelona. Her critical and ethnographic research examines linguistic diversity (policy, practice, ideology, and discourse) in Catalonia (Spain). Her most recent project dissects the multilingualisation of compulsory schooling against the backdrop of a neoliberalising educational market.

Alfonso Del Percio is Lecturer at UCL Institute of Education. His ethnographic research focuses on language, migration, and governmentality. He also studies the links between language, work, and social inequality as well as the intersections between language and political economy.

Noelia Fernández-González is a PhD student at the Universidad Autónoma (Madrid, Spain). Her line of research draws on different approaches (politics, sociology, and pedagogy) to address current processes of educational reform. Her work focuses on privatisation policies and the new discourses on education, the meanings that these policies introduce in education, and the type of subject these policies construct.

Nelson Flores is an associate professor of educational linguistics at the University of Pennsylvania Graduate School of Education. His research seeks to denaturalise raciolinguistic ideologies that inform current conceptualisations of bilingual education.

Monica Heller is Professor at the Ontario Institute for Studies in Education and the Department of Anthropology, University of Toronto. She is a Fellow of the Royal Society of Canada. Her work focuses on changing ideologies of nation, state, and language in late capitalism, with a focus on francophone North America.

Elisa A. Hidalgo McCabe is a PhD student at Universidad Autónoma (Madrid, Spain). Her research focuses on the impact of streaming on learning opportunities in bilingual/CLIL contexts. She is a certified English as a Second Language (ESL) and Spanish teacher in the state of Massachusetts, USA, and has worked with English language learners at the primary level.

Kamilla Kraft is a postdoc at the University of Copenhagen. Her research on multilingualism in workplaces is positioned within the fields of critical sociolinguistics and sociology of language. She focuses on processes of labour migration, social mobility, and social stratification. Kraft looks at how multilingualism is constructed, regulated, and at times instrumentalised, as well as the implications of these practices.

Luisa Martín Rojo is Professor in Linguistics at the Universidad Autónoma (Madrid, Spain). She was former President of International Association Discourse Studies and Society (EDiSo), and member of the International Pragmatic Association Consultation Board (2006–2017). She leads the Research Group MIRCO on multilingualism, racism, and social inequality, from a discursive, sociolinguistic, and interactional perspective.

Joan Pujolar (Olot, 1964), Llicenciat (U. Autònoma de Barcelona), MA/PhD (Lancaster University), Professor in Sociolinguistics (U. Oberta de Catalunya) leads the Research Group on Language, Culture and Identity in the Global World and is chair of the Catalan Sociolinguistics Society Sociolinguistics. He studies how languages in Catalonia are mobilised in the construction of identities and its implications for access to resources.

Andrea Sunyol is a PhD candidate at Universitat Autònoma de Barcelona. Her thesis explores the discursive and semiotic construction of internationality in elite schools in the area of Barcelona. It focuses on the relationships between multilingualism, privilege, and ideologies of globalism in the production and reproduction of social advantage.

Bonnie Urciuoli is Professor Emerita of Anthropology at Hamilton College. She has written on race/class ideologies of Spanish–English bilingualism in the United States, the discursive production and marketing of 'skills,' and the construction and marketing of studenthood and student diversity in US higher education. Publications include *Exposing Prejudice and The Experience of Neoliberal Education* (edited volume).

Jacqueline Urla is Professor of Anthropology, University of Massachusetts Amherst. She is author of *Reclaiming Basque: Language, Nation and Cultural Activism* (2012).

Sze Wan Vivian Wong holds a MA in Applied Linguistics from UCL Institute of Education. Her research focuses on language and employability programmes for NEETS in East London. Vivian currently works as an English teacher in Hong Kong.

Acknowledgements

This volume emerged out of a series of conversations we were privileged to have. It began in 2014 in Barcelona at the First Whole Action Conference of the Cost Action New Speakers in a Multilingual Europe, when Jacqueline Urla gave a plenary on Language and Governmentality and several of us engaged in a public conversation on new ways of articulating the question of language and power. These initial conversations continued, with a slightly different set of participants, at a workshop organised at the University of Sorbonne nouvelle Paris III in 2016 as well as at the Second Whole Action Conference of the Cost Action New Speakers in 2016 in Hamburg. The papers were further developed and improved at EDISO 2017 in Barcelona and at the Sociolinguistics Symposium 23 in Auckland. We are grateful for these opportunities, and for the many conversations in and out of the meeting rooms that they inspired. We also would also like to acknowledge the support of the Cost Action New Speakers in a Multilingual Europe, which allowed us to fund these workshops, events, and panels and which enabled us to raise the questions underlying this volume in the first place. The seminar series – Foucault 13/13 – extended over the full 2015–2016 academic year at Columbia University was also fertile ground for this book. The actual preparation of the volume could not have been done without the support of all anonymous reviewers as well as the help of Jacqueline Urla, who read many of the manuscripts carefully more than once, and who helped shape them in many ways. Thanks as well to the series editor David Block and to Joan Pujolar for their feedback on several versions of our introduction. Also thanks to our contributors for their patience and perseverance and for their inspiring chapters.

Whilst every effort has been made to trace copyright holders, this has not been possible in all cases. Any omissions brought to our attention will be remedied in further editions.

1 Neoliberalism, language, and governmentality

Luisa Martín Rojo and Alfonso Del Percio[1]

Language and neoliberal rationality

Under current conditions of capitalism, neoliberalism has become much more than an economic policy, evolving into a form of governance which extends the logic of the market throughout public and private life. Principles such as globalisation, free markets, deregulation, quality, quantification, freedom, flexibility, and competition now permeate virtually all areas of social behaviour, including education, work, human rights, culture, the media, urban planning, migration, public administration, security, and health. These principles also affect language policies and speakers' trajectories and practices.

Educators and students have witnessed how academic institutions are becoming increasingly responsive to business logic, in which the overriding priority is coming to be that of satisfying the needs of the market. As citizens, we are viewed as "clients" of services that are funded by our taxes but which at the same time are obliged to profit from our patronage. As researchers, we are called upon to produce knowledge at a pace that barely allows reflection, and to compete for resources, in accordance with a business logic that is turning us into entrepreneurial scientists. As workers, flexibility, mobility, and insecurity are our constant companions. As individuals, we strive to overcome these market conditions (although at times we barely survive) through the persistent accumulation of skills and certifications, maximising performance in our respective fields of competence.

What has made these developments possible, when for centuries the search for knowledge has been considered quite separate from economic concerns? To what extent is colonisation by business logic impacting on linguistic trajectories and practices? What role is played by discourse and language ideologies, and by linguistic disciplinary knowledge as a material resource in this economic takeover? How do economic principles affect the ways in which institutions and individuals view themselves and others, and how individuals present themselves in society? In everyday life, how are market principles colonising social life? How and why is this process endorsed and reinforced (and also contradicted and contested) in the daily practice of social agents and individuals, each with their own agenda and occupying unequally-valued positions in our social order? What do these circumstances tell us about power and how it is viewed and exercised under the present conditions of capitalist expansion and of neoliberal principles, ideologies, and knowledge?

These questions are at the core of the present volume. They are the product of our concerns about contemporary regimes of power and control, and about their effects on the ways in which we understand language, subjects, and social life. The authors contributing to this volume seek a better understanding of the processes that make such colonisation possible, how it takes place, the role of language, and whether there exist any loopholes for resistance. They also examine the effects of this colonisation on speakers, on how they view themselves and others, and on their ability to acquire social, material, and emotional comfort.

We employ the term "neoliberal governmentality" as a conceptual lens for addressing these issues from critical, sociolinguistic, and discursive standpoints. Our objective is to grasp how neoliberal governmentality is constructed, reproduced, strengthened, and disseminated via discourse by means of daily institutional practices (accompanied by techniques of self-presentation and self-knowledge employed by institutions and individuals). As a further goal, we examine how this form of governance affects the ways in which language is seen, used, and governed, and consider the roles played around the world by language and communicative practices in the neoliberalisation of institutions, in diverse socio-political contexts. Finally, we consider whether any opposition to this rationality, despite the inescapable logic of neoliberalism (encapsulated by the motto *"There Is No Alternative"*),[2] is emerging and, if so, what forms may be taken by such resistance and what alternatives are offered.

The understanding of neoliberalism put forward in this book is different from that prevailing in studies of language and political economy (for an overview, see Allan, 2018; Allan and McElhinny, 2017). Scholars of neoliberalism in the language disciplines have foregrounded how neoliberal ideology governs language (Block, Gray, and Holborow, 2012; Holborow, 2015), as well as how neoliberalism, inequality, and social class mediate language in societal issues (Block, 2018). In addition, scholars have sought to understand the circumstances through which shifting conditions of political economy have turned languages into economic resources, which then poses new/old questions as to what counts as legitimate language, who counts as a legitimate speaker, and who benefits from the linguistic resources produced (Duchêne and Heller, 2012; Park and Wee, 2012).

Departing from past theorisations of language and neoliberalism (see Allan and McElhinny, 2017; Dlaske et al., 2016; Flubacher and Del Percio, 2017), this volume propels the study of language and neoliberalism in a new direction. Drawing on a Foucauldian theorisation of the microphysics of power and on more recent developments of Foucault's concept of "governmentality", we examine how language and communication intersect with all-encompassing regimes of power. Neoliberalism is then understood as a political rationality that informs the contemporary governance of populations, institutions, and practices, including language and subjects. This approach is related to recent contributions in sociolinguistics and linguistic anthropology to the study of governmentality by authors such as Urla (2012), who focuses on language policies; Flores (2013), Urciuoli (2010), and Gao and Park (2015), on education and language learning, and teaching; Barakos (2016), in private sector businesses; Urciuoli (2008), Dlaske et al. (2016), in the domain of work; Del Percio (2016), on the activities of nongovernmental organisations (NGOs); and Rampton (2014; see also Charalambous et al., 2015), on security and securitisation; McIlvenny, Klausen, and Lindegaard (2016), in discourse studies, among others. Within this frame, this volume places more decisively subjects at the heart of the analysis. Thus, we study not only how language becomes commodified but also how speakers can accumulate language and communication skills as a personal asset; and we not only address the question of how population is governed within a neoliberal frame but also how neoliberal rationality produces and transforms subjectivities. We share the conviction that understanding, rigorously analysing, and conducting a radical critique of how neoliberalism shapes subjectivities could be the first step in triggering resistance.

Thus, informed by eight empirical studies investigating the workings of neoliberal governmentality in diverse educational and work settings, in a variety of geographical contexts, the present volume makes several novel contributions.

First and foremost, this volume examines the processual nature of this political rationality, that is, *how* and with what effects neoliberal governmentality is exercised, and by means of which power techniques. Second, we consider the practices and circumstances in which neoliberalism as a political rationality is constructed and circulated through discourse. Our analysis focuses on the concrete practices adopted in education and in the workplace whereby economic principles associated with neoliberalism, such as competitiveness, freedom, quality, flexibility, and internationality, are reinforced, naturalised, and inculcated into people's minds. The successive chapters in this volume show that the implementation of these new practices and processes is transforming our understanding of language and speaking. Third, we study how neoliberalism as a political rationality produces specific subjectivities, that is, specific ways of understanding the self, that affect the ways in which individuals exert control on their own (linguistic) conduct and monitor that of others. Thus, we study how these neoliberal subjectivities are actually produced, that is, how and via which practices individuals are interpellated by specific personae and invited to socialise themselves into specific modes of being and speaking. Fourth, this book presents a new understanding of how neoliberalism as a global rationality becomes entrenched with local, longer-standing histories of colonialism, modernity, and capitalistic exploitation and dispossession. Finally, we study how institutions and actors dialectically engage this political rationality, and to what extent this logic is reproduced and challenged by their peers with different (linguistic) agendas.

In summary, this edited volume provides both a theoretical framework and a significant methodological "tool-box", one that is offered to "users" rather than "readers" (Foucault, 1994: 523–524), enabling them to critically detect and understand the impact of neoliberalism on everyday social spheres, particularly in relation to language.

In the following sections, we first define the concept of neoliberal governmentality, understood as a specific form of political rationality, focusing on the kinds of knowledge and discourses it generates, and on the techniques of power that it mobilises. We then explain the rationale for the volume, and how the two parts in which it is organised respond to two of the main processes by means of which neoliberalism is colonising other areas of our social and personal life, beyond the economy, that is, the neoliberalisation of institutions and the production of neoliberal subjects. To do so, we reflect on the production of neoliberal rationalities that shape our current understanding of languages, skills, and competences, and how this is affecting social classes and ethnic groups in social fields such as education and the labour market. In the final section of this chapter introduction, we consider the extent to which the expansion and naturalisation of neoliberal rationalities is changing forms of subjectivity, thus producing neoliberal subjects who are also neoliberal speakers, trained to accumulate language skills and capital in order to survive in a world of competition, strenuous life-long education, and increased productivity.

Neoliberal governmentality

In this volume, neoliberalism is seen as both a practice and a form of governance, and so the first contribution presented seeks to understand how this governing *happens* and how it is *conceived* (Foucault, 2008: 319), approaching these questions from the standpoint of language. In order to develop this approach, we take as a starting point Foucault's "governmentality". This concept first appeared in two of the courses imparted (*Security, Territory and Population*, 1978; *Naissance de la biopolitique: Cours au Collège de France*, 1979) as part of a series of public lectures given between 1970 and 1984. These lectures advanced his work in this field, and were later edited and summarised from audio recordings by Michel Senellart. Unlike other concepts, which, either as "discipline" or as "biopolitics", can be precisely located at the heart of his main books, the notion of neoliberal governmentality is sometimes fuzzy and its place within the Foucault universe is not always apparent.

The concept of governmentality was broached in *Security, Territory and Population* in 1978, when its author professed the ambition to abandon "institutional analysis only to be enjoined to enter into another type of institutional analysis in which, precisely, the State is the stake" (Foucault, 2007: 164). Subsequently, governmentality was held up as representing "to the State what techniques of segregation were to psychiatry, what techniques of discipline were to the penal system, and what biopolitics was to medical institutions" (Foucault, 2007: 166). In the 1978 course, the concept of governmentality was developed in a precise, historically determinate sense, referring to the techniques of government deployed in the eighteenth century, underpinning the formation of the modern state and enabling the question of the State to enter the scope of analysis of micro-powers (see Senellart in Foucault, 2007: 494).

As Senellart explains, subsequent to 1979, the concept came to be viewed in more abstract terms. It "no longer only designates the governmental practices constitutive of a particular regime of power (police state or liberal minimum government)", but "the way in which one conducts people's conduct", thus serving as an "analytical perspective for relations of power" in general (Senellart, 2007: 495). The framework for studying governmentality in the 1979 course was that of liberalism around the world, including an overview of the latest developments. This shift in the understanding of governmentality is the source of frequent confusion: although the term "governmentality" has been applied to a variety of historical periods and to different regimes, it is often used (by other scholars and by Foucault himself) in reference to "(neo)liberal governmentality". In other words, it is used to refer to a particular type of governmentality that characterises advanced liberal democracies, one that has displaced other forms of governance like sovereignty and discipline.

Although neoliberalism is currently generating more privatised, marketised, and increasingly dispersed modes of governmentality than any envisioned by Foucault (Fraser, 2003: 166), the liberal frame explored by this author has made the concept of governmentality particularly appealing and useful for authors in the fields of social sciences, political economy, and political theory. As the present volume shows, it is now also used in the fields of sociolinguistics and linguistic anthropology as a means of understanding neoliberal forms of government.

The first definition of "governmentality" provided by Foucault refers to:

> the body of institutions, procedures, analyses, reflections, calculations, and tactics that facilitate the exercise of this very specific (albeit complex) form of power, which has the population as its target, political economy as its principal form of knowledge, and the 'apparatuses of security' as its essential technical instrument.
>
> (Foucault, 2007: 144–145)

In order to understand how governmentality operates, we now examine the key elements involved in its definition: "population as a target", "political economy as its principal form of knowledge", and the "apparatuses of security".

"Population", "political economy", and the "apparatuses of security"

Foucault observed a significant shift in the eighteenth century, from sovereignty over the territory to the regulation of populations. Population, which in the 1978 lectures was associated with the theme of "biopower", was understood as a set of procedures, or relations, that manipulate the biological features (for example, the birth rate and fertility) of the human species and thus shape a political strategy for governing an entire population. The concept of population was presented as a novel and key concept to understand the functioning of political power. According to Sokhi-Bulley (2014), "population" in this sense refers not simply to "people" but also to phenomena and variables, such as birth rate, mortality, and marriage. As Foucault highlights population gives rise to a mass of juridical, political, and technical problems that have a disruptive effects in the field of economic reflection and practice (Foucault, 2007: 107). Population needs then to be analysed by the field of economic theory and be managed by the government's economic-political action within liberalism and neoliberalism. Individuals and the series of individuals, who were the target of disciplinary power, are no longer pertinent as the objective, but simply as the instrument, relay, or condition for obtaining something at the level of the population (Foucault, 2007: 55; see also Castro-Gómez, 2010: 76). Thus, the term "population" encompasses then the whole field of "the social", and describes both the network of social relationships and also the site at which political power operates. By this means, political power becomes omnes et singulatum – "of all and of each".

Moving further towards the concepts involved in Foucault's definition, the issue of population is related to security, in the sense of techniques specific to the management of populations, which Foucault considers a feature of modern liberal society. In relation to security, Foucault sees a very important change within liberalism and neoliberalism. The problem within neoliberalism is:

مرا کردن/جدا کردن

> no longer that of fixing and demarcating the territory, but of allowing circulations to take place, of controlling them, sifting the good and the bad, ensuring that things are always in movement, constantly moving around, continually going from one point to another, but in such a way that the inherent dangers of this circulation are cancelled out.
>
> (Foucault, 2007: 93)

These mechanisms (for example by restricting mobility through the control of borders), do not tend to a nullification of phenomena in the form of the prohibition, "you will not do this", nor even, "this will not happen", but in the form of a delimitation of phenomena within acceptable limits, rather than the imposition of a law that says no to them (see Castro-Gomez, 2010: 73ff.). The goal of security is then to protect the collective interest against individual interests. For Foucault, the "apparatuses of security" are exercised to provide society with a feeling of economic, political and cultural well-being, particularly through the control of risk, for example by calculating probabilities with statistical instruments.

Finally, under Foucault's definition of the term, the principal form of knowledge informing governmentality is political economy. In the current phase of capitalist expansion, political economy as a body of knowledge postulates the predominance of market mechanisms and restricted action by the State. It emphasises the logic of pure competition within the economic terrain, and seeks to extend the rationality of the market to domains hitherto considered to be non-economic (as manifested in the theory of "human capital") (see, in Foucault, 2008, an analysis of the different kinds of neoliberalism). Among the elements of this regime of truth of political economy, Foucault includes the *homo oeconomicus*, that is, he analyses as part of political economy the economic behaviour of producers and consumers.

If we focus now on the interplay of all the elements examined earlier and encompassed by Foucault's definition, we will then understand how, since neoliberal rationality is about increasing the production effectiveness, it targets the managing of large populations, of life and society, and the managing of huge information databases, surveillance techniques, and statistical management by the state, as well as by corporations and civil society actors, and finally it also targets individuals to act in a particular way, as a form of action of the "self on self".

Governmentality is then understood as the "art or practice of government" in a broad sense, referring not only to political structures or to the management of States, but also to the ways in which the conduct of individuals or groups might be directed – that is, the government of children, of souls, of communities, of the sick ... (Foucault, 2007: 126 and ss.). To govern, in this sense, is to control the possible field of action of others (Foucault, 2002: 341). Thus, in Nosál's words, governmentality encompasses "*a wide range of control techniques, and that applies to a wide variety of objects, from one's control of the self to the 'biopolitical' control of populations*" – in other words, the control of customs, habits, health, reproduction and many other aspects of society (Nosál, 2009: 117). Furthermore, and this is one of the most significant features of (neo)liberal governmentality, this "conducting of conduct" is not enforced by violent means but often acquires the compliance and even agency of social actors and institutions, the very objects of governmentality.

Foucault's understanding of power is based on the assumption that it is exercised only over free subjects, and only insofar as they are free. As we see in the following fragment from Foucault's The Subject and Power, it is precisely this complex relation what gives also place to resistance:

> By this we mean individual or collective subjects who are faced with a field of possibilities in which several ways of behaving, several reactions and diverse comportments, may be realized. Where the determining factors saturate the whole, there is no relationship of power; slavery is not a power relationship when man is in chains. (In this case it is a question of a physical relationship of constraint.) Consequently, there is no face-to-face confrontation of power and freedom, which are mutually exclusive (freedom disappears everywhere power is exercised), but a much more complicated interplay. In this game <u>freedom may well appear as the condition for the exercise of power</u> (at the same time its precondition, since freedom must exist for power to be exerted, and also its permanent support, since without the possibility of recalcitrance, power physical determination).

The relationship between power and freedom's refusal to submit cannot, therefore, be separated (Foucault, 2002: 77).

However, as Lilja and Vinthagen (2014: 121) note, while so far several researchers have explored how power mechanisms are exercised within a neoliberal governance, it is less clear what are the options or ongoing practices and their effective application to avoid this managing of population policies and institutions. Resistance in this case tries to avoid the managing of population by acting differently, in subcultures, and by cultivating a different set of values, practices, and institutions, and take on the challenge and develop non-productive forms of life and biological existence. At this point the ability of governmentality to generate knowledge and discourses, and mobilise techniques of power is revealed. An ability that can be always neutralised by resistance, given that, as Dean (2010) notes, knowledge, discourse, and power mechanisms can always be reversed. All of this will be approached in the next section.

Neoliberal governmentality as a political rationality

Beyond laws and rules, what makes (neo)liberalisation possible is a "mentality" that becomes hegemonic and rationalises the exercise of this kind of government (Foucault, 1997: 74).[3] Under this mentality, for example, it may be considered that a necessary and foreseeable ambition for an educational institution is that it should be economically profitable; or that a cost-benefit logic should be applied to education and language learning, to make individuals competitive in their subsequent careers. In the view that neoliberalisation is both the origin and the effect of a ruling mentality, we assume that there is no single founding act of reason or a unique "rationality", but instead that there are specifically political rationalities, which emerge in particular times or spaces. The neoliberal order has acquired a global outreach, but there are significant differences in how it has taken root in different contexts, and in the circumstances and knowledge that have contributed to this process. The present volume highlights similarities, but also identifies and discusses how neoliberal rationales become intertwined with longer, locally-anchored histories of colonialism, modernism and capitalist exploitation. In this respect, the authors examine how social life and policies in institutions are re-presented or re-cast in market terms, and how "enterprise" is held up as the model that all institutions and individuals should follow. Languages, too, are strongly involved in these processes and have become an object of attention for neoliberal rationality (in this volume, see Flores, 2017 and Urla, 2012; see also Martín Rojo, 2017; Codó & Patiño-Santos, 2018; Gao & Park, 2015; Relaño-Pastor, 2018). Finally, the social effects of this rationality are examined, via questions such as how it produces new forms of inequality and reproduces old ones, how it leads people to live within an illusion of social mobility, thus forestalling challenges to the system, and how it redefines the hierarchies of languages, compelling people to accumulate them as part of social completion.

From this standpoint, neoliberal rationality is just another rationality. In order to highlight the relevance of neoliberal rationality to the goals established for the present volume, in the next section we will steer a course guided by the Foucauldian triad of discourse-knowledge-power. We consider how governmentality is constructed in discourse, what knowledge is generated thereby and what technologies of power are employed to do so. And we will illustrate these powerful dynamics by reference to several processes taking place within the current neoliberal order, which are also analysed in this volume.

Economicist discourses, knowledge, and governmental power

The visions of competition and self-interest as a guarantee of success, and of cooperation as a procedure prone to failure, are part of the knowledge production within a neoliberal rationality. This knowledge, as we will see, not only becomes hegemonic or dominant, but it also "counts as truth" or enter the "game of truth". Furthermore, this first element of the knowledge-discourse-power triad extends and reinforces, in this case, the prevalence of an economic outlook that permeates the discourse of educational institutions and workplaces, which is addressed in the chapters of this volume. The second contribution of this volume is precisely to show how this knowledge is constructed and circulated in discourse, that is, an "economicist discourse" that evokes the neoliberal principle of the law of supply and demand. Discourses, the second element of the knowledge-discourse-power triad, encompass certain terms (such as *quality, profitability, surplus*), lexical collocations ("*the need to compete*") and mottos or slogans ("*Compete or die*" in the case of schools, or "*Compete to be profitable*", in the case of individuals) that are constantly evoked by social actors and institutions in accounting for their practices and trajectories. Furthermore, given the changes brought about by global capitalism in the role played by languages in the economy and in enabling the mobility of capital, goods and people, competition frequently mobilises the accumulation of linguistic resources (such as languages and registers), to "make a success" of people's lives, or to achieve their "objectives". Therefore, terms and concepts such as "language as capital", "language as economical resources", "language investment", and "language accountability" form part of the discourses analysed in this volume.

Taking into account these considerations, and in order to articulate forms of resistance, we seek to understand how the neoliberal discourse has infiltrated society to a hitherto unknown degree, to the point that there appears to be no good alternative. This profound transformation is partly explained by the success with which neoliberal discourse has parasitised culturally-rooted terms such as "freedom", "quality", "effort", and "lifelong learning", via a gradual process of semantic slippage. Hence, the meaning of the term "freedom" (of action, of thought, of ideas, of creation) has now become tightly restricted, and it is commonly used to refer to "neoliberal freedoms" (individual ones such as freedom to choose schools, doctors, etc., and the individual freedom to conduct their own behaviour conforming to economic principles), based on competition; "quality" has come to be measured, not by the support of the state towards its institutions, but by the results presented in rankings; and "training" has mutated into the perpetual obligation to accumulate skills and certificates.

These considerations bring us to the third element of the knowledge-discourse-power triad, i.e., the question of what kind of power regime results from the knowledge produced by neoliberal rationality. The concept of "governmentality" embodies the potential of Foucault's understanding of power, encompassing not only the top-down power of the State, but also the ways in which social control is exercised in disciplinary institutions (such as schools, hospitals and psychiatric institutions), and how knowledge and discourses are produced and subsequently internalised by individuals to guide the behaviour of entire populations (in a process that Foucault describes as the "conduct of conduct"). These forms of behaviour are those which tend to be promoted by corporations and by careers advisers: they represent specific forms of knowledge and practice that individuals are encouraged to adopt. The outcome is a more efficient form of social control, with individuals using this knowledge for self-governance.

As shown in some of the chapters in this volume (see Del Percio & Wong, Kraft, Sunyol & Codó, Martín Rojo, and Pujolar), "the conduct of conduct" is a kind of power which links the normalising objectives of neoliberalism – profitability, competitiveness, flexibility and mobility – to the subjects' self-created ideals (Hook, 2004: 262). But also, as Foucault claims, it links them to freedom. As Dardot and Laval explains this government requires liberty as its condition of possibility:

to govern is not to govern against liberty, or despite it; it is govern through liberty – that is, to actively exploit the freedom allowed individuals so that they end up conforming to certain norms of their own accord.

(Dardot & Laval, 2014: 11)

Thus, contemporary forms of governance make use of "self-governing" strategies based upon particular constructions of "subjectivity". It is on this point that our volume highlights the decisive role played by the existence of "models of success" of individuals and of speakers, in relation to the mechanisms of power. As part of this second contribution of this volume, we show how an entrepreneurial model is configured as one of success par excellence, for governments, institutions and individuals, who all rely on the knowledge that is produced by neoliberal rationality and that circulates via hegemonic discourse to choose among their options.

Individuals, as entrepreneurs of the self, discipline their tongues to produce the languages of economic dominance, which they prize as giving them an edge in a globalised labour market. Through self-care and self-reflection, they compare their own skills and resources with those presented in a model of success that in turn is defined by the enterprise model, according to which there are only winners or losers, and where only the former are valued, valuable and profitable. Furthermore, when individuals attempt to make themselves profitable by the application of self-reflection, self-knowledge and self-examination, this brings about what Foucault termed "technologies of the self". In his words, these technologies

… permit individuals to effect by their own means or with the help of others a certain number of operations on their own bodies and souls, thoughts, conduct, and way of being, so as to transform themselves in order to attain a certain state of happiness, purity, wisdom, perfection or immortality.

(Foucault, 1988)

As Lemke points out, the internalisation of dominant discourses imposes a high degree of responsibility on subjects, making them view social risks such as illness, unemployment and poverty not as the responsibility of the State, but as residing in the domain for which the individual is responsible and transforming the problem into one of "self-care" (Lemke, 2001: 201). In this respect, the practice of lifelong education, of accumulating skills and languages, can be seen as one outcome of responsibilisation, of the expression of our own responsibility to find a job, to work and to create security for our dependents. Rankings, surveys, curricula and a vast body of discourses create a framework for the functioning of institutions. This framework is then internalised to generate a power-knowledge regime and hence a neo-liberal rationality (Dean, 1994: 181–187). However, power techniques, such as internalisation, can be also be reversed. People will be then also able to modify themselves differently and/or resist the processes of internalising power through alternative modes of self-making.

Language and the neoliberalisation of institutions

In their consideration of contemporary forms of governmentality, the authors in this volume address three of the essential tasks which, according to Fraser (2003: 167), should be performed in order to understand neoliberal rationality. First, the initial chapters highlight the transnational character of neoliberal governance: despite differences in the historical, socio-political and economic processes present in the various contexts studied, it is apparent that a similar strand of logic is applicable to institutions in different countries. Secondly, the chapters examine the ways neoliberalism relies on increasingly dispersed and marketised modes of governmentality, that is, through intermediation different types of institutions and actors. Finally, the contributing authors analyse the key elements that might define this kind of political rationality, including its characteristic objects of intervention, modes of subjectification and technologies of power.

In order to explain how neoliberal economic principles colonise other spheres of social life and how this rationality becomes a form of governance, most of the chapters consider, as the first step in their analysis, the neoliberalisation of institutions. They go on to show how this process particularly affects institutions in the fields of education and employment, and emphasise the resemblance observed between the forms of logic that currently govern educational institutions and work places. This proximity, in part, arises from the transformation of education, which now more than ever serves the interests and needs of the market, particularly those of the labour market. Both education and work serve as crucial spaces for the inculcation of neoliberal principles as well as sites of production of the type of worker needed for a neoliberalised economy.

The hallmarks of neoliberalism, "*deregulation, privatisation, and withdrawal of the state from many areas of social provision*" (Harvey, 2005: 3), are undoubtedly present in the contexts studied in this volume. Institutions have not only become amplifiers of these principles, but also, in their implementation, construct social and political environments that actively encourage neoliberal rationality.

One of the contexts that most affected by neoliberalisation is the labour market. This is of course due to the central role of work in a society governed by principles of quality, competitiveness and entrepreneurship. The chapter by Kamilla Kraft shows, in this respect, how neoliberal logic is present and influential in the Norwegian construction industry. In particular, neoliberal principles of deregulation impact on staff flexibilisation, whereby workers are leased on temporary contracts rather than hired permanently. Flexibilisation and employment liberalisation are presented as inevitable for an industry that competes internationally. Flexibilisation and liberalisation however are risk factors and the causes for accidents and insecurity at work. It is at this point that language enters the scenario: the workers who are hired permanently are Norwegians whereas most of the temporary, flexible workers come from Poland. In order to create the conditions for the securitisation of a neoliberal model that relies on flexibilisation and deregulation, language regulation becomes object of regulation and control. All work sites are required to have just one official language, preferably Norwegian. Linguistic homogeneity is considered a key resource to resolve the tension between reducing labour costs and maintaining job security. Kraft concludes that welfare and neoliberal logics co-exist in the Norwegian context discussed, and that security practices actually legitimise the existence of flexibility in the industry, by creating a form of "safe flexibility". However, the internalisation of this rationality by contractors, who systematise and severely restrict language in the workplace, drastically reduces (Polish) temporary workers' access to professional mobility and recognition, and compels them to expand their linguistic competences.

In this context of neoliberalisation, after the labour market, the social field of education is of particular importance. The neoliberal principle that Fraser termed "desocialization" is transforming the Fordist welfare state into a post-Fordist "competition state". This evolution is manifested in efforts to privatise social services, either shifting them onto the market or devolving them to the family, thus destructuring the zone of "the (national) social" (Fraser, 2003: 166). One of the main effects of desocialisation is that funding cuts are imposed on public education, thus obliging institutions to search for strategic alternatives. Among these, external funding, market-applied research and the sale of teaching materials are often employed in order to generate additional revenue (Saunders, 2010). Changes are taking place in the discourse of institutions, which now reflect a neoliberal logic, summarised in entrepreneurial slogans featuring "competition", "quality", "efficiency", "innovation", "quality", and "flexibility" (Wilkins, 2012). Thus, the humanist separation between education and work is being eroded, and a previously hidden curriculum, focused on meeting the needs of capital, is now voluntarily exposed and embraced (Aronowitz, 2000; Saunders, 2010: 61). Education institutions are of primordial importance in shaping and preparing a future elite workforce for a flexible, delocalised labour market, by assuring future employers of their international and multilingual orientation (see Hidalgo & Fernández-González, Martín Rojo, and Urciuoli in this volume). Educational institutions are however also important as producers of the working class subjects who are able to cope with the flexibility and precarity produced by the neoliberal economy. These subjects are willing to accept the idea that lifelong learning and processes of continuous self-development are crucial for social mobility and individual freedom. Among the main strategies employed to meet the needs of the labour market, and expected to increase the institution's competitiveness, are those of designing applied language programmes (dual or bilingual), providing training in language register and developing degree programmes for mobile workers.

In this particular context, although authors have observed a common orientation in schools, certain differences are also apparent. With respect to the United States, Nelson Flores presents a genealogy of the neoliberalisation of language education, analysing the initiatives adopted, and showed that while some US States banned bilingual education in 1998, others promoted it in 2016. This analysis reveals a very significant shift from a "nationalist framing", in Flores's terms, which positions bilingual education as a threat to the production of national subjects, towards a "neoliberal framing", according to which bilingual education is part of a broader project producing neoliberal subjects to fit the political and economic needs of global capitalism. This shift explains why, in the United States, language programmes often present bilingualism as a skill that can make the speaker more competitive in the global marketplace. Such programmes have grown exponentially over the past 15 years.

In this same context of the neoliberalisation of education, Elisa Hidalgo McCabe and Noelia Fernández-González analyse the ways in which the ideologies and the discourses of language policies respond to new economic principles that have transformed public education and schooling, foregrounding risk and fluidity in a framework that resembles the flows of markets. These authors focus on the neoliberal principle of individual and market freedom – by means of which "competitiveness" is transforming schools' policies and practices to make them profitable. Linked to notions such as quality and democratic freedom, parental choice is presented as accessible to all without exception and is largely formulated as a right of families, entitled to choose any school within a wider zone. Within this competitive context, many schools and teaching staff in Spain implement Spanish-English bilingual programmes (BP). This choice is presented in interviews as the result of a conscious calculation of possibilities, risks, cost and benefits. However, for the teaching staff this transformation is also based on the assumption that there is no real alternative: in order to compete, adopting a BP is the only way for their schools to survive. In this case, the extension of parental choice acts as a neoliberal principle giving rise to a new model by which school practices, programmes and activities are organised. The analysis by Hidalgo and Fernández-González goes on to reveal some distinctive features of neoliberal freedom, which is viewed only in terms of consumer choice, among specific, predetermined options. The authors show that this parental choice in fact heightens inequality in access to education. In modern-day Spain, however, only social movements and activists defending public education continue to uphold the ideal of education as a universal right, and to argue that quality should not be judged by inter-school rankings or competition but derived from the sustained allocation of resources and from high-quality training.

A far-reaching effect of "desocialization" and of the "competition order" in education is the implementation of new communicative training programmes that are said to respond to the needs of neoliberal capitalism. In this volume, Urciuoli shows how communication skills training, particularly when oriented towards transformational leadership ("bringing change"), has moved forcefully into higher education in the United States, blossoming into a higher-education industry of experiential learning programmes, with a multitude of organisations entering into partnerships with colleges and universities. Such skills are presented to liberal arts undergraduates as crucially important to their future success. They are heavily promoted in workshops and in instructional materials, and connected to neoliberal models of subjectivities. However, Urciuoli notes, this neoliberal register (or pseudo-register as Urciuoli calls it) is never used outside of the training programme and therefore seems to be useless for many of the students enrolled in these programmes. Further, many students seem to ignore this transformational power, which raises the question of why the supposed need to make oneself more competitive.

In addition to showing how the process of neoliberalisation takes place, the chapters in this section address other issues related to the consequences of neoliberalisation, such as the increase in inequality that it brings. All these chapters reveal mechanisms that tend to increase inequality within the labour market or within education. Kamilla Kraft describes the neoliberal turn and the discrimination suffered by foreign workers who, as well as being subject to flexibility and precarity, are required to acquire self-training. In consequence, they are not deemed to be, from a linguistic point of view, as well qualified as "Norwegian" workers, which restricts the tasks they are allowed to perform and the training they receive. As a result, their professional qualifications are often not taken into account, and they are limited to performing unskilled work. A similar expression of aggravated inequality is presented by Hidalgo and Fernández-González, who show that in the transition from primary to secondary bilingual education, a streaming process is applied, by which students are channelled into one of two academic paths according to their level of English proficiency. This chapter's analysis of the principle of freedom of choice, in which fairness and equal opportunity are held up as paradigms of neoliberal rationality in the terrain of public education, reveals a marked degree of social selection. The realisation that inequality is constitutive of neoliberal rationality explains why Flores' chapter ends with an exploration of alternative framings of bilingual education that resist both nationalist and neoliberal framings by positioning bilingual education as part of the broader political and economic struggles of minoritised communities.

A further effect observed is that of the successful efforts made to promote new conceptions of what it means to be an individual and an agent within neoliberal governance (Harvey, 2005: 42). In each of the chapters in this volume, it can be seen that individuals are targeted. Flores, for example, studies the shift from a punitive system, which threatens parents and urges them and their children to accept particular options in language programmes, to an entrepreneurial frame that introduces competition into schools and calls on them to adapt to global market needs and to be well equipped to be chosen by parents (this question is also addressed by Hidalgo and Fernández-González). This process effectively reflects the way in which neoliberal governmentality works. Finally, Urciuoli shows how students take part in workshops and attend mentoring sessions and conferences, but do not necessarily emerge from these activities identifying themselves as agents of neoliberal values, or even employ the discourse of leadership. Nevertheless, despite students' disinterest, lack of understanding and even overt resistance, higher education institutions and their partner organisations continue to invest in and maintain these programmes.

Language and the neoliberal subject

Harvey argues that neoliberal policies have necessarily been accompanied by relatively successful efforts to promote new conceptions of what it means to be an individual and an agent (Harvey, 2005: 42). As discussed earlier, this transformation is part of the knowledge that is produced within a neoliberal rationality and is also the objective of power technologies. Accordingly, the second step in extending neoliberalism, which explains how neoliberal principles can become a form of governance, is that of subjectivation. In the same way as for the neoliberalisation of institutions, the third contribution of this volume is to generate complex knowledge about how neoliberal governmentality produces specific types of subjects within education and the workplace. These subjects are structured by particular tendencies, preferences and motivations, and bearing a particular responsibility towards their own skills and traits, which are viewed as "a collection of assets that must be continually invested in, nurtured, managed, and developed" (Martin, 2000: 582).

The chapters presented in this volume make an important contribution to a better understanding of governmentality, highlighting three elements as crucial to enabling the knowledge produced by the neoliberal rationality to affect its subjects through the application of power techniques such as discipline and self-observation. These elements are neoliberal agency, the existence of behavioural models (especially that of linguistic behaviour) and the performance/pleasure apparatus.

The defence of market freedom has as a corollary individual freedom, which is understood as the ability to act on one's own calculations and to increase advantages, capabilities and resources, and thus to become more profitable (Gershon, 2011: 540). Thus, within neoliberalism, the subject is conceived as an active, and calculating individual, who looks out for better opportunities. This agency is made apparent in the ways in which speakers act and design their linguistic trajectories, within elite educational programmes, for example by increasing the number of languages they speak, adapting to the migratory situation or committing themselves whole-heartedly to employability programmes (even though success in this respect is far from guaranteed).

The role of neoliberal agency is examined by Pujolar, in whose chapter migrants in Catalonia narrate experiences and employ concepts illustrating how effectively they have been caught up and trussed in the spider's web of neoliberalism. However, their trajectories and practices are not homogeneous, as the living conditions, resources enjoyed and the positions adopted seem to vary considerably. Furthermore, the practices and discourses presented could potentially be mobilised to enable and explain alternative, more egalitarian, configurations of discourse and action. In fact, it was the socially more privileged group that expressed the most critical discourses on economic and linguistic inequalities. Pujolar claims that while notions such as "projects of the self", "choice", and "self-improvement" express dimensions of contemporary life that have been brought about by capitalist relations of production, liberal legal systems and governance practices, technological innovations and the emergence of a middle class no longer tied to an economy of subsistence, these notions can also be viewed as being incorporated within alternative visions of society and governance, which seek to attain more egalitarian political projects.

The second element considered is that of behavioural models, such as those of professional and personal success and of neoliberal speakerhood. It is the existence of such a model that guides the agency of the subjects studied and which drives them to exert diverse power techniques on themselves. In this volume, the models are analysed with respect to the liberal model of *homo œconomicus* and its entrepreneurial version. The classical *homo œconomicus,* derived from economic liberalism, has been updated by neoliberalism, with the introduction of changes that give rise to the construction of the subject as entrepreneur (Foucault, 2008: 225–226; a more detailed analysis of these changes is given in Brown, 2015: 79–111). According to Dardot and Laval, this is the main point at which the current model of *homo neoliberal* diverges from the liberal model of *homo œconomicus:*

> It is the efficient, competitive individual who seeks to maximise his human capital in all areas, who not only seeks to project himself into the future and calculate his gains and losses like the old economic man, but above all seeks to work on himself so as constantly to transform himself, improve himself, and make himself ever more efficient.
>
> (Dardot & Laval, 2014: 295)

In the case of neoliberalism, the crucial point is that the enterprise is promoted to the rank of model of subjectivation: everyone is an enterprise to be managed and represents a capital that must bear fruit.

The potential of these models was highlighted in Sunyol and Codó's study of the International Baccalaureate Diploma Programme (IB), which was initially a curriculum designed to attract a specific population (the children of expatriate families), but which over time has become a much-desired educational credential for post-nationally-oriented national elites (Resnik, 2012). In a context where consumption practices – including educational ones – have become increasingly status-oriented, IB credentials are now convertible into the types of economic and cultural capital that enable students to acquire better positions in their endless race towards a brilliant future. In the new neoliberal scenario, the IB humanist-liberal goal of educating the "whole person" (and not just students' intellects) has gradually been transformed into a neoliberal technology of citizenship aimed at subjectifying students to embody neoliberal selves. Essentially, this is the creation of citizen-workers who are always anxious to outperform in every respect, to become not just "A-students" but "A-people", brilliant academically but also excellent self-carers and disciplined affective selves. Their ultimate goal is to become agents of (neoliberal) change, people who can transform places into positive environments in which everybody can feel happy to work more (and thus enhance efficiency and productivity). These individuals are inculcated with the values and settings of the corporate world; they are encouraged to imagine themselves as separable pieces, as sets of mainly soft skills, which they should strive to improve in order to achieve perfection, come what may. In schools and workplaces, the effects of this neoliberal rationality are summarised in diverse mottos expressing the notion that self-knowledge leads to self-betterment, and thus push students to take a step beyond (*"anar més enllà"*, in Catalan).

In another educational context, that of Madrid universities, Martín Rojo examines how neoliberal rationality is constructed, supported and disseminated in higher education, and illustrates this process with an analysis of the accounts offered by Madrid university students of their experiences in language and communication. Following a critical pedagogy approach, Martín Rojo conducted a series of tasks designed to highlight students' problems and experiences in relation to language and to increase awareness of the process of internalising the power relation to which we are subjected. These activities were based on the assumption that self-techniques are not only power mechanisms, but effective means for resistance, and for this reason they were mainly based on self examination, including questions, narratives and exchanges of experiences, and reflections. The main aim was not only to reveal how the power techniques are exercised in transforming subjectivities, but also to show how can they be mobilised as part of a processes of exploring alternative modes of self-making. Analysing students' accounts, the chapter explains how neoliberal rationality connects external and internal forms of governance, shaping subjectivities. Thus, this analysis shows, firstly, how students in their assignments evoke a particular model of speaker, the "self-made" speaker, which is the linguistic correlate of the neoliberal subject (or entrepreneurial subject). In them, the students describe how they manage language capital and competences, calculate costs and benefits, render accounts, and at the same time seek "self-realisation" and hence security and self-satisfaction. In spite of the fact that linguistic performance is bound to the speakers' agency and their scenario of success, which is embodied in a particular model of conduct and life, the complexity of the motivations revealed in students' discourses shows that performance is not the only important factor; self-satisfaction must also be taken into account. The "performance/pleasure" apparatus proposed by this chapter operationalises governmentality, and at the same time integrates and explains this complexity. Furthermore, it is precisely through the analysis of this complexity and even contradictions that Martín Rojo illustrates how neoliberal rationality reaches into the very grain of individuals, showing how in this neoliberal context the technologies of power -such as internalisation, normalisation, self-surveillance, free choice and external and internal accountability, self-discipline, and self-training- become self exercised. And it is precisely the self-made speaker model, what articulates the intersection between the domination exercised by others and that exercised on oneself, helping us to understand the role of language in relation to neoliberal governmentality. Secondly, in relation to power technologies and specifically to technologies of self, this chapter also shows how the neoliberal governmentality not only produces specific types of subjects, but also how consent and thus governmentality can be eroded by developing with speakers tools to examine the extent to which neoliberalism drains their subjectivity. Thus, the awareness-raising exercises and the overall context of a collective exchange of experiences that was established in the classes have contributed in this case to find new ways of understanding and practice languages.

The effects of the "performance/pleasure" apparatus are also revealed and highlighted in the chapter by Del Percio and Wong. The two authors discuss how hope and neoliberal rationales get enmeshed in an employability programme provided by a London-based charity. Through an ethnographic account examining how such programmes contribute to the making of neoliberal subjects, the two authors demonstrate that poverty in East London is managed through a set of disciplining techniques that target peoples' minds, souls and individuals' capacity to be affected and dream about a better future. These training programmes ask people to bring their subjectivities in alignment with principles of quality, competitiveness and self-development. Along with Gershon (2011: 540) who argues that "According to the neoliberal perspective [...] agents are responsible for their own futures [and] regardless of their disadvantages and the unequal playing field [...] are maximally responsible for their failures (Brown, 2003)", in Del Percio and Wong's ethnographic account unemployed subjects are interpellated as autonomous, self-responsible and entrepreneurial subjects, that can achieve freedom, independence and success if only they are willing to subject themselves to the live ethics imposed by neoliberalism. Del Percio and Wong note that the neoliberal promise of agency through self-discipline and self-development is powerful, because it is anchored in authoritative assumptions about the self, society and the (labour) market that naturalise the type of disciplining work that individuals are asked to do on their selves and that in the same time erase the structures of power and inequality that these processes of self-disciplining and self-regulation contribute to sustain. Further, and along with this volume's forth contribution to an understanding of neoliberalism's entrenchment with alternatives histories of modernity and theories of society, Del Percio and Wong note that that the principles of self-discipline, self-regulation and self-responsibilisation is effective since it bears the traces of older, but not less persuasive discourses of progress, inclusion, equality, emancipation and change that for many decades have framed the material support provided by local charities. This discourses are now used to convince young people that social and economic inclusion can be fostered through reflexivity, self-management and resilience. Indeed, as several chapters in this volume show the neoliberal principles are not only dialectically engaged with on the ground by different actors, occupying unequally valued position in society and pursuing different agendas. Neoliberal rationales and modes of governmentality are also entrenched in a complex way with longer histories of modernity, capitalism and class stratification (see, e.g., Kraft, Flores, Hidalgo & Fernández-González, Pujolar, and Sunyol & Codó)

Conclusion: On "the how" of governmentality

This volume focuses on how neoliberal governmentality *happens,* on how it is *thought* (Foucault, 2008: 319) and on the role of language as ideology and practice in each of these processes. To do so, the approaches considered in this volume are framed within a study of the interplay between discourse, knowledge and power. By this means we extend our understanding of the neoliberal governmentality and of how it can transform dimensions and aspects of our existence. The contributors to this volume have opened up new lines of research, creating new concepts and testing earlier ones such as neoliberalism, governmentality, neoliberal agency, power techniques and subjectivation in the light of a new understanding. The authors of these chapters draw on a variety of research methods, including observation and the analysis of practices and discourses produced in educational institutions and in the workplace. These analyses reveal that such practices are in fact shaped by neoliberal principles. Discourse analysis also enables the authors to trace the history of the concepts used by institutions to "conduct the conduct" of students or workers. In some cases, the roots of these concepts are located in humanism or in postulates of social democracy, i.e. prior modes of thought that were later appropriated and placed within a neoliberal framework. By examining how previous knowledge has thus been appropriated (see Sunyol & Codó), and how neoliberal principles (with their corresponding contradictions, see Hidalgo and Fernández-González; also see Urciuoli) have taken root, we expand the scope of the present volume, to extend its view beyond the economy to include the history of the ideas that underpin and inform neoliberal rationality.

As shown in some chapters (see Del Percio & Wong, Kraft, Sunyol & Codó, Martín Rojo & Pujolar), "the conduct of conduct" is a kind of power which links the normalising objectives of neoliberalism – profitability, competitiveness, flexibility and mobility – to the subjects' self-created ideals (Hook, 2004: 262). Thus, contemporary forms of governance make use of "self-governing" strategies based upon particular constructions of "subjectivity". To study the processes of subjectivation, the authors in this volume allow us to hear the subjects' voices, and thus understand how they are permeated by neoliberal rationality, and how they apply power techniques to themselves in order to accumulate new resources and to prepare for success. Interviews and class activities are seen, following Talmy, as social practices, and so the researcher's aim is not to determine what the interviewees "really think" or what they "have really experienced" (Talmy, 2010: 31), but rather, by viewing the interviews as social practices, to show how they are co-constructed interactively. Thus, normative positions are negotiated (i.e., the interviewees deliver what they believe the interviewer expects to hear or what they expect to supply a socially positive image) and the interview is adjusted to match the conditions and contradictions of its existence. Interactions during the interview often reveal the tensions felt by the interviewees with their normative positions and with the hegemonic discourses experienced, and it is interesting to observe whether these discourses are reproduced or resisted (Briggs, 1986).

The method used by the authors to detect critical positions towards neoliberalism is that of ethnography. Some postures are very subtle, such as those detected by Martín Rojo among the students of anthropology, or by Urciouli, among students who choose not to adopt these registers, by Hidalgo and Fernández-González, among schools' teachers, or by Pujolar, regarding the different linguistic trajectories that speakers may present. Further study in this area is needed. Martín Rojo's action research methodology, designed to reflect critically upon the power-knowledge relations and to engage in practices of self-transformation, is based on the assumption that resistance is a particular form of power whose targets should be to curb the infiltration of these neoliberal principles within subjects and then reverse the knowledge, discourses and power techniques produced by them. This resistance, however, cannot be individual, but requires the construction of an alternative discourse and another rationality, of new hegemonies that help create new subjectivities. In this respect, new social movements can contribute by advancing new models of subjectivity, such as those of cooperative subjects (see Martín Rojo, in preparation), in contrast to the entrepreneurial model that demands continual self-examination and improvement. This volume, nevertheless, is innovative in centring attention on the subject in general, and on speakers in particular. By revealing the attacks made on speakers, making them entrepreneurs of their own capital, and the forms of subjectivity that emerge in this context, we show how this should be the starting point for problematising consent. In addition, we raise the questions of consciousness and of agency, whether individual or collective. In short, this volume provides the reader with a tool kit, one that encourages further reflection on the question of neoliberal governmentality, on how to prevent neoliberal discourses from infiltrating their subjectivity, and on how to act in search of alternatives.

Notes

1 This work was supported by the research project "Linguistic Mudes: an ethnographic approach to new speakers in Europe", Ref. FFI2015-67232-C3-1-P, funded by the Spanish Ministerio de Ciencia e Innovación, and by the project "Linguistic superdiversity in peri-urban areas. A scalar analysis of sociolinguistic processes and metalinguistic awareness development in multilingual classrooms", funded by FEDER/Ministerio de Ciencia, Innovación y Universidades – Agencia Estatal de Investigación. Reference: ffi2016-76425-p. This chapter has also benefitted from regular discussions by the first author during a visiting professorship at the Advanced Research Center (CUNY), and participating at the seminar series – Foucault 13/13 – at Columbia University.

2 The phrase was used to represent Thatcher's claim that the market economy is the only system that works, and that further debate on this question is meaningless. One commentarist characterised the slogan as meaning that "Globalised capitalism, so-called free markets and free trade were the best ways to build wealth, distribute services and grow a society's economy. Deregulation's good, if not God" (see Flanders, 2013).

3 Political rationality is the term used by Foucault to describe the conditions, legitimacy and dissemination of a particular regime of power-knowledge that centres on the truths organising it and the world it brings into being (Dean, 1994: 181–187).

References

Allan, K. (2018). Critical political economic approaches to the study of language and neoliberalism. *Journal of Sociolinguistics*, 22(4), 454–469.

Allan, K., & McElhinny, B. (2017). Neoliberalism, language and migration. In S. Canagarajah (Ed.), *The Routledge handbook of migration and language* (pp. 79–101). New York: Routledge.

Aronowitz, S. (2000). *The knowledge factory: Dismantling the corporate university and creating true higher learning.* Boston: Beacon Press.

Barakos, E. (2016). Language policy and governmentality in businesses in Wales: A continuum of empowerment and regulation. *Multilingua*, 35(4), 361–391.

Block, D. (2018). *Political economy and sociolinguistics.* London: Bloomsbury.

Block, D., Gray, J., & Holborrow, M. (2012). *Neoliberalism and applied linguistics.* London: Routledge.

Briggs, C.L. (1986). *Learning how to ask.* Cambridge: Cambridge University Press.

Brown, W. (2003). Neoliberalism and the end of liberal democracy. *Theory and Event*, 7(1), 37–59.

Brown, W. (2015). *Undoing the demos: Neoliberalism's stealth revolution.* Cambridge, MA: MIT Press.

Castro-Gómez, S. (2010). *Historia de la gubernamentalidad: Razón de Estado, liberalismo, neoliberalismo en Michel Foucault.* Bogotá: Siglo del Hombre Editores, Potificia Universidad Javeriana-Instituto pensar, Universidad Santo Tomás.

Charalambous, C., Charalambous, P., Khan, K., & Rampton, B. (2015). Sociolinguistics & security. *King's College Working Papers in Urban Language and Literacies,* 177, 2–22.

Codó, E., & Patiño-Santos, A. (2018). CLIL, unequal working conditions and neoliberal subjectivities in a state secondary school. *Language Policy,* 17(4), 479–499.

Dardot, P., & Laval, C. (2014). *The new way of the world: On neoliberal society.* London: Verso Books.

Dean, M. (1994). *Critical and effective histories: Foucault's methods and historical sociology.* New York: Routledge.

Dean, M. (2010). *Governmentality: Power and rule in modern society.* 2nd ed. London: Sage.

Deleuze, G. (1995). Postscript on control societies. In *Negotiations, 1972–1990* (pp. 177–182). New York: Columbia.

Del Percio, A. (2016). The governmentality of migration: Intercultural communication and the politics of (dis)placement in Southern Europe. *Language and Communication,* 51, 87–98.

Dlaske, K., Barakos, E., Motobayashi, K., & McLaughlin, M. (2016). Languaging the worker. *Multilingua,* 35(4), 345–359.

Duchêne, A., & Heller, M. (2012). *Language in late capitalism.* London: Routledge.

Flanders, L. (2013). "At Thatcher's funeral, bury TINA, too". *The Nation.* www.thenation.com/article/thatchers-funeral-bury-tina-too/. Retrieved 8 February 2019.

Flores, N. (2013). The unexamined relationship between neoliberalism and plurilingualism: A cautionary tale. *TESOL Quarterly,* 47(3), 500–520.

Flores, N. (2017). From language as resource to language as struggle: Resisting the coke-ification of bilingual education. In M.C. Flubacher & A. Del Percio (Eds.), *Language, education and neoliberalism: Critical studies in sociolinguistics* (pp. 62–81). Bristol: Multilingual Matters.

Flubacher, M.C., & Del Percio, A. (2017). *Language, education and neoliberalism: Critical studies in sociolinguistics.* Bristol: Multilingual Matters.

Foucault, M. (1988). Technologies of the self: Lectures at University of Vermont Oct. 1982. In L.H. Martin, H. Gutman, & P.H. Hutton (Eds.), *Technologies of the self* (pp. 16–49). Amherst: University of Massachusetts Press.

Foucault, M. (1994). Prisons et asiles dans le mécanisme de pouvoir. In *Dits et ecrits,* Vol. 2 (pp. 523–524). Paris: Gallimard.

Foucault, M. (1997). Ethics: Subjectivity and truth. In P. Rabinow (Ed.), *Essential works of Foucault, 1954–1984.* Vol. 1. New York: New Press.

Foucault, M. (2002). The subject and power. In J. Faubion (Ed.), *Power: Essential works of Foucault 1954–1984.* Vol 3 (R. Hurley, trans.) (pp. 326–348). London: Penguin.

Foucault, M. (2007). *Security, territory, population: Lectures at the Collège de France, 1977–78.* New York: Palgrave Macmillan.

Foucault, M. (2008). *The birth of biopolitics: Lectures at the Collège de France, 1978–1979.* New York: Palgrave Macmillan.

Fraser, N. (2003). From discipline to flexibilization? Rereading Foucault in the shadow of globalization. *Constellations*, 10(2), 160–171.

Gao, S., & Park, J.S.-Y. (2015). Space and language learning under the neoliberal economy. *L2 Journal*, 7(3), 78–96.

Gershon, I. (2011). Neoliberal agency. *Current Anthropology*, 52(4) (August), 537–555.

Harvey, D. (2005). *A brief history of neoliberalism*. Oxford: Oxford University Press.

Holborow, M. (2015). *Language and neoliberalism*. London: Routledge.

Hook, D. (2004). Governmentality and technologies of subjectivity. In *Critical psychology* (pp. 239–271). Cape Town: Juta and Company.

Lemke, Th. (2001). "The birth of bio-politics": Michel Foucault's lecture at the College de France on neo-liberal governmentality. *Economy and Society*, 30, 190–207.

Lilja, M., & Vinthagen, S. (2014). Sovereign power, disciplinary power and biopower: Resisting what power with what resistance? Journal of Political Power, 7(1), 107–126.

Martin, E. (2000). Mind-body problems. *American Ethnologist*, 27(3), 569–590.

Martín Rojo, L. (2017). Neoliberalism and linguistic governmentality. In J.W. Tollefson & M. Pérez-Milans (Eds.), *The Oxford handbook of language policy and planning* (pp. 544–567). Oxford: Oxford University Press.

Martín Rojo, L. (in preparation) The quiet revolution of the commons: The collective construction of discourses and practices in commoning (manuscript).

McIlvenny, P., Klausen, J.Z., & Lindegaard, L.B. (2016). New perspectives on discourse and governmentality. In P. McIlvenny, J.Z. Klausen, & L.B. Lindegaard (Eds.), *Studies of discourse and governmentality* (pp. 1–70). Amsterdam: John Benjamins.

Nosál, I. (2009). Governing abandoned children: The discursive construction of space in the case of "babybox". In A. Galasinska & M. Krzyzanowski (Eds.), *Discourse and transformation in Central and Eastern Europe* (pp. 114–136). London: Palgrave Macmillan.

Park, J.S., & Wee, L. (2012). *Markets of English linguistic capital and language policy in a globalizing world*. London: Routledge.

Rampton, B. (2014). Gumperz and governmentality in the 21st century: Interaction, power and subjectivity. *Working Papers in Urban Language & Literacies*, 136, 1–19.

Relaño-Pastor, A.M. (2018). Bilingual education policy and neoliberal content and language integrated learning practices. In J.W. Tollefson and M. Pérez-Milans (Eds.), *The Oxford handbook of language policy and planning* (pp. 505–525). Oxford: Oxford University Press.

Resnik, J. (2012). La programme du baccalauréat international et la formation (humaniste?) des élites internationales de demain. In C. Magnin & C. A. Muller (Eds.), *Enseignement secondaire, formation humaniste et société (XVIe–XXIe siècle)* (pp. 253–269). Geneva: Slatkine.

Saunders, D.B. (2010). Neoliberal ideology and public higher education in the United States. *Journal for Critical Education Policy Studies*, 8(1), 41–77.

Senellart, M. (2007). Course context. In M. Foucault, *Security, territory, population: Lectures at the Collège de France, 1977–1978* (pp. 477–507). London: Palgrave Macmillan.

Sokhi-Bulley, B. (2014). Governmentality: Notes on the thought of Michel Foucault. http://criticallegalthinking.com/2014/12/02/governmentality-notes-thought-michel-foucault/. Retrieved 8 February 2019.

Talmy, S. (2010). Qualitative interviews in applied linguistics: From research instrument to social practice. *Annual Review of Applied Linguistics*, 30, 128–148.

Urciuoli, B. (2008). Skills and selves in the new workplace. *American Ethnologist*, 35, 211–228.

Urciuoli, B. (2010). Neoliberal education. In C. Greenhouse (Ed.), *Ethnographies of neoliberalism* (pp. 162–176). Philadelphia: University of Pennsylvania Press.

Urla, J. (2012). *Reclaiming Basque: Language, nation, and cultural activism*. Reno: University of Nevada Press.

Wilkins, A. (2012). Neoliberalism, pedagogy and the curriculum: A global perspective. Journal of Pedagogy, 4(1), 5–10.

Part I

Language and the neoliberalisation of institutions

2 Linguistic securitisation as a governmentality in the neoliberalising welfare state

Kamilla Kraft

A neoliberal industry in a welfare state

In the Nordic welfare states – Denmark, Finland, Iceland, Norway and Sweden – neoliberal logics are often understood as being in stark political contrast to the traditional welfare state logics of these countries. A major point of this ideological conflict is employment liberalisation (Peck, Theodore, & Ward, 2005), especially employee leasing which refers to the practice of companies hiring staff on a day-to-day basis from staffing agencies. This conflict is waged between left-wing and right-wing politicians, but is also significant for trade unions as well as employer and business organisations that hold significant influence in the Nordic welfare state model (Gösta Esping-Andersen, 1990). By opponents, employee leasing is seen as a trademark of neoliberalism, linked to growing deregulation and flexibilisation of labour. Such processes have been described by Richard Sennett (1998) as characteristic of a new form of capitalism and by Nancy Fraser (2003) as a post-Fordist governmentality. The critique of flexibilisation and employment liberalisation is first and foremost that risks which used to affect companies are now instead redistributed to the employees. For example, should a company experience decreased productivity or be under financial pressure, management can fire employees with no or highly limited notice to decrease costs. This is part of the business model known as "just-in-time" or "lean" production which aims to increase profit by reducing costs (Kotler, 2003, p. 226), including employee costs. Proponents understand this flexibility as an essential means of ensuring that companies can survive and profit in a market dominated by steep competition.

The construction industry is a central object of this struggle since it is one of the most deregulated areas of the labour market. It is also an industry which relies heavily on employee leasing. The Norwegian construction industry, which will be the object of analysis in this chapter, is the largest area by far in the staffing industry; 32% of all workers in staffing agencies are being leased as builders by contractors (NHO, 2016). A substantial part of the leased workers is from Poland, currently constituting the biggest group of work migrants in Norway.[1] Norwegian work sociologists explain this as an outcome of two interrelated processes (Friberg, 2016). (1) In 2004, Poland joined the European Union which Norway had been collaborating with as a member of the European Free Trade Association (EFTA) since 1994. This meant that work migration from Poland to Norway, in addition to work migration from the other Nordic countries with which Norway had had free mobility agreements since 1954, increased significantly (Friberg & Eldring, 2013; Friberg & Golden, 2014). (2) The 2004 EU expansion coincided with a deregulation of the Norwegian labour market in 2000, which had made employee leasing legal in all areas of the labour market (Alsos, Bråten, & Trygstad, 2016; Ødegård & Andersen, 2011). This resulted in a situation where staffing companies got easy access to a labour force of mobile workers from Poland, who in turn got access to work or to better paid work.

Attacks on employee leasing – often spearheaded by trade unions and left-wing politicians – are frequent and emphasise how leased workers are economically disadvantaged compared to their permanently employed colleagues, how they have fewer rights and worse employment conditions, and also how they are more vulnerable in terms of accidents (cf. e.g. Prestegård [2015] and Bals [2017]). One of the most frequent critiques of leasing is related to the latter point, namely safety. The construction industry tops the annual statistics for fatal and severe accidents (Arbeidstilsynet, 2017; Byggeindustrien, 2014a, 2015) and hence security and safety become weighty arguments for regulation aimed at securitisation. Not surprising then, both employer and employee organisations commit themselves to the common cause of ensuring safety and security for both Norwegian and migrant workers. Especially the latter group has received considerable attention since the Norwegian Labour Inspection Authority as well as industry stakeholders have identified these workers as particularly exposed to risks (Arbeidstilsynet, 2012; Byggeindustrien, 2014b).

Studies from the European Agency for Safety and Health at Work as well as reports from the Norwegian Labour Inspection Authority (Arbeidstilsynet, 2012) identify various causes for accidents at work: long work hours, high-risk industry and high-risk tasks, different cultures, language and communication, as well as employee leasing which entails that workers often do not have the time to acquire enough knowledge about safety procedures in the various workplaces to which they are sent. These reasons, however, are not emphasised equally in the process of making the industry safer and more secure. While these studies have identified employee leasing as one, if not the biggest, cause of accidents amongst migrant workers, language and communication often feature more prominently in safety and security debates and initiatives. This contributes to leasing, the very core of the industry's flexibility, becoming less visible within securitisation debates. Hence, the practice can remain relatively uncontested, and maintain its status as an inevitable part of the construction industry. Meanwhile, the focus on language and communication as part of ensuring safe workplaces and work conditions for all shows commitment to conducting business under flexible, yet safe conditions.

The aim of this chapter is to analyse how, why and with what consequences language and communication are constructed as conditions for the securitisation of flexible labour in the Norwegian construction industry. It will also discuss the management and control of workers and work. Conceptually, the analysis will draw on Michel Foucault's concepts of "governmentality" and "technology of power" in particular. These will allow for a demonstration of how institutions and agents through various practices, rationalities and techniques (re)produce a system of governance based on security in the construction industry. This governance is not coercive, rather it shapes conditions that require companies and workers to internalise practices and logics to uphold constant securitisation. This "governmentality" and especially its "technologies of power", such as securitisation procedures, analyses and reflections, shape the conduct of workers and make them act in ways that are beneficial to themselves as well as to society at large (Foucault, 1988, 1991). Foucault's concept of governmentality underscores power as multi-centric and productive; it produces specific logics, which become the basis of interventions, social relations, subjectivities, as well as material objects. Moreover, this process takes place on different levels, in different context, and with different agents.

To conduct this analysis, I will draw on ethnographic data generated between 2014 and 2018 in Norwegian construction sites. The data set consists of fieldnotes from observations and conversations, video-recorded interactions of employees' and managers' daily work, recorded interviews, and various materials, including legal documents and news articles, on safety and security. Such a broad data set is an advantage when dealing with studies of governmentality, since these kinds of studies must provide an understanding of both government and mentality, that is, insights into institutional as well as individuals' logics. Different methodologies are used in the analysis of these data, including interactional sociolinguistics for the recordings (Goffman, 1983; Gumperz & Cook-Gumperz, 2012; Rampton, 2014) and text and multimodal analysis (Kress & Van Leeuwen, 2001; Skovholt & Veum, 2014) for the written texts.

This chapter will be ordered in the following way. The next section engages with theories of neoliberal and welfarist governmentality, flexibilisation, and securitisation. This theoretical outline will demonstrate, (1) how the logics of both welfarism and neoliberalism have been part of forming government, and (2) how these logics are invested in the macro level of policies as well as the micro level of individuals' orientations and common sense. The theoretical framework is followed by the analysis, which is presented in three sub-sections to show construction, circulation and consequences of the language, safety and security discourse. The concluding section discusses how certain logics about safety and language become a system of governing logics – a governmentality – that may provide for the co-existence of a welfare state and a neoliberalising labour market.

Welfarism, neoliberalism, securitisation

Since the early 1900s, welfarism has been a dominant political rationality that has governed labour and society in Norway. Based on a utilitarian idea about the well-being of the collective, welfarism operates through a social contract between the state and the individual. The state has to provide socio-economic welfare and stability, while citizens in return have to work and provide the state with income through taxes. In Norway, welfare benefits are considered universal, i.e. all citizens are entitled to them. This is based on a political rationale of decommodification of welfare. This decommodification is ensured through active labour market policies aiming at full employment and a coordinated market economy, making the regulations of the labour market and social insurance policies "core areas of welfare policy" (Larsson et al. 2012, p. 4). Larsson et al. (2012) argue that the Nordic welfare model has been designed as a governmentality that ensures maximum compromise and minimal conflict between state, business and labour as well as low levels of government coercion. Accordingly, the labour market has historically been regulated by tripartite negotiations between government, business (represented by employer organisations) and labour (represented by trade unions) (Gallie, 2007; Gösta Esping-Andersen, 1990, 1999).

Welfarism is often considered the contrast to neoliberalism as this ideology aims at minimal state intervention, deregulation of markets, and individual responsibility. Its philosophical foundation is liberalism, strongly emphasising individual freedom and choice. Neoliberal supporters have criticised welfarism as a form of governance that makes citizens dependent on the state. Thus, neoliberalism can be summed up as a governmentality that argues in favour of free, self-regulating markets and individuals who are themselves responsible for their choices and trajectories (Harvey, 2005; Willig, 2009).

While increasing deregulation and flexibilisation may be understood as signs of the dwindling influence of the welfare state and of take-over by a neoliberal system, scholars investigating the history of the Nordic welfare states (Larsson et al. 2012) argue that the welfare states are at most neoliberalising, since they maintain clear welfare state logics too. The authors' point is that the Nordic welfare states have moved from strict social control of the population aimed at ensuring a utilitarian aim of what is best for most, to increasing individualisation. However, they also underscore that the waxing and waning of welfarism and neoliberalism is a historically on-going process. This is in line with Rose et al.'s (2006) argument that the so-called neoliberal mode of government is not a contrast to, but rather a continuation of the welfare states that characterised Europe and North America after the Second World War. They suggest that a more accurate understanding would be to view liberalism, welfarism and what they call advanced liberalism, rather than neoliberalism, as historical continuities, which implies that contemporary modes of government contain traces of all these ideologies. The transformations of states may be in pursuit of neo-liberal logics, but these co-exist with logics of welfarism and liberalism.

An example of a process where neoliberal and welfare logics struggle and combine is what is often described as the shift from welfare to workfare. This shift was initiated with the labour parties' "third way" which included more privatisation and deregulation of markets (Larsson et al. 2012, p. 8), and challenged the principle of universalism, yet without dismantling the Nordic welfare model (Torfing, 2009). Increased flexibilisation of work and the workforce is changing the stability of livelihoods in the universal welfare states. Still, flexibilisation and stability, represented, for example, by temporary contracts and permanent appointments respectively, both operate in the labour market. Yet, in the construction industry they predominately target different groups of workers, namely "migrants" and "locals" respectively (Friberg & Haakestad, 2015).

As described in the introduction, flexibilisation, especially employee leasing, has been criticised for being connected to safety risks. The combination of the industry's reliance on employee leasing and the critique of this practice as risk-inducing has led to a situation where safety and security can legitimise the regulation of the construction industry. On the one hand, regulations may satisfy welfarist demands about taking responsibility for the well-being of all, also in a deregulated and flexibilised labour market and industry. On the other hand, safety and security regulations become a justification of the continued use of neoliberal flexibilisation practices. In this way these two logics combine to create a governmentality of securitisation.

Securitisation has been studied as a tool used by the state to control its population, especially under globalising conditions. In securitisation and migration studies it has been argued that securitisation allows for enforcing restrictions on one's own and other countries' populations, particularly the latter, at the same time as states can engage in global mobility and the global economy (Lazaridis & Wadia, 2015). Charalambous et al. (2015) argue that securitisation is an "institutional process" which incorporates regulations so as to avoid threats to the

> existence of the state and other bodies [...]. Throughout this process, discourse plays a crucial part, both in declaring a particular group, phenomenon or process to be an existential threat, and in persuading people that this warrants the introduction of special measures.
>
> (Charalambous et al., 2015, p. 2)

To take such measures necessitates the identification of risk groups and processes, and subsequently the introduction of regulations.

Securitisation through language

The discursive construction of language as part of securitisation

In order to argue that discourses on language and securitisation become a technology of the management of risk, the first aim of this analysis is to demonstrate how language and the communicative competence of specific workers are discursively constructed as interlinked with questions of safety and security in the construction site. Organisations that represent the (supra-)national level as well as organisations that represent the industry both take part of this construction. I will begin by analysing the former.

The Norwegian Labour Inspection Authority is the principle institution concerned with matters of safety and security in Norwegian workplaces. It is a governmental agency under the Ministry of Labour and Social Affairs.[2] The institution has to ensure that employers uphold the legislation on Health, Work Environment, Safety and Security (HESS) in their workplaces. Furthermore, it disseminates HESS legislation, evaluates HESS practices in workplaces, and makes recommendations for new standards.[3] This particular institution is, in other words, a crucial part of enforcing government power.

The English version of the Labour Inspection Authority's website, under the header "Safety and Health" states:

> **Foreign workers have a higher risk of work accidents than their Norwegian colleagues. Workers in the industry and construction sector are exposed to the highest risk, regardless of nationality.**
>
> The reasons why foreign workers have a higher risk of work accidents are many and complex. The reasons are for instance: language barriers, that they more often are employed in sectors with high risks, many are hired labor and therefore not an integrated part of the safety culture at the work place. Foreign workers often work long hours, which might be another risk factor. (emphasis in original[4])

"Foreign workers", the majority of whom are leased workers, is the first category that is activated in this text. Moreover, construction workers in general, but especially "foreign" workers, are assessed as being at risk. The list of reasons for this is long, and "language barriers" features prominently as the first point. That they are "hired labour", that is, leased, is also mentioned though with the causal conjunction that they do not become part of "the safety culture at the work place", that is, it is explicitly mentioned that the issue is not the practice of employee leasing in and of itself. This point is the only item on the list that is not presented as self-explanatory as to why "foreign workers" labour under more risk. In contrast, "language barriers" is a point that is not modified, nor explained.

Interestingly, the Norwegian version of website looks rather different. While language also appears here under the Safety and Health section, it is much further into the text, and it is simply one point on one out of three lists explicating different risk factors in construction sites. "Språk- og kommunikasjonsproblemer" [*Language and communication problems*] is mentioned as the ninth reason out of ten as to why so-called "unwanted situations" may occur.[5] The focus on "foreign workers" and the role of language and communication seem to be emphasised in the version of the website which is arguably addressed to "foreign" employees. This then means that the Labour Inspection Authority on its website creates different risk constructions targeted at different addressees, and that it pays special attention to interrelations between language, risk and "foreign" workers.

The link between "foreign workers", language and safety is not only visible on the Labour Inspection Authority's website but also in a range of documents and initiatives. Many of these are co-authored or co-founded by other stakeholders in the industry. An example of such a cooperation is the brochure "*Forstår du hva jeg sier? Krav til språk og kommunikasjon på bygge- og anleggsplassen*" [Do you understand what I am saying? Requirements for language and communication in construction sites] (Arbeidstilsynet, 2014) which is co-authored by The Confederation of Norwegian Construction Industries and the three biggest trade unions for construction workers. The brochure provides an overview of all language and communication regulations related to safety and security at work. The brochure addresses the responsibilities of clients, viz. those who order and pay for a construction project, employers and employees. In particular, "foreign" employers and employees are addressed. The first line of the opening paragraph reads: "With many foreign employees and companies in the construction industry lack of communication in the workplace may pose a significant risk" [org. "Med mange utenlandske arbeidstakere og virksomheter i bygge- og anleggsbransjen kan mangel på kommunikasjon på arbeidsplassen utgjøre en betydelig sikkerhetsrisiko"] (Arbeidstilsynet, 2014, p. 3). Hence, from the beginning, this brochure establishes a connection between the categories "foreign workers", "lack of communication" and "safety risks".

That the brochure is indeed a cooperation between institutions that normally have rather different interests, for example, workers' rights versus production affordances, attests to a joint understanding of how safety challenges in the industry are connected to language and communication. It could be considered a manifestation of the tradition of negotiation between state, business and labour, and this kind of cooperation is in fact rather visible in the securitisation of the construction industry. Another major initiative called *Charter for en skadefri bygge- og anleggsindustri*[6] [Charter for a construction industry with no injuries] was launched in 2013 and signed by several unions, contractors, the Confederation of Norwegian Construction Industries, and the state as well as one university, charged with conducting research on HESS. The explicit aim of the charter was to create a more safe and secure industry and to decrease fatal accidents. The charter was signed anew in 2017[7] by all parties, and the new version of the document read: "To avoid injuries it is required that all parties take on responsibility and that we through mutual involvement create a joint effort supported by everyone in the industry. A collaboration for safety and security!" [org. "Det å unngå skader krever både at den enkelte part tar et selvstendig ansvar og at vi gjennom gjensidig involvering skaper en kollektiv innsats fra alle i næringen. Et samarbeid for sikkerhet!"]. The discourse is crystal clear: the labour market parties take a joint stance on the importance of safety and security.

Part of the cooperation outlined in the charter is to continually monitor developments in accidents and injuries and to disseminate the results in annual reports. Currently there are three reports that cover 2015, 2016 and 2017. All of these reports, though in different ways, include language and/or communication as reasons for accidents or near-accidents in building sites. The first report, published in 2015, does not mention "language" as a category in itself, rather it mentions "lack of communication" twice, and it does not activate categories such as "foreign workers". An example from the report of how lack of communication can lead to accidents is in relation to workers being run over by machines. The report concludes that this "is often due to lack of communication between the driver and workers on the ground [...]" [org. "Ofte skyldes dette mangel på kommunikasjon mellom maskinfører og arbeidstakere på bakken [...]" (Arbeidstilsynet, 2015, p. 22). A couple of pages later, "lack of communication between persons and between workers from different companies" [org. "Manglende kommunikasjon mellom personer og mellom arbeidstakere fra ulike virksomheter"] (Arbeidstilsynet, 2015, p. 24) is also mentioned as one of the reasons for accidents. The 2016 and 2017 reports both explicitly mention languages and poor command of "the language" as risk factors. The 2016 report has a section entitled "Communication" where it reads that "Problems with communication [...] may include that one has a poor command of the language, does not wish to communicate for various reasons, and leaders who do not want to communicate." [org. "Problemer med kommunikasjon [...] kan inkludere at man behersker språket dårlig, ikke ønsker å kommunisere av ulike grunner og ledere som ikke ønsker å kommunisere." (Mostue, Winge, & Gravseth, 2016, p. 26). Lack of command of "the language" is fronted despite the fact that both reports also identify language and communication as the cause of the fewest number of accidents compared to other causes. The 2017 report specifically emphasises the connection between accidents and foreign workers' lack of command of "the workplace language". Overall, it identifies four factors common in accidents: age, length of employment with the same employer, language, and employment status (leased or permanent contract with contractor). It also shows how "Norwegian" and "foreign" workers are affected to different degrees by these factors. Interestingly, the report also mentions that due to data limitations it is difficult to assess precisely to what extent language deficits cause accidents (Arbeidstilsynet, 2017, pp. 8, 43).

These reports are authoritative texts that in a longitudinal perspective create expert knowledge about risks and language and which are used to advance specific views on proper behaviour in building sites and for workers. They identify lack of communication as a source of risk, and throughout the reports, lack of communication is constructed not as a general issue among workers, but as one caused by "foreign" workers in the sites. At the same time, they also construct these workers as more prone to suffer accidents and injuries. While working conditions are also identified as a cause of risk, language figures as an increasingly central explanation, which is interesting as these reports identify language and communication as the least risk-inducing factors. The emphasis on language and communication means that these, without being particularly well defined, can be used as arguments in a powerful discourse on safety and security. In the following, I will turn to how this discourse is brought into and circulated in the actual construction sites as part of everyday work life and logics.

The circulation of discourses on language and securitisation in construction sites

Interfaces between securitisation discourses and practices

The legislation, joint industry initiatives and related studies along with best practice recommendations discussed in the previous section are mediated through various media, notably the industry's news magazine, *Byggeindustrien* [The Construction Industry]. This is published early every morning and provides an overview of news relevant to the industry. I became aware of the magazine in 2014 as a project leader emailed me a link to a news item from *Byggeindustrien* about the then recently published *Do you understand what I am saying* brochure which outlined language and communication requirements in the construction industry. The project leader asked if I had seen the brochure, hence indicating that he read the daily *Byggeindustrien* and believed the brochure to be relevant to me. The news magazine is thus one way for the state, unions and employer organisations to disseminate regulations and best-practice recommendations to practitioners.

Another place of circulation is the annual Health, Environment, Safety and Security (HESS) conference. Here, the aforementioned parties meet to discuss developments, challenges and new initiatives within HESS in the industry. Over the years, managers within the HESS area have mentioned these conferences to me, especially highlighting talks by representatives from staffing agencies who provide insights into language and culture challenges when leasing Polish employees. For example, describing how she managed groups of "Nordic" and "Polish" workers, a HESS counsellor told me about one such talk which she had found particularly useful.

She subsequently sent me the power-point presentation which was based on a newly released research report, commissioned by The Federation of Norwegian Construction Industries and carried out by SINTEF, a research centre specialised in technology and industry research. According to this research report, employers consider "foreign" workers first and foremost a source of flexible staff (Kilskar, Wasilkiewicz, Nygaard, & Øren, 2017, p. 7). In addition, it is reported that most contractors considered language a central challenge when employing transnational workers. The study also finds that while employers may understand language as a central issue for collaboration, only few consider it a factor in security and safety breaches and risks (Kilskar et al., 2017, p. 7). A major point in the report is that Norwegian and Polish work cultures are different. Put briefly, the report ventures that Norwegians are used to flat structures and independence, whereas Polish workers are used to hierarchical structures and orders (Kilskar et al., 2017, pp. 24, 25, 36). This is also a highly common discourse in the sites where one can frequently encounter the "wall story". Basically, this story is about how Polish workers do not understand inferences. A Norwegian manager once summarised the story like this: "If you say to a Pole, 'go and have a look at that wall there', then five Poles will go and look at the wall, but that was obviously not what we meant" (fieldnotes, June 27, 2014). This is explained as a linguistic problem of not understanding the inference, but also as a cultural problem since Polish workers are depicted as dependent on micromanagement and as showing little ability for self-management. This discourse is rather similar to historical discourses on "foreign" workers as can be seen from Kulczycki's (1989) study of how Polish workers' attitudes and behaviour were identified as the cause of accidents in the mining industry in the Ruhr area in the late 19th Century, as well as Lahiri's study of Indian seamen serving on British ships from the mid-1880s to early 1900s. As Lahiri shows, while these historical stereotypes may be very similar to the ones encountered today, the reasons for difference in behaviour and attitudes were back then not attributed to culture or language, but to differences in the races' cognitive abilities (Lahiri, 2000, p. 159).

In short, securitisation discourses resonate historically and within the actual sites. Furthermore, in the sites they manifest as practices related to HESS.

Management measures

Securitisation and the discourse on language and communication as a major risk factor directly affect the management of work processes and workers. Main contractors are legally responsible for organising HESS strategies and rules, and sub-contractors are obligated to follow these. If they do not, they can be sanctioned in different ways, for example, receiving fines or having to do more frequent internal controls which equals a lot of extra work. In the sites where I did fieldwork, dissemination of safety information, written and oral, to all workers took high priority. Dissemination efforts were typically focused on written safety manuals and oral introduction courses, both directed primarily at new workers in the sites. This fulfilled a legal requirement that all new workers must receive information about safety and security procedures and sign a personal declaration of safety before they start working in a new construction site. When signing the declaration, the worker would attest to having been informed about and having understood safety regulations.

In one site, safety manuals were available in Norwegian, English, Polish and Lithuanian, languages that together represented the majority of speakers in the site. The English, Polish and Lithuanian versions were translations of the Norwegian original. The English translation was rather poor, containing mistakes as well as complicated sentence constructions, which were often due to direct translations of passive structures in the Norwegian text. According to a Polish linguist I asked to help me look at the Polish translation, this text was quite good, though some of the language was rather old-fashioned and complex. In general, the manuals were dense, filled with technical language, showing an orientation towards providing the required safety information and rules of conduct rather than providing easily accessible information. Still, the site management could and did refer to their written multilingual safety information. Furthermore, this site operated with oral safety courses, obligatory for all who needed to access the construction site. These courses were provided in either English or Norwegian, and if new workers understood neither, the contractors that employed or leased these workers had to provide them with interpreters. The power point slides used for the safety course were with little or no language. This was a deliberate choice made by the course presenters. By minimising written text and instead using a lot of pictures, the opposite strategy of the manuals, their aim was to increase understanding. The importance of ensuring, and documenting, understanding was also visible from the personal safety declarations used in this particular site. As per usual these had to be signed after the oral safety course by new workers, but in addition to standard declarations, interpreters too were obligated to sign and agree that the worker had understood all safety rules (cf. Figure 2.1, fields "Signed by employee" and "Sign. av ansvarlig tolk" [Signed by the interpreter responsible]).

Breach of safety rules
I am aware that breach of the safety rules results in fines and warnings from ▆▆Prosjekt AS and possibly ejection from the construction site.

Place and date	Signed by employee:	Sign. av ansvarlig tolk:	Sign kursholder
▆▆: ..../.......20.......			

Figure 2.1 Fields "Signed by employee" and "Sign. av ansvarlig tolk" [Signed by the interpreter responsible]

According to the leader responsible for the course, this feature had been incorporated into the declaration as yet another way to underscore the importance of understanding, and informing about, safety regulations. So, while manuals and declarations were meant to inform workers about safety and security, they also contained a strong element of providing proof, viz. they were material objects providing evidence of the contractors meeting their HESS responsibilities. All of this signifies how safety and language is not a matter taken lightly – and how important it is for contractors to continuously assign responsibility and demonstrate that it has been fulfilled.

In another site, the main contractor had decided that understanding safety and security rules was so important that written safety rules must be in as many languages as required for all to understand them. In addition, all "foreign" workers must have a Norwegian-speaking contact person. This was reported in *Byggeindustrien*, the industry's news magazine, as a very high standard for language and safety. The level of interpretation and translation required to fulfil these requirements entailed considerable costs – ultimately to an extent where the cost for interpreters became so high that the main contractor, who had made a public announcement on how they wanted all communication translated and interpreted due to safety concerns, softened the demands for interpretation considerably.

In other sites, contractors relied more on pictures than on written or spoken texts. For them, a useful source of materials was a project that turned HESS regulations into self-explanatory drawings. This project was funded by The Scheme of Regional Safety Representatives with 645,000 NOK (around 70,000 €) and its aim was to "reduce accidents and injuries within the industry. To affect attitudes to dangerous work in an easily comprehensible way through good illustrations/drawings of good and bad work situations." [Org. "Redusere ulykker og skader innen næringen. Påvirke holdninger til risikobetont arbeid på en lettfattelig måte gjennom gode illustrasjoner/ tegninger av gode og dårlige arbeidssituasjoner."].[8]

The trend of reducing, rather than translating or interpreting, language was also visible in other sites' HESS information courses which consisted of videos explicating safety routines. A project secretary would show the video to newcomers, who subsequently signed a personal declaration of safety. It was not checked if the workers actually understood the video's message. Moreover, it is unlikely that the project secretary, not being trained within construction or HESS work, would have been able to answer their questions or concerns. Such safety courses might end up primarily being procedures where a product, for example, a signed personal declaration, is produced to attest to the proper conduct of the contractor.

Managers also reported that they received aid from Polish-Norwegian-speaking workers to translate Job Safety Analyses, that is, reports about how a dangerous task is best carried out to minimise risks, and other written materials, so that they could ensure the legal standards. With less important texts, managers might also try to use Polish themselves. A HESS coordinator had produced a sign showing how not to prepare materials for crane-lifting. He showed me the sign (cf. Figure 2.2) and explained how he had tried to accommodate to the linguistic diversity in the site. In Norwegian he had written in a red box (left): "This is not how we do it! This is strictly prohibited", and then in a separate green box (right) he had written the instructions for how to mount materials properly. The red box also had a "Polish" text, "NJET DOBSJE". While this would be recognised by a Polish speaker as meaning "not good" the correct rendering would be "niedobrze". In fact, "njet" is closer to a transliteration of Russian "Нет" than Polish "nie".

Figure 2.2 In Norwegian he had written in a red box (left): "This is not how we do it! This is strictly prohibited", and then in a separate green box (right) he had written the instructions for how to mount materials properly

As was also the case with the written manuals, the sign represents little concern with the correct linguistic form. It is therefore questionable who the intended addressees are; the "foreign" workers or the contractor themselves and their partners.

Arguably, the form and use of safety declarations, manuals and introduction courses indicate that they are not only objects and activities to ensure effective dissemination of safety and security rules, but also function as documentation for the contractors' safety and security routines. In short, they display how the contractors take their responsibility seriously.

Logics about language, safety and "the other" in daily discourse

In daily interactions, discourses of language and securitisation also manifest in workers' conversations. These are often versions of "the wall" story and they have a double narrative: (1) safety and/or efficiency are dependent on language and communication, and (2) language and "foreign" workers may cause problems.

Below is an excerpt from a meeting between a foreman representing the project's main contractor and two representatives from a surveillance company.[9] One of the surveillance representatives (SUR) asks for a Health, Environment, Safety and Security (HESS) plan. The foreman (FOR) hands him a map of the site indicating where important points are located, e.g. first-aid stations. This is technically not what SUR asked for, but this is passed without notice. Instead, SUR comments that earlier he saw the employees' HESS representative pick up these maps and had asked him whether he had remembered to translate them into more languages (ll. 2–4).

```
01   FOR:   and one xxx (space) xxx [(cars)]
02   SUR:                          [well I saw] that he picked them up
03          (xxx)? so I asked,
04          have you: translated them into more languages?
05   SUR:   ha ha ha ha ha [ha ha]
06   FOR:                  [yea:, this is] (0.8) these::, yes [they are in English]
07   SUR:                                                     [yes here is is], here it
08          is in English.
            ((ll. 09-11 omitted))
12          (1.5)
13   SUR:   because it is of course: (0.4) he thought, that sometimes there are
14          communication problems
15   FOR:   certainly
16   SUR:   and:: (0.4) one (0.6) thing that I at least have noticed is the
17          problem that they (0.2)
18          say yes? (1.1) and then they have not quite erm: (0.2) understood
19          the instructions that have been given
20   FOR:   no
21          (0.8)
22   SUR:   and then they have carried out the task regardless
23   SUR:   [erh]
24   FOR:   [mm]
25   SUR:   the way that they thought and understood that it must be [done]
26                                                                  [hm]
27   SUR:   and then they haven't quite understood the message after all
```

An immediate observation here is how SUR and FOR pass from the topic of a HESS plan to that of language, emphasising how closely safety and language are connected, at least for SUR. FOR replies to SUR's indirect question about multiple languages (line 4) by looking at the map and stating that it is in English (line 6). SUR quickly aligns with this answer but does not abandon his narrative which he continues in lines 13 and 14. Here, he reframes the question of multiple languages to one of problematic communication, but does not present this as his own observation, or opinion, but rather as that of the aforementioned employee representative. FOR aligns strongly with this claim (l. 15) and SUR then pursues this topic in lines 16–19. The interactional caution that SUR exhibits up until this point reflects how the question of language, safety and migrant workers is not uncontested and that a certain measure of agreement needs to be established first. However, after having established joint agreement on the topic, SUR changes footing once again as he presents it as his own observation that "they" do not always quite understand the instructions that they are given. The introduction of the othering category "they" in line 17 is completely unmarked and unquestioned. It is significant that it is never made explicit who "they" refers to, not earlier in the interaction nor later, yet SUR and FOR seem to understand who the referent is regardless. "They" represent a problem because of their lack of understanding combined with their behaviour, that is, even if they do not quite understand a task, they carry it out regardless. These three turns produce an account that moves from the question of use of multiple languages, presumably in order to ensure understanding, to a statement about communication problems, to an observation about this being caused by "them", which arguably indexes migrant workers. In this way, the responsibility of ensuring understanding moves from the managers who produce the signs to the workers who do not understand them. Moreover, the "foreign" workers' lack of understanding, according to the above narrative, entails that work is not carried out correctly. In short, language and safety turn into matters of professional skills and language too.

Consequences of the language and safety discourses and practices

Lack of language (i.e. Norwegian or English) and misunderstandings amongst workers in the sites were the reasons reported as to why certain restrictions on communication had been introduced in the various sites and by various contractors. In short, the discourse and practices on language and safety produced and reproduced in both legislation, recommendations and daily conversations do have direct effects. Most contractors had a policy about only offering permanent hire to workers who spoke Norwegian, or another Scandinavian language, or English, simply because they needed to be able to communicate with their permanent staff. Moreover, one main contractor had a policy to hire only Scandinavian-speaking managers on all management levels (cf. Lønsmann & Kraft, 2018). This practice was indeed based on a rationale about ensuring understanding, as the contractor's HESS leader believed that communication would become complicated and opaque if it were to be conducted in English. As he commented, "Norwegian is complicated enough" (interview, June 17, 2014). Being able to ensure understanding is a constant issue for management, part of the reason being their obligation to disseminate safety procedures. The translation of written safety instructions mirrored this concern too. Yet, as the linguistically problematic texts illustrated, contractors' aim of informing workers of safety and security regardless of their linguistic backgrounds is conflated with an implicit aim of adhering to legal requirements so as to avoid being sued for misconduct or lose their good reputation.

Another example of restrictions was a site where all radio communication had been limited to Norwegian-only because of minor accidents with materials being lifted by crane. The cause of the accidents had been identified as miscommunication between the Norwegian crane controller and the Polish workers on the ground who used "a combination of Norwegian, German, English and Polish" (fieldnotes, September 29, 2014, HESS course). This story was told by an instructor at a HESS introduction course as an explanation of why there were certain language regulations on tasks and training in that particular site. The participants, three Norwegians and one Dane, did not react in any particular way to this story, which seemed to be their general level of participation throughout the course. However, before the course started, and before the Danish participant had arrived, there had been general complaints about how few Norwegians worked in construction these days. This had been a reaction to the teacher's observation that no "foreign" workers were signed up for the course, which was highly unusual. One of the participants commented, "It is hopeless to be in Norwegian construction sites these days. No one speaks Norwegian", which led another to narrate how he had at some point needed to order a crane, and had reached a Pole, "who spoke neither Norwegian nor English" (fieldnotes, September 29, 2014, HESS course). Safety, then, is only one aspect of construction work where language and "foreign" workers may be activated as problematic. Yet, it is the most consistent one on state, institution, industry and local levels, and it is also the one that can legitimate practices that entail different opportunities for different types of workers, such as language requirements for certain tasks or positions.

Concluding remarks

The regulations and recommendations introduced by powerful state and private institutions, covering employer, employee and government interests, shape a discourse on the interdependence of language and safety with regard to "foreign" workers. The discourses are backed up by expert knowledge, carried out in collaboration with universities and researchers, though the points that the industry focuses on can be a rather select version of the scholarly findings. The resulting discourses can be seen as technologies of power aimed at disciplining the industry, and in turn the contractors, in order to ensure conditions for safe flexibility in the construction industry. Such a discourse can ultimately also contribute to the legitimisation of employee leasing. Regulations of and recommendations for language as part of a securitisation process are necessary to become part of and be taken seriously in the industry. Moreover, they are necessary for contractors to avoid economic sanctions and getting a bad reputation for not complying with safety standards.

The desire to be seen as seriously committed to safety and to avoid sanctions leads contractors to internalise language and safety demands and recommendations: they spend resources – time as well as money – on different strategies and materials that will ensure that the regulations and recommendations for language are followed. They frequently emphasise the need for this as part of HESS work. However, the format and content of especially written materials make it questionable whether creating understanding is the primary purpose or whether their internalisation of these demands leads them to focus more on "doing being" a serious agent. Moreover, language regulations can at times be bent or softened if they become too economically costly. What is internalised amongst the Norwegian contractors and their managers are then perhaps first and foremost that it is important to show investments into language and securitisation, and that it is important that all legal responsibilities are upheld. This concern is visible from, for example, the practice of having interpreters sign personal safety declarations. In other words, they uphold an idea and discourse on safe flexibility.

While securitisation is evident in the discourses and practices of the contractors, the internalisation of language and securitisation is not limited to managers' language and safety strategies, initiatives and materials. The discourse stated most clearly in the *Do you understand what I am saying?* brochure about how "foreign workers" often do not understand Norwegian and how this can lead to "lack of communication" and subsequent "safety risks" also permeates everyday conversations between co-workers, signifying a certain strength to the discourse. This is the case even if a substantial amount of reports and research shows that it is very difficult to assess the relationship between language and accidents, or even that this relationship hardly plays any role, at least compared to practices such as short-term employee leasing. Moreover, the daily discourses may actively problematise the "foreign" or "Polish" worker due to their lack of language competences and hence lack of understanding. In such interactions, the discourse on language deficits becomes a discourse on professional deficit too because workers without the "right" language and culture are presented as carrying out work incorrectly, with the consequent understanding that their tasks need to be restricted to something rather simple.

These internalisations – that language and security are deeply entrenched, and that lack of language poses a safety risk and/or a professional deficit – by the Norwegian contractors and their staff mean that certain restrictions on language are implemented in the construction sites. These restrictions entail that workers must accept that they are not likely to get permanent employment if they do not speak Norwegian, or at least English, depending on the contractor. If they do not possess Norwegian or English language skills, their primary value is as a flexible workforce. Some, but relatively few, workers do discipline themselves, that is, they self-invest in language competences to obtain language skills, hence also accepting that they need to be language workers in addition to workers who are qualified professional builders. Regardless, the majority remains satisfied with their temporary leasing, or at least the promise of stability does not persuade them to pursue language as a road to permanent employment. Internalisation of the securitisation logics with regard to self-management or self-skilling is modest.

The primary impact of disciplinisation and internalisation then lies with the contractors and more broadly the practices of the neoliberalising industry. If the advocates of welfarism cannot stop deregulation of the labour market and employment liberalisation, they can at least control the neoliberalisation. Since most leased workers are migrant workers, regulations on language become an efficient tool. Overtly, the motivation is to protect these workers, as well as their Norwegian co-workers, through language regulations. While everything indicates that quitting leasing would be the most optimal way of ensuring a safe working environment in the industry, this would compromise the industry's business model – having a competitive edge through staff flexibilisation – and hence this form of neoliberal governance seems to be untouchable. What is not untouchable is the safety argument aimed at ensuring the welfare of all, especially in a state where workers' rights remain a central part of the labour market and welfare state. The industry needs to show that it functions according to neoliberal logics of competition, just-in-time production, and profit maximisation, but that it is still *safe* for all, that is, it takes care of a basic welfare principle and quiet (some of) the critique of the links between employee leasing, language and safety for workers. A side effect of this truce between neoliberalism and welfarism through securitisation is, however, the limitations on "foreign" workers' opportunities and value in the workplace.

Notes

1 www.imdi.no/om-integrering-i-norge/innvandrere-og-integrering/innvandrerbefolkningen-i-norge/ (accessed September 17, 2018).
2 From arbeidstilsynet.no, English version www.arbeidstilsynet.no/en/about-us/ (accessed August 22, 2018).
3 From arbeidstilsynet.no, Norwegian version www.arbeidstilsynet.no/om-oss/ (accessed August 22, 2018).
4 www.arbeidstilsynet.no/en/safety-and-health/ (accessed August 22, 2018).
5 www.arbeidstilsynet.no/hms/hms-i-bygg-og-anlegg/ (accessed August 22, 2018).
6 www.bnl.no/globalassets/dokumenter/hms/charter_bnl_4sider_3nov-2.pdf (accessed August 22, 2018).
7 http://eba.no/globalassets/signert-charter-for-en-skadefri-bygge--og-anleggsnaring.pdf (accessed August 22, 2018).
8 https://ba.rvofond.no/visualisering-av-god-hms (accessed August 29, 2018).
9 The original conversation was in Swedish and Norwegian. The English text is the author's translation.

References

Alsos, K., Bråten, M., & Trygstad, S. C. (2016). *Sjatteringer av likhet: Evaluering av reglene om likebehandling av utleid arbeidskraft* (Fafo-rapport). Oslo: Fafo.
Arbeidstilsynet. (2012). *Arbeidsskader blant utenlandske arbeidstakere* (Kompass No. 2). Trondheim: Arbeidstilsynet.

Arbeidstilsynet. (2014). *Forstår du hva jeg sier? Krav til kommunikasjon og språk på bygge- og anleggsplassen* (Arbeidstilsynets publikasjoner). Trondheim: Arbeidstilsynet.

Arbeidstilsynet. (2015). *Skader i bygg og anlegg: Utvikling og problemområder* (Kompass No. 4). Trondheim: Arbeidstilsynet.

Arbeidstilsynet. (2017). *Helseproblemer og ulykker i bygg og anlegg* (Kompass No. 1). Trondheim: Arbeidstilsynet.

Bals, J. (2017). *Hvem skal bygge landet?* Trondheim: Cappelen Damm.

Byggeindustrien. (2014a). Ekstra vanskelig HMS-arbeide i bygg og anlegg. Retrieved from www.bygg.no/article/116297

Byggeindustrien. (2014b). Utenlandske arbeidstakere utsettes for større risiko. Retrieved from www.bygg.no /article/1194219

Byggeindustrien. (2015). Ingen nedgang i antall dødsulykker. Retrieved from www.bygg.no/article/1235316

Charalambous, P., Charalambous, C., & Rampton, B. (2015). De-securitizing Turkish: Teaching the language of a former enemy, and intercultural language education. *Applied Linguistics, 38*(6), 800–823.

Esping-Andersen, G. (1990). *The three worlds of welfare capitalism.* Cambridge: Polity Press.

Esping-Andersen, G. (1999). *Social foundations of postindustrial economies.* Oxford: Oxford University Press.

Foucault, M. (1988). Technologies of the Self. In: Hutton, P.H., Gutman, H., & Martin, L.H. (eds.). *Technologies of the self: A seminar with Michel Foucault* (pp. 16–49). Amherst: University of Massachusetts Press.

Foucault, M. (1991). Governmentality. In G. Burchell, C. Gordon, & P. Miller (Eds.), *The Foucault effect: Studies in governmentality* (pp. 87–104). Chicago: The University of Chicago Press.

Fraser, N. (2003). From discipline to flexibilization? Rereading Foucault in the shadow of globalization. *Constellations, 10,* 160–171.

Friberg, J. H. (2016). *Arbeidsmigrasjon: Hva vet vi om konsekvensene for norsk arbeidsliv, samfunn og økonomi?* (Fafo-rapport No. 2). Oslo: Fafo. Retrieved from www.fafo.no/index.php/zoo-publikasjoner/fafo-rapporter/item/arbeidsmigrasjon

Friberg, J. H., & Eldring, L. (2013). *Labour migrants from Central and Eastern Europe in the Nordic countries: Patterns of migration, working conditions and recruitment practices* (TemaNord No. 570). Denmark: Norden. Retrieved from http://norden.diva-portal.org/smash/get/diva2:702572/FULLTEXT01.pdf

Friberg, J. H., & Golden, A. (2014). Norges største innvandrergruppe: Historien om migrasjon fra Polen til Norge og om andrespråkskorpuset ASK. *NOA Norsk Som Andrespråk, 30,* 11–23.

Friberg, J. H., & Haakestad, H. (2015). Arbeidsmigrasjon, makt og styringsideologier: Norsk byggenæring i en brytningstid. *Søkelys På Arbeidslivet, 31*(3), 182–205.

Gallie, D. (2007). Production regimes and the quality of employment in Europe. *Annual Review of Sociology, 33*(1), 85–104.

Goffman, E. (1983). The interaction order: American Sociological Association, 1982 Presidential Address. *American Sociological Review, 48,* 1–17.

Gumperz, J. J., & Cook-Gumperz, J. (2012). Interactional sociolinguistics: Perspectives on intercultural communication. In C. B. Paulston, S. F. Kiesling, & E.S. Rangel (Eds.), *The Handbook of intercultural discourse and communication* (1st ed., pp. 63–76). Oxford: Wiley.

Harvey, D. (2005). *A brief history of neoliberalism*. Oxford: Oxford University Press.

Kilskar, S. S., Wasilkiewicz, K., Nygaard, B., & Øren, A. (2017). *Flerkulturelle arbeidsplasser i byggenæringen: Kartlegging av muligheter og utfordringer* (No. 2017:00352). Trondheim: SINTEF.

Kotler, P. (2003). *Marketing management* (11th ed.). Upper Saddle River, NJ: Prentice Hall.

Kress, G., & Van Leeuwen, T. (2001). *Multimodal discourse, the modes and media of contemporary communication*. London: Arnold.

Kulczycki, J. J. (1989). "Scapegoating" the foreign worker: Job turnover, accidents, and diseases among Polish coal miners in the German Ruhr. *Polish American Studies*, 46, 42–60.

Lahiri, S. (2000). Patterns of resistance: Indian seamen in Imperial Britain. In A. J. Kershen (Ed.), *Language, labour and migration*. Aldershot: Ashgate.

Larsson, B., Letell, M., & Thörn, H. (2012). Transformations of the Swedish welfare state, from social engineering to governance. Basingstoke: Palgrave Macmillan.

Lazaridis, G., & Wadia, K. (2015). Introduction. In G. Lazaridis & K. Wadia, *The securitisation of migration in the EU: Debates since 9/11*. London: Palgrave Macmillan.

Lønsmann, D., & Kraft, K. (2018). Language in blue-collar workplaces. In B. Vine (Ed.), *Handbook of language in the workplace* (pp. 138–149). Abingdon: Routledge.

Mostue, B. A., Winge, S., & Gravseth, H. M. (2016). *Ulykker i bygg og anlegg i 2015* (Kompass No. 8) (p. 46). Trondheim: Arbeidstilsynet.

NHO. (2016). *Bemanningsbarometeret 2016: Bemanningsbransjens årsstatistikk*. NHO Service/Prognosesenteret.

Ødegård, A. M., & Andersen, R. K. (2011). *Østeuropeisk arbeidskraft i hotell, verft, fiskeindustri og kjøttindustri* (Fafo-notat No. 21). Oslo: Fafo.

Peck, J., Theodore, N., & Ward, K. (2005). Constructing markets for temporary labour: Employment liberalization and the internationalization of the staffing industry. *Global Networks*, 5, 3–26.

Prestegård, S. (2015, November 18). Ap: Ingen skal dø på jobben. *Dagsavisen*. Retrieved from www.dagsavisen.no/oslo/ap-ingen-skal-do-pa-jobben-1.458601

Rampton, B. (2014). Gumperz and governmentality in the 21st century: Interaction, power and subjectivity. *Working Papers in Urban Language & Literacies*, 136, 1–19.

Rose, N., O'Malley, P., & Valverde, M. (2006). Governmentality. *Annual Review of Law and Social Science*, 2, 83–104.

Sennett, R. (1998). *The corrosion of character: The personal consequences of work in the new capitalism*. New York: W.W. Norton.

Skovholt, K., & Veum, A. (2014). *Tekstanalyse: Ei innføring*. Livonia: Cappelen Damm Akademisk.

Torfing, J. (2009). Fra welfare til workfare: Nye udfordringer til velfærdsprofessionerne. *Gjallerhorn*, 10, 6–12.

Willig, R. (2009). Self-realization options: Contemporary marching order in the pursuit of recognition. *Acta Sociologica*, 52, 350–364.

3 Producing national and neoliberal subjects

Bilingual education and governmentality in the United States

Nelson Flores

The 1980s witnessed a national assault on bilingual education in the United States. This assault culminated in successful efforts to ban bilingual education in California in 1998 followed by Arizona in 2000. In 2002 another successful effort to ban bilingual education occurred in Massachusetts alongside an unsuccessful attempt in Colorado (Escamilla, Shannon, Silviana & García, 2003). Surprisingly, the fifteen or so years since this national mobilization seeking to ban bilingual education has witnessed a new nationwide expansion of these programs albeit with one major difference. While previous models of bilingual education had for the most part been transitional in nature and were typically reserved only for students officially designated as "English Learners" this new wave of programs, known as *dual language programs*, are open to all students with the hope that approximately half of the students will be English dominant and half of the students will be dominant in the other official language of instruction. As was the case with the previous transitional models of bilingual education, the vast majority of these programs have Spanish as the other official language of instruction (US Department of Education, 2015). In spite of the banning of bilingual education in three states, these dual language programs have continued to grow exponentially (Wilson, 2011). The growth in the popularity of dual language education even helped spearhead repeals of the ban on bilingual education in California in 2016 and Massachusetts in 2017 (Mitchell, 2017).

In order to examine this seemingly abrupt change in fortune for bilingual education in the United States, in this chapter I will analyze two different initiatives pertaining to bilingual education in the state of California as a point of entry for understanding the points of convergence and divergence between nation-state/colonial governmentality that seeks to produce subjects who conduct themselves in ways that align with the interests of the nation-state and neoliberal governmentality that seeks to produce subjects who conduct themselves in ways that align with the interests of transnational corporations. The first of these initiatives is Proposition 227, a state initiative that voters approved in 1998 that banned bilingual education and was informed primarily by nation-state/colonial governmentality. The second of these initiatives is Proposition 58 that voters approved in 2016 that repealed

Proposition 227 and was informed by neoliberal governmentality. I will examine the text of the two initiatives in order to reveal the shift from nation-state/colonial governmentality that positions bilingual education as a threat to the production of national subjects toward neoliberal governmentality that positions bilingual education as part of a broader project of producing neoliberal subjects to fit the political and economic needs of transnational corporations (Katznelson & Bernstein, 2017). I will pay specific focus to the differences in linguistic conduct promoted by both initiatives, with Proposition 227 promoting monolingualism and Proposition 58 promoting bilingualism while also illustrating the common underlying racial project that they both share. The chapter ends with an exploration of alternative framings of bilingual education that resist both nationalist and neoliberal framings by positioning bilingual education as part of broader political and economic struggles of racialized communities.

The metadiscursive regime of nation-state/colonial governmentality

In order to fully contextualize the contemporary context related to bilingual education in the United States, it is first necessary to situate it within the broader sociopolitical context that has allowed for its emergence. Extending Foucault's concept of governmentality, Flores (2013) proposes *nation-state/ colonial governmentality* as a framework for conceptualizing the production of governable national and colonial subjects that fit the political and economic needs of modern society. As Foucault (2003) notes, a key element in the rise of nation-states was the need to defend society from supposedly deviant populations who were deemed a threat to the purity of the national polity. Postcolonial scholars have further developed this analysis by pointing to the key role that colonialism placed in producing discourses of deviancy primarily through the production of racial categories as forms of social differentiation (Fanon, 1967; Mignolo, 2000; Said, 1978). Stoler (1995) illustrates the ways that the production of deviant populations examined by Foucault within the European context was inextricably connected to the production of racialized others as part of European colonialism. These othering processes have served to naturalize the social inequalities associated with the exploitation of the proletariat in European nations and the robbing of colonial lands from racialized populations for their raw materials.

Language played an integral role in the production of these deviant populations. For one, discourse was the primary conduit for the production of the idealized and deviant subject positions of nation-state/colonial governmentality. Specifically, Foucault (1978) describes discourse as producing a *grid of intelligibility* that legitimizes certain *subject positions,* or ways of being in the world, and delegitimizes others. In addition, particular metadiscursive regimes "that drew on assertions regarding the nature of language in regulating linguistic conduct and imbuing some ways of speaking and writing with authority while rendering other modes a powerful source of stigma and exclusion" (Baumann & Briggs, 2003, p. 32) were instrumental in the production of these legitimate and illegitimate subject positions. In short, discourse is the primary vehicle for the production of subject positions associated with nation-state/colonial governmentality with discourse about language (i.e. metadiscursive regimes) being one mechanism in these broader processes of subject formation.

The metadiscursive regime associated with nation-state/colonial governmentality has two major components. For one, it relies on a *language-as-entity paradigm* that abstracts language from the practices in which people engage into an entity that people can possess (Park & Wee, 2012). It connects this language-as-entity paradigm with *monoglossic language ideologies* that produce an idealized monolingualism as the norm to which all should aspire (García, 2009). At the core of the metadiscursive regime associated with nation-state/colonial governmentality is the need to protect the purity of the national language by imposing monoglossic norms on the entire national population (Flores, 2013). Those deemed to not have mastered these monoglossic norms receive social sanctions and are often excluded from mainstream society (Lippi-Green, 1997).

Importantly, these social sanctions are not typically the result of top-down policies that mandate conformity with particular forms of behaviors – a form of power that, while certainly present, cannot fully encompass the working of power in modern society. Instead, as Foucault (1995) notes, power in modern society can be understood using the metaphor of the Panopticon, a prison design proposed by Jeremy Bentham in the eighteenth century that allows one prison guard to observe the entire prison while barring prisoners from observing whether the prison guard is, in fact, observing their cell at any particular time. The idea is that prisoners will monitor their own behavior and conform to the prison rules because of the threat that they are possibly being observed and could be punished if they deviate from the prison rules. In a similar way, monoglossic language ideologies have become so embedded within mainstream institutions that they are able to mold the populace into conformity by ensuring the self-policing of language.

As an example, the United States never adopted an official language. Nevertheless, throughout US history and into the present English has been the dominant language, with the expectation being that all people residing in the United States master the language (Wiley, 2000). Yet, it wasn't any form of English that was promoted as the standard that all should aspire to. It was Midwestern speech patterns associated with the so-called American Heartland that was deemed racially pure and free of foreign contamination that became the standard all were expected to achieve (Bonfiglio, 2002). In this way, the liberal democracy associated with the United States and other modern societies is produced through the same racializing metadiscursive regimes that are associated with more blatantly coercive colonial relations of power (Flores, 2014). A key difference is that subjects of liberal democracies are expected to discipline themselves into conformity rather than be disciplined by top-down decrees.

Yet, as Foucault (1978) notes, "where there is power there is resistance, and yet, or rather consequently, this resistance is never in a position of exteriority in relation to power" (p. 95). In other words, the subject positions produced by the grid of intelligibility are never completely determined, and localized forms of resistance occur in everyday interactions that can eventually also lead to changes in the grid of intelligibility (Martín Rojo, 2017). In the case of the metadiscursive regime of nation-state/colonial governmentality, monoglossic language ideologies have often been re-appropriated by racialized communities in ways that challenged their oppression. In the case of the United States, one example of this resistance can be found in struggles for bilingual education that emerged within the context of the US Civil Rights Movement (Donato, 1997; Flores & García, 2017). It is to this resistance and the backlash against it that I now turn.

Re-appropriating the metadiscursive regime of nation-state/colonial governmentality

The struggle for bilingual education that emerged in the 1960s in the United States can be understood as a re-appropriation of the metadiscursive regime of nation-state/colonial governmentality in ways that sought to counter the marginalization of racialized communities. One of the first bilingual programs to be implemented in the United States during this time period was spearheaded by Cuban refugees to Miami shortly after Fidel Castro came to power. Because the Cuban refugees were still perceived to be foreign nationals who would soon return to their native country, it was deemed appropriate that they should maintain their national language (Crawford, 1992). Therefore, rather than being in opposition to nation-state/colonial governmentality, the first bilingual education program that emerged in the 1960s was made possible through the same grid of intelligibility. A similar re-appropriation of nation-state/colonial governmentality can be found in battles for bilingual education among Mexican American activists in the Southwest (Trujillo, 1996) and Puerto Rican activists in New York City (Del Valle, 1998) as both of these communities relied on nationalist discourses as they fought for maintenance models of bilingual education that sought to support students in maintaining Spanish as they learned English.

These efforts to re-appropriate the metadiscursive regime of nation-state/colonial governmentality in ways that advocated for bilingualism, as opposed to monolingualism, were hindered by the continued of the discursive construction of the Latinx[1] community as a racialized other within the grid of intelligibility. This can be seen in the discourses circulating among federal policymakers as they debated the passage of the *Bilingual Education Act*, which would provide federal funds to states and districts interested in developing bilingual education programs to serve Latinxs and other bilingual communities. Latinx community activists typically positioned bilingual education within broader demands for the economic development of Latinx communities (Flores, 2016). In contrast, the predominantly white male liberal politicians who developed and advocated for the passage of the Bilingual Education Act adopted the dominant policy framing of the era as encapsulated in the War on Poverty that posited that poverty was the result of deficiencies within racialized communities that needed to be remedied rather than a natural product of structural forces associated with racialized capitalism (Goldstein, 2012). From this perspective, bilingual education was framed as providing necessary remediation that would address the supposed cultural and linguistic deficiencies of Latinx students and allow for their social mobility (Sung, 2017). That is, discourses produced as justification for the institutionalization of bilingual education within US schools did not challenge the discursive construction of the Latinx community as a racialized other. On the contrary, support for bilingual education among policymakers relied on this discursive construction as part of their efforts to frame bilingual education as a tool for remediation of the supposed cultural and linguistic deficiencies of the Latinx community. From this perspective, the root cause of racial inequalities is the individual deficiencies of Latinx students rather than structural barriers confronting the Latinx community.

Divorcing bilingual education from broader political struggles also served to reframe these programs away from the maintenance model favored by many community activists toward a transitional model where Spanish was only to be used as a temporary tool for the sole purpose of developing English. The first line of attack against maintenance models of bilingual education was for the federal government to explicitly mandate that federal funds for bilingual education be provided only for programs focused on transitioning students into English as quickly as possible (Crawford, 2000). This same stance was adopted by states such as New York (Del Valle, 1998) and Texas (Blanton, 2004) where original efforts to develop maintenance models of bilingual education were undermined through the institutionalization of transitional models of bilingual education. A similar mandate for transitional bilingual education was passed in California in 1976 though mandatory bilingual education was ended in 1987 with districts left to decide for themselves what language programs they wanted to offer (Johnson & Martinez, 2000). Unsurprisingly, California districts typically opted for English-Only instruction with most of the bilingual programs available adopting a transitional model (Krashen, 1999).

For many bilingual education activists these transitional programs were a difficult but necessary compromise to ensure that some form of bilingual education was available for Latinx students (Reyes, 2006). Yet, this compromise did not protect these programs from attacks by conservative critics hoping to maintain the hegemony of English. This attack culminated in the emergence of Proposition 227 in California. Dubbed "English for the Children" this proposition proposed to ban bilingual education in

California school and mandate instead that all schools offer a Structured English Immersion Program, not normally to exceed one year for any student (Crawford, 2000). In the next section, I use the framework of nation-state/colonial governmentality as a lens for situating the discourse of the proposition within the broader grid of intelligibility that has made it possible.

Nation-state/colonial governmentality and Proposition 227

The nation-state/colonial framing of Proposition 227 can be seen in the very first statement which states that English is "the national public language of the United States of America" and "is spoken by the vast majority of California residents". While the statements may have been technically true at the time the proposition was written both ignore the increasing multilingualism of US society. In fact, in the 2000 Census 40% of Californians over the age of five were reported to speak a language other than English at home instead of or in addition to English (US Census Bureau, 2002). Rather than framing this language diversity as an asset, the proposition argues that California has a "moral obligation and a constitutional duty to provide all of California's children … with the skills necessary to become productive members of our society" asserting that "and of these skills, literacy in the English language is among the most important". In short, the proposition frames the teaching of the English language as one of the primary functions of school while framing languages other than English as at best irrelevant and at worse a barrier to learning.

The idea that languages other than English may actually be a barrier to learning can be found in the ways that bilingual education is discussed in the proposition. Not only are these programs framed as ineffective, but they are also described as inflicting actual damage on immigrant children by denying them the English literacy skills that will allow them to "fully participate in the American Dream of economic and social advancement". As a result, the proposition allows for parents to sue "any school board member or other elected official or public school teacher or administrator who willfully and repeatedly refuses to implement the terms of this statute by providing such an English language educational option at an available public school". The proposition goes as far as to hold school personnel "personally liable for fees and actual damages by the child's parents or legal guardian". That is, district officials who defy the law by offering bilingual education instead of English-Only instruction are essentially criminalized with parents authorized to personally sue them for the harm they are said to be inflicting on their children.

In a continuation of discourses dating back to at least the Bilingual Education Act, the proposition frames the primary barrier confronting immigrant families as linguistic rather than economic. The proposition asserts that "immigrant parents are eager to have their children acquire a good knowledge of English" so that their children can "fully participate in the

American Dream of economic and social advancement". Further evidence of this linguistic framing of the challenges confronting immigrant communities are calls within the initiative to raise "the general level of English language knowledge in the community" through providing funds "for free or subsidized programs of adult English language instruction to parents or other members of the community who pledge to provide personal English language tutoring to California school children with limited English proficiency". In short, lack of proficiency in English is framed as the primary barrier to the upward mobility of immigrant communities, with investments in English seen as the primary solution to addressing this barrier. No mention is made of the long history of discrimination experienced by the Latinx community or the continued political and economic marginalization of immigrant communities at the time the initiative was being proposed. Instead, the basic premise of the proposition is that bilingual education is the cause of Latinx immigrant poverty and that English-only instruction was going to end the cycle of poverty.

In short, Proposition 227 can be understood as a backlash against efforts by Latinx community activists to re-appropriate the monoglossic language ideologies of nation-state/colonial governmentality to challenge the marginalization of Latinx students. It does this in two different ways. First, it rejects the notion that any language other than English should have a role in civil society. Second, it suggests that any efforts to incorporate languages other than English into civil society, especially in public schools, harm the immigrant communities that they purport to support. In this way the goal of public education is primarily charged with ensuring that immigrants students "have" English (reproducing the language as entity paradigm) through ignoring or even eradicating languages other than English (reproducing monoglossic language ideologies). The language-as-entity paradigm and monoglossic language ideologies coalesce in a way that suggests that the primary barrier to the social mobility of Latinx and/or immigrant communities is linguistic thereby continuing to reify a focus on remediating supposed individual deficits as opposed to dismantling the structural barriers these communities confront.

The majority of Californians found this nation-state/colonial framing compelling with the initiative easily passing with 61% of the vote (Johnson & Martinez, 2000). The success of Proposition 227 in California provided momentum for successful efforts at banning bilingual education in Arizona in 2000 and Massachusetts in 2002. This momentum dissipated with the rejection of a proposed ban in Colorado in 2002. One major reason for this defeat was a US$3 million contribution to the opposition campaign made by Pat Stryker, a millionaire whose daughter was attending a dual language program threatened by the possible passage of the amendment (Hubler, 2002). This serves as a prelude to the recent proliferation of dual language education that seeks to bring political cover to bilingual education through the incorporation of powerful white parents into the movement for bilingual education (see Hidalgo & Fernández, this volume for a similar political process occurring in Spain). The "two-way" model, such as the one that Stryker's daughter was is, which seeks to have a 50–50 balance of English dominant students alongside students who are dominant in a language other than English have received increasing attention in recent years and have witnessed exponential growth (Wilson, 2011). While the shift toward dual language education may have been politically expedient in a context where bilingual education was under systematic attack, it also marked a shift away from bilingual education as a program that serves the needs of Latinx and other racialized communities toward a program that serves the needs of affluent white communities (Petrovic, 2005). It is to a more thorough examination of this shift that I now turn.

The metadiscursive regime of neoliberal governmentality

In this section I seek to contextualize the recent proliferation of dual language education within the broader grid of intelligibility associated with the *neoliberal governmentality* in which it has emerged. While nation-state/colonial governmentality seeks to produce governable national and colonial subjects, neoliberal governmentality seeks to mold populations to fit the needs of transnational corporation. These two processes are not incompatible with one another. The interest of nation-states, especially imperialistic ones like the United States, often overlap with the needs of transnational corporations. In a similar vein, a governable national subject can overlap with a governable neoliberal subject in that both subjects are made possible by a grid of intelligibility that has global capitalism as its foundation. Therefore, I am not suggesting a neat linear development that is gradually moving away from nation-state/colonial governmentality toward neoliberal governmentality. On the contrary, it is the continued racialization processes that were produced as part of the grid of intelligibility of nation-state/colonial governmentality that allows neoliberal governmentality to maintain the racial status quo.

While the grids of intelligibility of nation-state/colonial and neoliberal governmentality are not incompatible they are also not identical. In particular, Deleuze (1992) argues that whereas disciplinary systems associated with nation-state/colonial governmentality were closed systems, transnational corporations associated with neoliberal governmentality are open systems connected through discursive networks of power. Under nation-state/colonial governmentality, the assembly line was the norm, and docile workers produced through disciplinary mechanisms that Foucault described using the metaphor of the Panopticon were the ideal. Monoglossic language ideologies were part of the production of this Panopticon that ensured disciplined subjects. However, in the service economy currently emerging in many industrialized nations, docility is no longer ideal. Instead, constantly bettering oneself is desired – so long as this self- improvement can be commodified and marketed (Hardt & Negri, 2000). That is, while under closed systems associated with nation-state/colonial governmentality the ideal subject is one that passively accepts their prescribed role on the assembly line, in the open systems associated with neoliberal governmentality the idea subject is one who actively works for continual self-improvement (see Rojo, this volume for more information on the mechanisms of self-improvement associated with neoliberal governmentality).

Flores (2017a) extends Pariser's (2011) discussion of the *filter bubble* to illustrate the shifting governance entailed in the move from national to neoliberal subjects. The filter bubble is a term that Pariser uses to describe the current workings of the internet. In a nutshell, the filter bubble uses probability in an attempt to decipher the user's desires and interests and uses this information to try to sell products to the user. The filter bubble provides a useful metaphor in conceptualizing neoliberal governmentality. People no longer need to be static subjects who self-discipline in response to the Panopticon at the core of the grid of intelligibility of nation-state/colonial governmentality. Instead, they become reduced to a series of clicks on a screen, which become an ever-changing algorithm that attempts to sell them products. As clicks on the screen indicate new interests, new products can be advertised. Therefore, in contrast with the grid of intelligibility of nation-state/colonial governmentality, the grid of intelligibility of neoliberal governmentality offers spaces for the incorporation of diversity with increased diversity offering new market niches that transnational corporation can exploit through discourses of *neoliberal multiculturalism* (Melamed, 2011; Martín Rojo, this volume refers to this process of subject formation as *homo economicus*).

As is the case with nation-state/colonial governmentality, there is a particular metadiscursive regime that is part of the production of neoliberal subjects. In contrast to the monoglossic language ideologies associated with nation-state/colonial governmentality at the core of neoliberal governmentality are *heteroglossic language ideologies* that develop conceptualizations of language that take bi/multilingualism as the norm (García, 2009). A range of terms have emerged within sociolinguistics in recent years that attempt to describe the more fluid conceptualizations of language that emerge from this perspective. The common thread between all of these terms are that they seek to denaturalize linguistic boundaries and refocus attention on the ways boundaries are negotiated and resisted by interlocutors (Jacquemet, 2005; Pennycook & Otsuji, 2015; Rymes, 2014). In their embrace of the inherent fluidity and dynamic nature of communication, heteroglossic language ideologies offer a direct challenge to the bounded notions of language that lie at the core of monoglossic language ideologies and offers ways of expanding the grid of intelligibility to develop new subject positions (García & Wei, 2014).

Yet, while embracing fluidity offers a direct challenge to monoglossic language ideologies, fluid language practices are not inherently incompatible with neoliberal governmentality. Indeed, neoliberal governmentality relies on fluidity as part of its efforts at the commodification of diversity (Kubota, 2016). In particular, a heteroglossic perspective can be mobilized as part of the production of neoliberal subjects through a continued reliance on the language-as-entity paradigm that suggests that one can possess language. The difference is that rather than being framed in terms of national identity this ownership over language is reframed as part of the accumulation of corporate profits (Heller & Duchêne, 2012). In this way, neoliberal governmentality extracts communication from practice and converts it into a commodity that one can both market and purchase (Canagarajah, 2016; see also Rojo, this volume). As Higgins (2009) describes it, "in a consumerist world, then, prescriptive attitudes towards purity in language and the maintenance of boundaries between languages are no longer relevant" (p. 120). In short, the neoliberal subject does not need to achieve an idealized monolingualism. Instead, the use of fluid language practices can provide corporations with successful marketing tools that continue to marginalize the target population while profiting from them. This is perhaps the key differences between nation-state/colonial and neoliberal governmentality. Whereas within a nation-state/colonial grid of intelligibility languages are bounded and separate and imposed monolingualism is the norm, within a neoliberal grid of intelligibility languages can co-exist in more fluid ways with multilingualism desirable as a mechanism for increasing corporate profits. Nation-state/colonial desires for monolingualism and neoliberal desires for multilingualism can place them into tension with one another as seen in recent debates surrounding Coca-Cola's celebration of multilingualism in the United States (Flores, 2017b).

The commodification of language is certainly not new and has always been integral to the working of global capitalism as people struggle to sell their labor, including their linguistic labor, on the job market (Holborow, 2015). Indeed, even Proposition 227, framed almost exclusively within the grid of intelligibility of nation-state/colonial governmentality, nodded to this commodification when it describes English as "the leading world language for science, technology, and international business, thereby being the language of economic opportunity". What is new, at least in the US context, is the commodification of language being the primary rationale for supporting bilingual education. Valdés (1997) offers an early cautionary note about the political implications of such a move, pointing to the dangers of relying on such an approach in a context fraught with racial inequalities and a continuing legacy of deficit perspective of Latinx communities. Petrovic (2005), writing several years later, documents the beginnings of Valdés' caution coming to fruition as supporters of bilingual education were beginning to rely on neoliberal discourses that refocused attention away from Latinx and racialized communities toward affluent white communities.

Both Valdés and Petrovic raised their cautions within a context that was witnessing the growth of dual language programs – growth that has continued in subsequent years (Wilson, 2011). While support for these programs has grown among bilingual education advocates, some scholars, taking Valdés' caution to heart, have continued to raise difficult questions about the contradictory role that the expansion of these programs has had in regards to addressing racial inequalities. For example, the availability of these programs have typically been unevenly distributed across communities, with affluent and/or gentrifying neighborhoods often having these programs much more readily available than low-income and segregated neighborhood (Morales & Rao, 2015; Valdez, Freire & Delavan, 2016; for a similar case in the context of Spain, see Higaldo & Fernández, this volume). Uncritical adoption of neoliberal discourse will do little to address these disparities since they are symptoms of broader societal inequities that are products of long histories of racial discrimination produced through the grid of intelligibility of nation-state/colonial governmentality (Varghese & Caryn, 2010). Despite these criticisms, the expansion of dual language programs continues unabated. As will be examined below, the passage of Proposition 58 points to a new direction to this shift as neoliberal discourses are now becoming codified into law.

Neoliberal governmentality and Proposition 58

In contrast to Proposition 227, Proposition 58 frames the linguistic diversity of California as an asset describing the state as "a natural reserve of the world's largest languages". The proposition argues that these languages, in particular "English, Mandarin, and Spanish" are "critical to the state's economic trade and diplomatic efforts". While Proposition 227 argues that bilingual education is damaging to immigrant students, Proposition 58 asserts that Proposition 227 "places constraints on teachers and schools, which have deprived many pupils of opportunities to develop multilingual skills". That is, while Proposition 227 frames bilingual education as damaging to the life prospects of immigrant students, Proposition 58 argues that being forced into English-only instruction is what is damaging to the life prospects of immigrant students.

The idea that English-only instruction is damaging to immigrant students has existed since demands for bilingual education surfaced in the 1960s within the context of the US Civil Rights Movement. However, earlier arguments were typically framed around the supposed psychological and cognitive effects of English-only instruction on immigrant students (Flores & García, 2017). Though this framing is somewhat present in Proposition 58, in particular where it points to the body of research that "has demonstrated the cognitive, economic, and long-term academic benefits of multilingualism" the primary thrust of Proposition 58 is that English-only instruction will hinder the economic productivity of immigrant students in ways that may undermine US political and economic interests. The proposition argues that multilingualism is necessary for filling the needs of "multinational businesses that must communicate daily with associates around the world". Specifically, the proposition argues that California employers "are actively recruiting multilingual employees because of their ability to forge stronger bonds with customers, clients, and business partners". Multilingualism is also framed as a resource for issues of national security with multilingualism described as "essential to conducting diplomacy and international programs". Therefore, bilingual education is framed throughout the proposition as primarily a tool for more effectively preparing *all* students for their role in the contemporary neoliberal political economy both through being productive workers domestically and supporting US national interests abroad.

Another significant shift from Proposition 227 to Proposition 58 is the changing role of parents in relation to the education of their children. In line with its nation-state/colonial framing, Proposition 227 frames lack of access to English as the primary barrier confronting immigrant communities with the solution being to offer English classes to immigrant parents so that they can support their children in further developing their English. In contrast, in line with its neoliberal framing, Proposition 58 frames lack of quality choices as the primary barrier confronting *all* parents. From this perspective, the solution becomes to offer more choices, with bilingual education being one choice that parents would have available to them. Specifically, Proposition 58 makes the case for the importance of offering parents "a choice and voice to demand the best education for their children". In particular, it argues that "parents now have the opportunity to participate in building innovative new programs that will offer pupils greater opportunities to acquire 21st century skills" arguing that multilingualism is one such skill. In this vein, the proposition argues that parents should have the choice to have "their children educated to high standards in English and one or more additional languages…thereby increasing pupils' access to higher education and careers of their choice" (see Codo, this volume, and Hidaldo & Fernández, this volume for other examples of choice and competition within neoliberal governmentality). Appropriating neoliberal discourses, the proposition asserts that allowing parents to choose language programs "will improve their children's preparation for college and careers, and allow them to be more competitive in a global economy".

While framed in terms of the need for more choices rather than the need for more English, a commonality between Proposition 58 and Proposition 227 is the continued framing of language as the engine of social mobility. For Proposition 227 the argument is that providing immigrant families access to English will ensure their future success. In contrast, for Proposition 58 the argument is that providing *all* parents with the option of high quality bilingual education will meet the needs of immigrant communities while providing much needed language skills for monolingual (predominantly white) communities. While on one level, this neoliberal discourse seems more progressive than nation-state/colonial discourses, on another level it continues to obscure the structural barriers confronting Latinx and other racialized communities through an assumption that these communities are on a level playing field with the white middle-class families these rebranded bilingual programs are seeking to attract. Yet, research in these programs indicate that this is not, necessarily the case, with white middle-class parents and their children often dominating in ways that contribute to the continued marginalization of Latinx and other racialized communities (Burns, 2017; Cervantes-Soon, 2014; Freire, Valdez & Delavan, 2017; Palmer, 2011). It also leaves unaddressed the intense policing of the language practices of racialized communities and the normalization of identical language practices within white communities (Hill, 1998). That is, it works from the assumption that the bilingualism of both Latinx and white students will be equally valued when in reality mainstream representations of Latinx bilingualism continue to be framed as a threat to national unity even as the bilingualism of white middle-class communities are increasingly celebrated (Flores & Rosa, 2015).

In summary, while Proposition 227 relies on national/state colonial framings of English as the national language that immigrant communities need access to in order to ensure their social mobility, Proposition 58 relies on neoliberal framings of multilingualism as a commodity that should be available to all communities. Both locate the root of the problem of racial inequalities within individuals thereby obscuring the structural barriers confronting Latinx and other racialized communities that have been produced through the dehumanizing of these communities that was integral to the production of the grid of intelligibility of nation-state/colonial governmentality. That is, while the neoliberal framing of Proposition 58 may offer a politically expedient way of countering attacks on bilingual education coming from the nation-state/colonial grid of intelligibility, it does so in ways that leaves the racializing processes at the core of this grid of intelligibility intact. At best, Latinx students become commodities who can be exploited by white middle-class families to further improve the economic prospects of their already privileged children (Burns, 2017). At worse, because of the entrenched racism of US schools and the broader society, they may be systematically excluded from these programs as they refocus their attention to the interests of affluent white communities (Morales & Rao, 2015; Valdez, Freire & Delavan, 2016). In short, neoliberal framings of bilingual education such as those produced within Proposition 58 do not get to the root of racial inequalities and, in light of this oversight, will do little to address and may actually exacerbate racial inequalities.

Proposition 58 passed in a landslide with 73% of the vote (Ulloa, 2016). What change from 1998 to 2016? It is important to point first to the tireless activism of bilingual education activists who have continued to struggle for bilingual education in spite of massive opposition. These activists have sought to mobilize a language-as-resource orientation (Ruiz, 1984) that frames the language practices of racialized communities as an asset for both schools and societies. This insistence on treating racialized language practices as a resource has transformed the grid of intelligibility in ways that have allowed for more spaces to emerge that value language diversity. Unfortunately, this discourse has also been taken up by the grid of intelligibility of neoliberal governmentality in ways that separate these discourses from broader political struggles in favor of superficial celebrations of diversity. Proposition 58 is a natural product of such a re-appropriation in that it completely divorces bilingual education from any discussion of equity for Latinx and other racialized communities through focusing on bilingualism as a commodity that should be available to all. By not bringing attention to the racialization processes that have shaped the foundation of the grid of intelligibility of nation-state/colonial governmentality, the grid of intelligibility of neoliberal governmentality reifies existing racial hierarchies. It is this failure to get to the root of the racialization of the Latinx community that likely made Proposition 58 so uncontroversial.

From accommodation to reconfiguration

Nation-state/colonial and neoliberal governmentality have different visions for the regulation of linguistic conduct. Whereas nation-state/colonial governmentality seeks to produce docile national subjects through imposed monolingualism, neoliberal governmentality seeks to produce dynamic neoliberal subjects who have competencies in multiple languages that can be used to maximize corporate profits. Yet, despite different visions for linguistic conduct both forms of governmentality build on the foundation of racialized capitalism that has marginalized racialized communities for hundreds of years and continues to shape their contemporary circumstances. In this way both the overtly racialized nation-state/colonial framing of Proposition 227 and the seemingly more progressive neoliberal framings of bilingual education obscure the root causes of the marginalization of Latinx and other racialized communities. In particular, both nation-state/colonial and neoliberal framings of bilingual education describe the educational challenges confronting Latinx and other racialized students as primarily a linguistic problem requiring linguistic solutions rather than as a political and economic problem requiring political and economic solutions. More generally, both framings perpetuate a meritocratic myth that places the burden on Latinx and other racialized students to overcome their political and economic marginalization while absolving the larger society from investing in the communities where these children reside. In this way, both reify the racialization processes that have lied at the core of the grid of intelligibility of modern society since the dawn of colonialism (Mignolo, 2000).

Both nation-state/colonial and neoliberal framings of bilingual education are limited in their ability to challenge these racialization processes because of their basis in an ideology of pragmatism that focuses on "getting the job done with no critical analysis of the consequences for the various parties" (Bensch, 2001, p. 27). This ideology of pragmatism leads both framings of bilingual education toward accommodation-oriented policies that "accept the existing structure … and seek to accomplish certain goals within that structure" (Park & Wee, 2012, p. 167). Left unaddressed are the racialization processes that lie at the core of the grid of intelligibility that has produced these structures. In contrast to the accommodationist stance, Park and Wee (2012) called for a reconfiguration-oriented stance. A reconfiguration-oriented stance connects advocacy work related to bilingual education with larger issues of social inequality produced by both nation-state/colonial and neoliberal governmentality. This stance has important implication for applied linguists who have typically taken language to be the center of our scholarly inquiry and have typically celebrated policies that promote multilingualism as inherently socially transformative. Indeed, many of the discourses associated with neoliberal governmentality, in particular the focus on promoting multilingualism as a necessary tool for our increasingly globalized society have strong parallels with the frameworks that exist in our field.

In order to resist the neoliberal impulse that is often at least implied in applied linguistics if not outright advocated, applied linguists need to engage in *epistemological vigilance* that consists of "questioning of our own assumptions about language and culture, which are at the root of the analyzes we produce" (Del Percio, Flubacher & Duchêne, 2017). This epistemological vigilance requires applied linguists to critically reflect on our own complicity in reifying the racialization processes that lie at the core of the modern grid of intelligibility. It entails taking seriously the claim that the root cause of the marginalization of Latinx and other racialized communities is not linguistic but racial and that bilingual education in and of itself cannot get to the root of the problem. While the idea that bilingual education is not a panacea is likely one that many applied linguists would agree with, efforts to address the marginalization of racialized communities that dominate our field typically focus on linguistic solutions. In this way, there is a disconnect between what applied linguists claim to know (that bilingual education is not a panacea) and what we propose (that bilingual education can empower racialized students). If we want to truly affirm the language practices of Latinx and other racialized students, bilingual education will never be enough. What we need is a fundamental transformation of the grid of intelligibility. That is, to shift our focus toward dismantling racialized capitalism rather than fixing the supposed deficiencies of racialized communities would require fundamental structural changes to the global political and economic order.

It is starting from this premise Flores and Chaparro (2018) building on the work of Melamed (2011) propose a *materialist anti-racist* framing of bilingual education. A materialist anti-racist framing of bilingual education still places bilingual education at the center of our scholarship and activism. Incorporating insights from what Pennycook (2015) has termed the "materialist turn" in applied linguistics a materialist anti-racism framing accounts for the ways that poverty, produced through capitalist relations of power, contributes to linguistic marginalization. It complements this with the incorporation of critical race scholarship that examines the material consequences of generations of white supremacy on racialized communities (Harris, 1993) and the role of these racialization processes in contributing to linguistic marginalization (Aggarwal, 2016; Baugh, 2003). Bringing language and race together, a materialist anti-racist framing of bilingual education critically examines the ways that poverty and white supremacy intersect to produce *raciolinguistic ideologies* that frame the language practices of racialized communities as inherently deficient (Flores & Rosa, 2015). Though these raciolinguistic ideologies have shifted over time from the early years of colonialism the underlying logic remains the same (Rosa, 2016). Yet, to analyze the contemporary instantiation of these raciolinguistic ideologies entails a focus on neoliberalism, which has shifted educational reform away from federal interventions focused on remediating racialized communities toward a focus on market-based reforms designed to improve choices with diversity becoming a commodity that can be sold on this marketplace of choices (Dumas, 2013).

Of course, these efforts to denaturalize and challenge the contemporary grid of intelligibility confront many challenges. Attempts to challenge the existing grid of intelligibility are fraught with their own relations of power and often serve to simultaneously reinscribe hegemonic subject positions while working to resist them (Butler, 1993). This is especially true for academics who have typically either intentionally or unintentionally served to reify racialization processes thereby contributing to the continued marginalization of racialized communities. Yet, by being more reflective about how we frame out scholarship and advocacy work we can ensure that we continue to focus on developing a reconfiguration-oriented stance that helps to imagine the social change necessary to develop the "democracy to come" – the unknowable, unpredictable, open-ended, and contingent movement toward a more just and less violent world order (Derrida, 1997).

Note

1 Latinx is a general neutral term used to describe people of Latin American origin. It is used as a way of resisting both the patriarchal assumptions undergirding the use of the masculine form Latino as an all-inclusive term and the heteronormative assumptions undergirding the use of the masculine and feminine form Latino/a or Latin@ that obscures nonbinary gender identities.

References

Aggarwal, U. (2016). The ideological architecture of whiteness as property in educational policy. *Educational Policy*, *30*(1), 128–152

Baugh, J. (2003). Linguistic profiling. In S. Makoni, G. Smitherman, A. Ball, & A. Spears (Eds.), *Black linguistics: Language, society, and politics in Africa and the Americas* (pp. 155–168). New York: Routledge.

Bauman, R., & Briggs, C. (2003). *Voices of modernity: Language ideologies and the politics of inequality*. New York: Cambridge University Press.

Bensch, S. (2001). *Critical English for academic purposes: Theory, politics and practice.* New York: Routledge.

Blanton, C. (2004). *The strange career of bilingual education in Texas, 1836–1981.* College Station: Texas A&M University Press.

Bonfiglio, T. (2002). *Race and the rise of standard America.* New York: Walter de Gruyter.

Burns, M. (2017). "Compromises that we make": Whiteness in a dual language context. *Bilingual Research Journal, 40,* 339–352.

Butler, J. (1993). *Bodies that matter: On the discursive limits of "sex".* New York: Routledge.

Canagarajah, S. (2016). *Translingual practices and neoliberal policies: Attitudes and strategies of African skilled migrants in Anglophone workplaces.* New York: Springer.

Cervantes-Soon, C. (2014). A critical look at dual language immersion in the new Latin@ diaspora. *Bilingual Research Journal, 37,* 64–82.

Crawford, J. (1992). *Hold your tongue: Bilingualism and the politics of English only.* Reading, MA: Addison-Wesley.

Crawford, J. (2000). *At war with diversity: US language policy in an age of anxiety.* Buffalo, NY: Multilingual Matters.

Deleuze, G. (1992). Postscripts on the societies of control. *October, 59,* 3–7.

Del Percio, A., Flubacher, M., & Duchêne, A. (2017). Language and political economy. In O. García, N. Flores, & M. Spotti (Eds.), *Oxford handbook of language and society* (pp. 55–75). New York: Oxford University Press.

Del Valle, S. (1998). Bilingual education for Puerto Ricans in New York City: From hope to compromise. *Harvard Educational Review, 68*(2), 193–217.

Derrida, J. (1997). *The politics of friendship.* London: Verso.

Donato, R. (1997). *The other struggle for equal schools: Mexican Americans during the Civil Rights era.* Albany: State University of New York Press.

Dumas, M. (2013). "Waiting for Superman" to save black people: Racial representation and the official antiracism of neoliberal school reform. *Discourse: Studies in the Cultural Politics of Education, 34*(4), 531–547.

Escamilla, K., Shannon, S., Silviana, C., & García, J. (2003). Breaking the code: Colorado's defeat of the anti-bilingual education initiative (Amendment 31). *Bilingual Research Journal, 27*(3), 357–382.

Fanon, F. (1967). *Black skin, white masks.* London: Pluto Press.

Flores, N. (2013). Silencing the subaltern: Nation-state/colonial governmentality and bilingual education in the United States. *Critical Inquiry in Language Studies, 10*(4), 263–287.

Flores, N. (2014). Creating republican machines: Language governmentality in the United States. *Linguistics and Education, 25,* 1–11.

Flores, N. (2016). A tale of two visions: Hegemonic whiteness and bilingual education. *Educational Policy, 30,* 13–38.

Flores, N. (2017a). Bilingual education. In O. García, N. Flores, & M. Spotti (Eds.), *Oxford handbook of language and society* (pp. 525–543). New York: Oxford University Press.

Flores, N. (2017b). From language as resource to language as struggle: Resisting the coke-ification of bilingual education. In M. Flubacher & A. Del Percio (Eds.), *Language, education and neoliberalism: Critical studies in sociolinguistics* (pp. 62–81). Bristol, UK: Multilingual Matters.

Flores, N., & Chaparro, S. (2018). What counts as language education policy? Developing a materialist anti-racist approach to language activism. *Language Policy*, 17, 365–384.

Flores, N., & García, O. (2017). A critical review of bilingual education in the United States: From basements and pride to boutiques and profit. *Annual Review of Applied Linguistics*, 37, 14–29.

Flores, N., & Rosa, J. (2015). Undoing appropriateness: Raciolinguistic ideologies and language diversity in education. *Harvard Educational Review*, 85(2), 149–171.

Foucault, M. (1978). *The history of sexuality, volume 1: An introduction.* New York: Vintage Books.

Foucault, M. (1995). *Discipline and punish: The birth of the prison.* New York: Vintage Books.

Foucault, M. (2003). *Society must be defended: Lectures at the Collége de France 1975–1976.* New York: Picador.

Freire, J., Valdez, V., & Delavan, M. (2017). The (dis)inclusion of Latina/o interests from Utah's dual language education boom. *Journal of Latinos and Education*, 16, 276–289.

García, O. (2009). *Bilingual education in the 21st century: A global perspective.* Malden, MA: Wiley-Blackwell.

García, O., & Wei, L. (2014). *Translanguaging: Language, bilingualism and education.* New York: Palgrave Macmillan.

Goldstein, A. (2012). *Poverty in common: The politics of community action during the American century.* Durham, NC: Duke University Press.

Hardt, M., & Negri, A. (2000). *Empire.* Cambridge, MA: Harvard University Press.

Harris, C. (1993). Whiteness as property. *Harvard Law Review*, 106(8), 1710–1791.

Heller, M., & Duchêne, A. (2012). Pride and profit: Changing discourses of language, capital and nation-states. In A. Duchêne & M. Heller (Eds.), *Language in late capitalism: Pride and profit* (pp. 1–21). New York: Routledge.

Higgins, C. (2009). *English as a local language.* Clevedon, UK: Multilingual Matters.

Hill, J. (1998). Language, race, and white public space. *American Anthropologist*, 100(3), 680–689.

Holborow, M. (2015). *Language and neoliberalism.* New York: Routledge.

Hubler, E. (2002, November 6). Bilingual-ed ban fails. *Denver Post*, E-01.

Jacquemet, M. (2005). Transidiomatic practices: Language and power in the age of globalization. *Language & Communication*, 25(3), 257–277.

Johnson, K., & Martinez, G. (2000). Discrimination by proxy: The case of proposition 227 and the ban on bilingual education. *UC Davis Law Review*, 33, 1227–1276.

Katznelson, N., & Bernstein, K. (2017). Rebranding bilingualism: The shifting discourses of language education policy in California's 2016 election. *Linguistics and Education*, 40, 11–26.

Krashen, S. D. (1999). *Condemned without a trial: Bogus arguments against bilingual education.* Portsmouth, NH: Heinemann.

Kubota, R. (2016). The multi/plural turn, postcolonial theory, and neoliberal multiculturalism: Complicities and implications for applied linguistics. *Applied Linguistics*, 37(4), 474–494.

Lippi-Green, R. (1997). *English with an accent: Language, ideology and discrimination in the United States.* New York: Routledge.

Martín Rojo, L. (2017). Language and power. In O. García, N. Flores, & M. Spotti (Eds.), *Oxford handbook of language and society* (pp. 77–102). New York: Oxford University Press.

Melamed, J. (2011). *Represent and destroy: Rationalizing violence in the new racial capitalism*. Minneapolis, MN: University of Minnesota Press.

Mignolo, W. (2000). *Local histories/global designs: Coloniality, subaltern knowledges, and border thinking*. Princeton, NJ: Princeton University Press.

Mitchell, C. (2017, November 27). Massachusetts law paves the way for more bilingual education. *Education Week*. Retrieved from www.edweek.org

Morales, P. Z., & Rao, A. B. (2015). How ideology and cultural capital shape the distribution of Illinois' bilingual education programs. Teachers College Record. Retrieved from www.tcrecord.org/content.asp?contentid=18139

Palmer, D. (2011). Middle-class English speakers in a two-way immersion bilingual classroom: "Everyone should be listening to Jonathan right now". *TESOL Quarterly, 43*, 177–202.

Park, J., & Wee, L. (2012). *Markets of English: Linguistic capital and language policy in a globalizing world*. New York: Routledge.

Pariser, E. (2011). *The filter bubble: What the Internet is hiding from you*. New York: Penguin Press.

Pennycook, A. (2015). Class is out: Erasing social class in applied linguistics. *Applied Linguistics, 36*(2), 1–9.

Pennycook, A., & Otsuji, E. (2015). *Metrolingualism: Language in the city*. New York: Routledge.

Petrovic, J. (2005). The conservative restoration and neoliberal defenses of bilingual education. *Language Policy, 4*(4), 395–416.

Reyes, L. (2006). The ASPIRA consent decree: A thirtieth anniversary retrospective of bilingual education in New York City. *Harvard Educational Review, 76*(3), 369–400.

Rosa, J. (2016). Standardization, racialization, languagelessness: Raciolinguistic ideologies across communicative contexts. *Journal of Linguistic Anthropology, 26*(2), 162–183.

Ruiz, R. (1984). Orientations in language planning. NABE Journal, *8*, 15–34.

Rymes, B. (2014). *Communicating beyond language: Everybody encounters with diversity*. New York: Routledge.

Said, E. (1978). *Orientalism*. New York: Pantheon Books.

Stoler, A. (1995). *Race and the education of desire: Foucault's history of sexuality and the colonial order of things*. Durham, NC: Duke University Press.

Sung, K. (2017). "Accentuate the positive; eliminate the negative": Hegemonic interest convergence, racialization of Latino poverty, and the 1968 Bilingual Education Act. *Peabody Journal of Education, 92*(3), 302–321.

Trujillo, A. (1996). In search of Aztlán: Movimiento ideology and the creation of a Chicano worldview through schooling. In B. Levinson, D. Foley, & D. Holland (Eds.), *The cultural production of the educated person: Critical ethnographies of schooling and local practice* (pp. 119–152). Albany: State University of New York Press.

Ulloa, J. (2016, November 8). California will bring back bilingual education as Proposition 58 cruises to victory. *Los Angeles Times*. Retrieved from www.latimes.com

US Census Bureau. (2002). *California 2000: Census 2000 profile*. Washington DC: U.S. Department of Commerce.

US Department of Education. (2015). *Dual language education programs: Current state policies and practices*. Washington, DC: U.S. Department of Education.

Valdés, G. (1997). Dual language immersion programs: A cautionary note concerning the education of language-minority students. *Harvard Educational Review, 67*(3), 391–429.

Valdez, V., Freire, J., & Delavan, M. (2016). The gentrification of dual language education. *Urban Review, 48*(4), 601–627.

Varghese, M. M., & Park, C. (2010). Going global: Can dual-language programs save bilingual education? *Journal of Latinos and Education, 9*(1), 72–80.

Wiley, T. (2000). Continuity and change in the function of language ideologies in the United States. In T. Ricento (Ed.), *Ideology, politics and language policies: Focus on English* (pp. 67–86). Amsterdam: John Benjamins.

Wilson, D. (2011). Dual language programs on the rise. *Harvard Education Letter, 27*(2), 4–5.

4 Framing "choice" in language education

The case of freedom in constructing inequality[1]

Elisa A. Hidalgo McCabe and Noelia Fernández-González

Introduction

The expansion of discourses on bi/multilingualism responds to new and shifting views on language learning and education as social practices within a contemporary neoliberal economy, drawn by increased mobility, delocalisation and the flexibilisation of markets (see Holborow, 2015: 14). Consistent with the first aim of this volume, the present chapter inquires on the ways in which the processes that govern markets colonise different social fields such as education – a key institution for social reproduction (Bourdieu & Passeron, 1977) – and language, imposing the need to be competitive and profitable. The case of the Madrid region shows how, in the last decade, a scenario of parental choice has progressively incorporated schools to a particular programme, the Spanish/English Bilingual Programme (BP) as their trademark and as a means to guarantee their survival in the educational market (Prieto & Villamor, 2012, 2016). Madrid is a single educational district since 2013, meaning that families can choose any school within the region, not only amid the private ones, but also among state and charter schools.[2] Notions such as quality, performance, transparency and accountability are keywords of parental choice discourses, and have arrived hand in hand with the introduction of standardised evaluations and school rankings as part of a global neoliberal reform that has changed the language of the public discourse (Fairclough, 2000). The public sector is now thought of and interpreted through the lens of the business world, colonising and changing its rationality and aims (Fairclough, 1993). Within this context, new economic principles have transformed the field of public education and schooling, bringing forward a frame of risk, fluidity and instability that resembles the flow of markets.

These shifting discourses, policies and ideologies shape educational goals in terms of profit, consumption and competition. Since 2004, the introduction of the BP in Madrid's compulsory school system has been endorsed by the conservative Popular Party (PP), bringing forward a new discursive construction in education that incorporates practices of social distinction. These discourses place English as a marker of social prestige among state and charter schools, which had traditionally been entrusted to Spanish-English language education programmes in elite schools (Pérez-Milans & Patiño Santos, 2014: 452). The BP is presented as the way to prepare students in their aspirations of "cosmopolitanism", that is, the idea that individuals should adapt to an international class of mobile citizenship (Block, 2002: 4). From the moment the BP was first launched, state schools have gradually taken part in this programme as a means to attract middle-class students and their families by reason of their transfer to private and charter schools in the previous decade, when the region received one of the largest waves of migration. This relocation had remained consistent throughout the 1990s as the regional state school system registered an unprecedented number of migrant students, shaping a new demographic reality. Even more so after the financial crisis in 2008, state schools have been confronted with budget cuts and have been obliged to "compete for students and resources" (Martín Rojo, 2017: 545). Consequently, a large number of schools have affirmed the benefits of the BP to enrol more students, especially those from more affluent families (see Flubacher & Del Percio, 2017, for a detailed analysis of how the role of language and of language programmes in schools is being affected by these developments).

The introduction of market principles in educational programmes has been promoted in the context of a "knowledge economy", by means of which education and knowledge – also referred to as "human capital" – are considered "aspects of productive labor with market value" (Urciuoli, 2008: 224; see Martín Rojo in this volume). This leads us to the second aim of this volume, which refers to the ways in which neoliberalism can become a practice of governance of individuals and population as a whole. In this direction, we follow the approach adopted by Laval & Dardot (2009/2013), who draw on Foucault's concept of governmentality, that is, understanding how power reaches at different levels of people's conduct until they become self-governed (Foucault, 1980, as cited in Martín Rojo, 2017). Mainly, we focus on two particular forms of neoliberal governmentality – individual freedom and market freedom – by means of which "competitiveness" emerges as a key principle, extending to "all sectors of public activity, and to all areas of social existence" (Martín Rojo, 2017: 547). In the Madrid region, competition among schools is harboured by the interplay between the BP and parental choice discourses that favour the application of other neoliberal principles such as accountability, certification and the law of supply and demand. These techniques are linked to what has been denominated as the "audit culture" (Strathern, 2000), which involves governing people and organisations through numbers (Shore & Wright, 2015; Strathern, 2000). Competitiveness shapes students too, whose trajectories are seen as a process of "self-capitalisation" (Rizvi & Lingard, 2010/2013; Martín Rojo, 2017), according to which individuals are encouraged to increase their knowledge and language skills in order to be "as profitable and competitive as markets" (Martín Rojo, 2017: 545; see also Sunyol & Codó in this volume for a detailed study of the role played by the International Baccalaureate Diploma

Programme in positioning schools and students in state schools across the city of Barcelona as more "marketable").

Under such conditions, the critical approach we take in this chapter addresses the problematic assumptions of freedom of choice, equity and equal opportunity taking place in the midst of the neoliberalisation processes in the sphere of public education. As reproduction theories from different approaches have pointed out since the 1970s (Bowles & Gintis, 1976; Bourdieu & Passeron, 1977), the segregating effect of the schooling system has always fulfilled dominant class interests in sustaining unequal access to knowledge-capital. The novelty we find in the ways these power mechanisms are exercised today responds to a neoliberal understanding of language – English – as a "source of symbolic added value" (Duchêne & Heller, 2012: 10) and the reasons to promote it are more closely linked to human capital theories, whereby education is mainly seen as a capital to better compete in the labour market. Whilst this logic highlights capital accumulation, it could potentially lead to inequality if a process of social selection takes place on the basis of students' "relative knowledge and competence in English" (Blommaert, 2010, as cited in Block, 2014: 134). To this effect, we employed an ethnographic approach as a "useful means of gaining in-depth descriptions and explanations" (Heller, 2008: 250) that inform our understanding of how our informants respond to these changing discourses in education. Our data comprises a total of 19 audio-recorded in-depth interviews[3] with school leaders, teachers, school counsellors and families in four state schools. For the purposes of this study, we focus on teacher and school leader interviews in three state schools in Madrid: *Promesas*, *Verde* and *El Campamento*. We were curious to examine participants' perspectives on the implementation of the BP at *Promesas* – a state-funded bilingual primary school – on the one hand, and the reasons behind the closing of *Verde* – a non-bilingual state secondary school – on the other. In the case of *El Campamento*, a bilingual secondary school, we study the effects of classifying students in different strands based on their level of English. These interviews have been accompanied by classroom observations in one of the schools and a deep examination of the legal documents that regulate the implementation of the BP and parental choice for a better contextualisation.

In making sense of the data, we paid special attention to the boundaries described by our informants in the wake of this competition scenario, which could grant or prevent students' access to symbolic capital "such as having access to learning languages, which can be converted into economic capital" (Martín Rojo, 2017: 550). Here, we can refer to capitalisation/decapitalisation (developed by Martín Rojo, 2010; based on Bourdieu's [1986] notion of capital) as acts of bestowing or withholding symbolic capital. In particular, we can observe how competition positions the schools with certain programmes such as the BP as "the better ones", placing other schools and programmes as "less valued ones". Moreover, streaming processes in the BP contribute to the hierarchisation of students at the secondary level upon the introduction of bilingual strands. In recent years, the symbolic power of language tests legitimises the classification of students in these strands according to their linguistic level (e.g. A2,[4] B1). These tests are delivered by external institutions of international prestige, which evaluate students' foreign language competence in different stages of schooling (Cambridge Tests, 2018).

Governing through freedom in Madrid, "a bilingual community"

Although parental choice is not a classical privatisation measure – that is, the replacement of the public service by a private provision – it is a form of endogenous or hidden privatisation, referring to "the importing of ideas, techniques and practices from the private sector in order to make the public sector more like business and more business-like" (Ball & Youdell, 2007: 9). Parental choice holds as its main feature the removal of restrictions in the area school district, allowing students to enrol in the school of their choice within a wider area. Hence, the proximity criteria is no longer relevant as had been the case of the previous attendance zone model, which required students to enrol in any school within their neighbourhood.[5] Linked to notions such as quality, deregulation and democratic freedom, parental choice is presented as accessible to all without exception and is largely formulated as a right of families, who are able to choose any school within a wider zone. As the area of choice increases, the scope of state and charter schools to choose from expands, generating higher competition among schools to attract students (Alegre, 2010). Schools are considered autonomous entities that must replicate the entrepreneurial organisation and, thus, are held accountable for their performance (Strathern, 2000). As a result, new subjectivities can be found: principals are conceived as managers (Merchán, 2012; Wilkins, 2015) and families are invited to participate in educational programmes as clients who seek a quality service (Jódar & Gómez, 2007).

One of the main features of parental choice is competitiveness, considered the featured principle of neoliberal governmentality (Brown, 2015/2016; Laval & Dardot, 2009/2013). The reasoning behind this competition is that the quality of any school improves when they compete with other schools. Competition is also closely interwoven with a discourse of freedom: the state must allow the market actors perform freely. Indeed, as Macedo, Dendrinos and Gounari (2003) reveal, the concept of freedom has for decades been cherished by neoliberal advocates who claim that "free markets are integral to human nature" (Macedo, Dendrinos & Gounari, 2003: 127). Milton Friedman (1962) embraced the notion of a minimum state, that is, minimum intervention and minimum regulation, in order to allow the market function freely. In *Free to Choose*, economic freedom is understood as "an essential requisite for political freedom by enabling people to cooperate with one another without coercion or central direction" (Friedman & Friedman, 1980: 2). As restrictions are removed, the market appears to be functioning freely and the state is conceived as "a mere watchman of the economy" (Block, Gray & Holborow, 2012: 45). Accordingly, parental choice is presented as the elimination of administrative restrictions in school attendance zones, which are considered obstacles that block the parents' democratic right to choose any school beyond the bounds of their neighbourhood school (Regional Education Department, 2013).

Nonetheless, as Karl Polanyi (1957/2016) highlights in his critique of the economic theory of liberalism, the fallacy of deregulation is confirmed by the artificial character of the free market: *laissez faire* markets are not natural, but the result of countless regulation enacted since 1830, when laws first favoured free market mechanisms in the context of England. Moreover, Macedo, Dendrinos and Gounari (2003) argue that freedom in capitalist economies "becomes a thing, a commodity, a product" (Macedo, Dendrinos & Gounari, 2003: 126). These authors highlight the preconditioned nature of freedom in Friedman's assumptions, which obviate the fact that choices, far from being universal, are accessible to individuals who experience the material conditions that enable them to choose. Here, it is important, again, following Foucault (2008), to emphasise the difference between classical liberalism of the eighteenth and nineteenth centuries and neoliberalism. While liberalism theory states that some matters should be managed by state whilst others should be dealt with inside the realm of the market and, in turn, governed by the *laissez faire* rules, the neoliberal purpose intends to expand its governmentality to all aspects of life. In this sense, freedom in the neoliberal order mobilises the subjects' desires upon an illusory variety of opportunities and choices. Bearing this in mind, Laval and Dardot (2009/2013) draw attention to the normative aspect of freedom of choice, arguing that individuals are invited to choose through particular techniques that orient their behaviour. In their own words, the logic of freedom of choice "consists in indirectly directing the conduct [of the subject]" (Laval & Dardot, 2009/ 2013: 218). Power is exercised by making individuals responsible for their choices in pursuit of their self-interest, acting as if it were their duty.

Language becomes central to articulating a neoliberal technology of freedom, allowing the market logic to colonise other spheres of individual's lives under the illusion of a variety of choices available (see Del Precio in this volume). In the Madrid region, the interplay between parental choice and BP discourses and policies presents language learning as a source of "profit" (Duchêne & Heller, 2012) and conceals the institutionalisation of English as a symbolic index of prestige, competitiveness and success. Promoted by the Local Administration as the "hallmark" of Madrid education (Regional Education Department, 2016: 80), the proliferation of state and charter schools that take part in the BP is supported by a growing national and international architecture that frames language education as a valuable capital (e.g. European Union). In 2004, the Regional Education Department introduced the BP in the compulsory school system, geared initially towards state primary schools.[6] That same year, 24 state primary schools took part in the BP. In 2007, the call for projects incorporated charter schools. Some years later, in 2009, this programme was also introduced in state secondary schools. In parallel with the introduction of BP, the Madrid

Regional Government has progressively introduced a model of parental choice intended to foster equality of opportunities among students regardless of their place of residence (Regional Education Department, 2013). The attendance areas were first broadened in 2005, meaning that parents could choose among a larger number of schools. Since then, a competition scenario has driven state schools to "go bilingual" as a branding strategy whilst language – English – has acquired a dominant role in the selection and streaming of students. These dynamics point to a virtuous and vicious cycle: the growing local reputation of a school attracts more outstanding students, which in turn is more attractive for middle and upper-middle class families who wish to avoid certain schools considered to have low performance (Maroy, 2008; Prieto & Villamor, 2012). That is, this cycle reveals the segregation consequences when competition among schools is introduced.

Nowadays, almost half of the state schools[7] in the Madrid region take part in the BP. Heightened by the Regional Government's ambitious slogan "Madrid, a bilingual community",[8] the rise in popularity of the BP has received attention from different perspectives on language policy and language ideology debates (Martín Rojo, 2013; Relaño Pastor, 2015), as well as from educational policy studies (Prieto & Villamor, 2012, 2016). After the financial crisis in 2008, discourses promoting the BP in Madrid have been redefined through particular associations that conform to the material or symbolic value of English at the expense of its broader social and political meaning. This transition implies that bilingualism and English are shifting from a humanistic concept of "citizenship" that contemplates English as "a necessary tool that enables students their effective integration as European citizens" (Regional Education Department, 2004: 12) to a more pragmatic vision that links bilingualism to employability, where English is seen as "an essential tool (…) that provides the education needed to compete in the labour world in the best conditions and achieve an excellent personal a professional future" (Regional Education Department, 2010: 1). In different advertisement campaigns designed by the Regional Education Department, students in the BP are portrayed as global cosmopolitans (Block, 2011, 2014), in this case as future high-level professionals (e.g. race mechanic, diplomat, scientist, pilot) who travel to different countries to develop their intercultural abilities. From these advertisements we can see how the schooling system "represents the means of entry to the job market and related social rewards" (Pérez-Milans, 2013: 166) and bilingualism is understood from a human capital frame as *the* tool to access a high standing job. Here, the BP fulfils the objectives of the European Union's new economic policy that was designed in the Lisbon strategy.[9] The discourses of this action link education and knowledge to economy, employment and trade through key notions such as lifelong learning and employability (Jessop, 2008). Moreover, the European Commission's multilingualism policy has gradually emphasised the important role of foreign language skills in "making young people more employable and equipping them for working abroad" (European Commission, n.d.).

In the following sections, we address how our participants frame these ideologies, discourses and policies in their specific educational contexts. For this purpose, we inquire on two axes: 1. the ways in which the expansion of the BP is experienced in particular schools in a context of parental choice; and 2. any potential inequalities engendered upon the introduction of new language demands and requirements in schools. Our framework of analysis comprises discourse analysis (Fairclough, 1995; Laclau & Mouffe, 1985/ 2001), and the stance taken by our interviewees (Du Bois, 2007; Gumperz, 1982; Martin Rojo & Molina, 2017). Stancetaking implies observing how participants evaluate and position themselves in relation to the content of their claims. The criteria adopted for the selection of the sites and our informants consisted in identifying different scenarios drawn by our corresponding research interests. Elisa Hidalgo's research on the BP addresses the impact of streaming on students' learning opportunities as they complete the transition from primary to secondary education. *Promesas*[10] and *El Campamento* school are two sites in which she conducted her fieldwork. As Noelia Fernández's research focuses on hidden privatisation dynamics of schools in Madrid, she selected *Verde* school, a critical case due to its closure as decided by the Regional Education Department.

"Go bilingual or die" in a scenario of parental choice

Villamor and Prieto (2012) highlight how, in the context of parental choice in the region of Madrid, the BP is perceived as: (1) a source of resources; (2) a strategic option to attract middle-class students; and (3) a way to increase student enrolment. Our shared interest in understanding how this rationality is felt at the level of the school motivated our ethnography, which entailed constructing an account of how our informants made sense of their context. Located in contrasting socioeconomic areas, *Promesas* and *Verde* school served as relevant agencies or sites that captured the tensions, contradictions and complexities involved in the coexistence of the BP and other education systems.

Situated in a municipality west of Madrid, a primarily upper-middle-class district, *Promesas* primary school incorporated the BP in the academic year 2007/2008. The school community is conformed mainly by local families. English-medium instruction takes place in approximately one third of the schooling hours in subjects such as history, science and educational art. Emphasis is placed on creating a "bilingual" atmosphere through different curricular and extracurricular activities. As they are called by the Regional Education Department, "native language assistants" facilitate the development of students' conversational skills in real and daily contexts. Moreover, the school launched an exchange programme with a twinned school in an English-speaking country, providing students who are interested in taking part in this programme the opportunity to establish close contact with other English-speaking children and learn about another culture. Elisa Hidalgo interviewed Jorge, the headmaster of the school, and Miriam, the head of studies, in June 2014. In the two extracts below, Jorge and Miriam negotiate the reasons behind the implementation of the BP. Jorge begins the conversation in Extract 1.[11]

Extract 1. "It was also a matter of marketing"

01	Jorge:	here there's / there's a lot of involvement / and it's from the
02		moment in which we launched the BP / that / here the demand for
03		places exceeded the number available I mean I at the beginning
04		when we arrived at the school / not only / I'm convinced that
05		bilingualism / is good because you learn other languages / and
06		also because children develop their intelligence more but well
07	Elisa H.:	hm / yes
08	Jorge:	that's another topic / eh: / I also saw it / a way to secure our jobs
09		because places would never be taken away and indeed after the first
10		year of bilingualism / this school transitioned / from having lost
11		the previous year at least one hundred places of people who went
12		to other schools (()) to / already / covering all its vacancies and to
13		leave on a waiting list with a number of students for example in
14		three years / to be able to have / eh: / two more classrooms and
15		to be the most demanded school in (()) of the state ones / already
16		the first year / I mean I also saw it not only as a matter / but /
17		something I was convinced because of the learning of languages
18		and for other reasons / but also because it was also a matter of
19		marketing / if with bilingualism it simply placing the sign means /
20		that in the environment where we're in / people value it.

Jorge's use of the term "demand" takes us to an economic frame of supply and demand, working thus as a recontextualisation (Fairclough, 1993) by means of which schooling is mainly understood from an economic lens. With respect to this frame, a stance is elicited: the BP increases the demand. However, this stance is not fully consolidated because right after there is a brief evaluative stance "bilingualism is good". The argument that follows is not economic but traditionally hegemonic in the field of education: the intellectual progress of students. Hence, this first intervention (lines 01–06) is an example of intertextuality (Fairclough, 1993; Martín Criado, 2014) that comprises a market logic perspective merged with a more pedagogical argument. In the second intervention (lines 08–20), the terms used by Jorge respond predominantly to an economicist discourse that evokes the neoliberal principle of the law of supply and demand. The key here is the term "secure", which evokes a frame of risk and fluidity: the school needs to survive far from the rotation and security of the state school system found in a previous social democracy order. The use of the noun "waiting list" (line 13) and of numeric terms strengthen this discourse, which is ended by Jorge's mention to "marketing" (line 19), another market principle.

In this vein, Miriam's perspective adds to Jorge's opinion on the positive value and benefits of the BP. Nonetheless, she brings to the forefront an additional viewpoint in the following extract, which takes place right after Jorge's intervention.

Extract 2. "It was also a demand on behalf of the families"

01	Miriam:	yes in fact / when the BP was requested / eh: well / it was requested
02		because / the school wa:s / convinced that it was going to be good
03		/ for our students a:nd for all the educational community for the /
04		for the school also >because of what Jorge was commenting< / but
05		also because / it was a demand of the parents / it was a demand of
06		our students' families / they / <u>wanted</u> that BP.
07	Elisa H.:	right.

Miriam brings forth an evaluative stance: "the BP is good for the school". Elements are added to this parallelistic structure through the organisation of the information ("good for our students and for all the educational community", lines 02–03). Even though she has clearly detected Jorge's stance and shows alignment, her co-positioning with respect to the BP is reframed through the information that is added immediately after: "it was a demand of the parents". In particular, Miriam's use of term "demand" (line 05) places the families as agents in the school's decision to incorporate the BP, rather than as mere outsiders (or consumers). Through the repetition of the phrase "it was a demand" it is inferred (Gumperz, 1982) that these demands are good for the school community and that it is convenient to follow the dictates of the families.

The analysis of Jorge and Miriam's discourses illustrates how the prosperity of *Promesas* school responded to a virtuous cycle that was accomplished by reason of the high student registration numbers in combination with a unified view of the BP as an added value to the school community. On several occasions, both school leaders mentioned to the researcher that parents' satisfaction with the BP was evidenced in their engagement in extracurricular activities such as holiday celebrations (e.g. Halloween, St. Patrick's Day) and musicals in English. Thus, positive partnerships were established between the school and the families due to the shared value of the BP as necessary to "build student skills and feelings of success" (Epstein, 1995: 702). The school administration was also proud of the positive results of a high-stakes English language test[12] students were expected to take at the end of primary. This test is no longer of indicative nature –as had been the case in previous years – and has become the sole benchmark for classifying students into two academic strands in secondary schools that participate in the BP.

By contrast, a vicious cycle could follow, as evidenced in the case of *Verde*, a secondary school located in a middle-class area in the western part of the city of Madrid. The school was closed in 2017 by decision of the Regional Educational Department, arguing as the main reason a progressive reduction in the number of students. The year before its closure, 290 students attended the school, a considerable percentage of which were of migrant origin – mainly from Latin America – as well as Roma minority students. *Verde* had offered a special education programme targeting 5 students with autism. This programme experienced some success inasmuch as it followed an inclusive model that favoured learning and autonomy in special education students, who attended mainstream classrooms whilst receiving individualised support. During the academic year 2016–2017, there was an open conflict between the headmaster, who supported the school closure, and those who were opposed to this finale, mainly students and families who believed that *Verde* school was necessary for the school community due to several reasons. In their view, fewer student enrolment numbers benefitted the students, who received more one-on-one attention and support. The surrounding schools were gradually becoming overcrowded due to the popularity of the programmes – the BP being one of them – and families at *Verde* were convinced that their school was a good option for their children. Moreover, parents perceived that, far from losing students, the enrolment numbers at *Verde* had remained stable in recent years. In June 2017, Noelia Fernández interviewed three teachers and the counsellor during the dismantling process. Extracts 3 and 4 belong to interviews with Carmen and Juan, both teachers. In extract 3, Carmen shares her view on the reasons that led the school to its closure.

Extract 3. "A Roma student can't be bilingual"

01	Noelia F.:	how many times did you apply for the BP?
02	Carmen:	<u>three times</u>
03	Noelia F.:	three times
04	Carmen:	in thr:ee / in three successive calls for projects / we applied for the
05		BP / and never was granted
06	Noelia F.:	when was the first / a:nd the last time?
07	Carmen:	well / the first time might be five or six years ago / something like
08		that // and the last time last year / and also rejected // the school
09		head / since I arrived here there's been the same headmaster / right?
10		// an o:ld man / a:nd well / he has retired quite o:ld and so on / but
11		about that point he was clear / he was clear that either they gave
12		us the BP / o:r / o:r we weren't going to <u>survive</u> / becau:se because
13		the children were going to leave / and most importantly / why do
14		children leave? / because this becomes a ghetto / see / a Roma student
15		can't be bilingual / they have no family structure to be bilingual / and
16		neither does a migrant student / so we end up with the students who
17		aren't bilingual / all together in the same place / forming a ghetto / so
18		the "<u>normal</u>" (makes a gesture of quotation marks with her hands)
19		student / normalised in quotation marks / their parents no longer
20		bring their children to that place because look you're going to be
21		surrounded by migrants by Roma students >and this and that< and
22		conflictive people // do you follow me? // so it's the fish that bites
23		its own tail / there isn't any way of getting: out of that loop // so
24		that's all / in the e:nd, we knew thi:s this situation had little time /
25		we knew it had little time / <u>we thought</u> / we all thought that ((*name
26		of another school)) was going to be closed first // because it had less
27		students than this one.

In this extract, Carmen situates the school in the same frame, in this case of subsistence ("survive", line 12), and it is conveyed that an injustice has been done. Emphasis on the phrase "three times" (line 02) allows us to infer that, even though the proposal to go bilingual was turned down, an effort was made. In addition, there is an example of intertextuality (Fairclough, 1993) in Carmen's formulation of the question "why do children leave?" (lines 13–14) that seems to evoke a dominant discourse in the school district area or among the students' families which rejects the presence of ethnic minorities. The prejudice that bilingualism is not for Roma or migrants is expressed, however, in an attenuated way by referring to the family structure (line 15). The mitigated evoking of prejudices requires the interviewee to confirm that the researcher is following this attenuated argument "do you follow me?", in line 22. For Carmen, the social composition of *Verde* school did not favour bilingualism, and in the opposite direction, bilingualism was not what their students needed. Therefore, it was the social composition of the school, in Carmen's view, that led to its closure.

Following this same logic, Juan, a teacher who spent one year at *Verde*, points to the competition with other schools in extract 4.

Extract 4. "Competition makes giants and kills the others"

01	Noelia F.:	why does this school have so few students?
02	Juan:	in the end it turns out to be like this doesn't it? / when you gain
03		the reputation of a special education school o:r the school where
04		it's easy to pass / that serves all types of needs / the:n this is
05		avoided / attendance is avoided / and also I think tha:t all this
06		is a bigger problem / after all / when every school has been able
07		to open more classes depending each year depending on their
08		enrolment petitions state schools have been led to compete
09		among them / and making state schools compete implies that
10		you begin to generate giants / while you kill those close to them
11		and here we have / we're surrounded by three secondary schools
12		that are becoming giants step by step / that they're being granted
13		programmes while we're not / we have a technology high school
14		here next to us where each student has a computer here we don't
15		even have a computer per classroom / I understand that parents
16		don't enrol here / we're surrounded by bilingual schools / here,
17		we applied and it was rejected / so / I don't know / this school
18		hasn't been granted any programme / or project it had applied for
19		/ and we're also surrounded by charter schools.

In this fragment, Juan's stance "state schools have been led to compete …" (line 08) refers to the neoliberal principle of competition that rules the state education system today. This stance is mitigated through the use of impersonalisation in the form of passive structures and the choice of the impersonal "you". The metaphors of war (to be surrounded, kill) and the repetition of the term "giants" (lines 10, 12) indicate that this competition does not take place under conditions of equity by reason of the existing asymmetries between schools with a large student population and minoritised schools. By evoking the discourse of the parents, whom Juan sympathises with ("I understand that parents don't enrol here", lines 15, 16), he does not seem to question the law of supply and demand but rather the existing conditions of inequality taking place this competence scenario takes place.

Albeit the sharply contrasting situation of both schools, from these interviews we are able to interpret how, in the context of parental choice in Madrid, the BP is perceived by our interviewees as one of the most attractive project schools can engage with. Our informants have highlighted the need for schools to invest a larger effort in fabricating a good reputation for themselves, paying much more attention to marketing strategies (Ball, 2003) to survive. As each administrative unit is considered autonomous, it must improve its own performance to justify its existence (Laval & Dardot, 2009/ 2013). In an affluent school such as *Promesas*, the request for the BP was shared by the school leadership team in alliance with the families and was a guarantee of success. Under these circumstances, language education fosters community partnerships and enhances learning. Inversely, the closing of *Verde* responded to a combination of factors: a growing adverse reputation of the school, the competition of nearby schools and the declined petition on behalf of the Local Administration to grant the school the BP. For Carmen and Juan, the school closure was part of a chain of interwoven elements alongside the competition generated by the surrounding schools taking part in popular programmes such as the BP or technology programmes. Here, both teachers draw on the inequality consequences that we also address in the following section.

English as a mediator of inequality in schools

The conditions that have been highlighted in the above section signal the introduction of the neoliberal principle of competition in the state school system, generating market dynamics that do not take place under conditions of equity, as our interviewees have described. The case of *El Campamento* bilingual secondary school shows how students were streamed into two academic strands – Bilingual Section and Bilingual Programme – which we will call High- and Low-Exposure, respectively. The former strand offers a higher number of content subjects taught through English-medium instruction (at least one third of the school time) in addition to 5 weekly hours of English, which is taught in the so-called "Advanced English Curriculum". The Low-Exposure strand comprises fewer hours of content instruction in English in addition to 5 weekly hours of English (Regional Education Department, 2017: 103). Placement in these strands is determined by the results of the high-stakes English language test at the end of primary, as mentioned in the previous section. Furthermore, students attending the Low-Exposure strand are also placed in different classrooms according to their English language abilities. Elisa Hidalgo interviewed two teachers at the school in order to address the impact of introducing bilingual strands on existing programmes (and hence, students). For over 25 years, *El Campamento* school has been acclaimed for promoting inclusive programmes. In previous years, the implementation of several educational initiatives included a "Welcoming Programme" for migrant students (see Martín Rojo & Alcalá, 2010; Mijares & Relaño Pastor, 2011) and compensatory classrooms targeting underachieving students. To this day, the school also offers a bus service to and from remote areas to provide schooling to migrant and ethnic minority students. The school had also taken part in a bilingual project that followed a Spanish-British curriculum.

Shortly after the BP was introduced at the school, the "Welcoming Programme" was removed and existing compensatory classrooms suffered budget cuts. Pedro, a teacher of Science in the Low-Exposure strand, argued that the allocation of the school's economic resources benefited High-Exposure students at the expense of some of his Low-Exposure groups. Laboratories had been dismissed and bus services had reduced their activity for students living in remote locations, who had no other means of transportation. The needs of underachieving students lost priority due a progressive lack of investment in professional teaching staff specialised in literacy development. According to Pedro, more social workers were needed to facilitate integration of ethnic and minority students. In his view, the overall implementation of different bilingual strands had an adverse effect on the academic achievement of these students. This perspective is developed by Pedro in the following extract.

Extract 5: "It makes you a bit angry … that resources are transferred on one side."

01	Pedro:	one thing that's ve:ry / very simple for example here there are
02		students who come from ((*name of deprived area)) en / en route
03		/ by bus // a:nd / and the bus picks them up at half past two / it
04		turns out that here we have class / on Mondays and Wednesdays
05		until / half past three / then these kids / since they live in ((*name
06		of deprived area)) / and if the bus doesn't pick them up then they
07		can't be picked up // well they miss / the seventh class on Mondays
08		and the seventh class on / Wednesdays / [a:nd]
09	Elisa H.:	[aha]
10	Pedro	for example I: / i-in this case: / I am the tutor of year 10 well I had
11		/ eh: / my groups had physics and chemistry class on Mondays
12		during the seventh class / a:nd physics and chemistry / on-only
13		take place two hours a week (.) which means that (.) a kid / who
14		comes from ((*name of deprived area))
15	Elisa H.:	[hmhm]
16	Pedro:	[only] (.) has taken fifty percent of the classes that correspond to
17		that subject / with music the same thing happened cause / music
18		also was two hours / it was taught on Wednesdays / then / well
19		maybe / being able to hire the buses that can come an hour later
20		/ well maybe / in schools where we have the seventh class [that]
21	Elisa H.:	[yes:]

22	Pedro:	well maybe it's no:t as costly but / the possibilities of students who
23		are also in social disadvantage are being undermined because they
24		come for far away / because they come from mo:re deprived areas
25	Elisa H.:	yes
26	Pedro:	then, it makes you a bit angry well that there could be: / that
27		resources are transferred on [one side] (to the High-Exposure strand)
28	Elisa H.:	[right]
29	Pedro:	and that sometimes / you see things like this right?
30	Elisa H.:	right / hmhm

Here, Pedro conveys the following stance: the allocation of economic resources at the school is detrimental to some of his Low-Exposure groups and, in particular, to students who live in deprived areas (line 24). This stance is elaborated through the anecdotal example that is provided, wherein Pedro describes the consequences of the lack of additional bus services for these students, who are not able to attend certain subjects. Pedro's affective statement "it makes you a bit angry" (line 26) outlines what has been said previously with respect to the unequal distribution of these resources, which is construed as favouring the segment of students who attend the High-Exposure strand ("are transferred on one side", line 27).

These considerations evidence the existing tensions with respect to the learning expectations of High- and Low-Exposure students. English proficiency confers High-Exposure students the status and distinction of the BP, legitimised by having passed the high-stakes English language test. Carlos, a teacher of Science in the High-Exposure strand, mentioned the additional demands tied to this subject by reason of the language of instruction, as Science is taught through English in the High-Exposure strand. That same year, Carlos had visited Germany with his High-Exposure group in year 11 as part of a mobility program organised by the school. He portrayed his High-Exposure students as remarkably responsible and highly engaged in the classroom activities. Moreover, he stressed the role played by the families of his students. In the following extract, Carlos refers to involvement of the families.

Extract 6: "I believe that there's a family standing behind."

01	Carlos:	the High-Exposure groups are much more / eh / they perform much
02		better [academically]
03	Elisa H:	[°hmhm°]
04	Carlos:	and obtain better results
05	Elisa H.:	okay: / a:nd=
06	Carlos:	=ah sorry (.) can I respond to [words]
07	Elisa H:	[yes yes yes] (.) pl- / ease
08	Carlos:	I believe that this situation / apart fro:m / apart from inner motivation /
09		which I also think is a bit created / it's created / by the family / to
10		the kid / eh: is that / I believe tha:t there's a family standing behind
11	Elisa H.:	hmhm

12	Carlos:	I mean I think this is because there's a family standing behind /
13		who: / who worries / about the student / and I also have to say /
14		tha:t / many of these students are lucky to be able to count / I su-
15		ppose / with a private teacher at home / in the High-Exposure I've
16		been able to see in these five-four years four years °of° / five years
17		>already in the BP<, / five years in the BP that / tha:t / that many
18		students have a private teacher at home / even / I have in my year 9
19		A group a student this year who scores all A's / all A's / wonderful /
20	Elisa H:	and I found out that he had a private teacher at home
21	Carlos:	hmhm
22		this kid is one of the advanced ones I mean tha:t / in year 11 he'll
23		take the *Advanced* (standardised English test) cause in year 9
24		students t-this year he took the *First* (standardised English) exam
25	Elisa H:	a:ha
26	Carlos:	bu:t a:nd well you mark an exam and you can't even if you act in
27		bad faith you can't °can't° correct anything because it's perfect and
28		(words)
29	Elisa H:	hmhm
30	Carlos:	°amazing° / but he has a private teacher / of English at home
31	Elisa H.:	a:ha

Carlos places his High-Exposure students on a comparative scale with respect to other groups ("perform much better", lines 01–02; "obtain better results", line 04) and assigns the responsibility for their academic and linguistic performance – and, to some extent, for their motivation – on the families and on their economy. Here, a stance is elicited: High-Exposure students have family support. The repetition of the structure "a family standing behind" (lines 10, 12) is used by Carlos to convey his stance to the researcher. The representation of these students as the "better achieving ones" is carried out by referring to the performance of a year 9 student ("amazing", line 30). Whilst this information is being shared, the student's performance is located in the frame of the family and their finance, which justify his academic success. By referring to this particular case, the point made by Carlos is that many High-Exposure students receive extracurricular support classes at home to improve their English (lines 17–18).

From these interviews we can witness how language plays a predominant role in regulating and legitimising political and economic spaces (Duchêne & Heller, 2012: 3). Linguistic value hierarchies consolidate the advantage of High-Exposure students by investing in the strands that are most likely to secure their access to symbolic capital. From the representations of these students as the "high achievers", particular categories are used in the understanding of their performance – for example, in terms of "their level of achievement set by standardised tests" (Martín Rojo, 2017: 560). Moreover, a close relationship is established with the ideal bilingual student model promoted by language education policies, linked to cosmopolitan views of language learning, travel and success. In this context, the value of academic hierarchies enables the academic institution to attract middle-class students and their families and language examinations become the "hidden criteria" (Bourdieu & Passeron, 1977: 154) for selecting these students. The opposition between those who "pass" and those who "fail" delineates the course of action in which disciplinary power is "rationalised" (Lemke, 2001: 191; see Martín Rojo, 2017). These dynamics sustain processes of "capitalisation" and "decapitalisation" (Martín Rojo, 2010) among students, which may impact their academic trajectories.

Discussion and conclusions

The context of Madrid serves as fruitful niche for understanding the interplay between parental choice policies and bilingual education as paradigm of a neoliberal rationality. English is presented as an indispensable skill and is equated with certain forms of "academic capital" (see Block, 2014) that will in turn grant access to social and material gain in a global competitive job market. In the Madrid region, we can observe a novelty in the ways these mechanisms of power are exercised as part of a neoliberal agenda: the introduction of a market logic in the educational terrain is carried out through particular techniques of governmentality – individual and market freedom – that champion a competitive model in schools. Language education discourses present the BP as the means to students "self-capitalisation" under the illusion of freedom of choice. These dynamics heighten inequality by strengthening "institutional processes of selection, streaming and competition" (Pérez-Milans, 2013: 88). The recounts of teachers and school leaders at *Verde*, *Promesas* and *El Campamento* school address how resources in specific locations have been allocated to the BP, and the hierarchisation processes taking place among schools and students under linguistic categories such as "bilingual".

Our study contributes to the discussion about the social and political impact of new educational programmes in a global era of neoliberalism. In this direction, Block (2014) raises awareness of the fact that the intersection between bi/multilingualism, social class and inequality needs to be critically examined for its social implications.

> As regards to the study of L1 + English bi/multilingualism, there is the need to consider not only how access to English is variable and this variability indexes class positions in society, but also how the acquisition of English language competence, usually by individuals who already possess a great deal of economic, cultural and social capital, serves to strengthen the dominant positions of the powerful in societies.
>
> (Block, 2014: 143)

Taking this passage as a starting point, we can consider how inequality and power relations introduced by parental choice and bilingual education policies are negotiated, resisted or challenged. Against this inescapable educational trend, several grass-roots movements involving mainly teachers are making efforts to counter privatisation processes in education. The association *Acción Educativa* has been developing a document to raise awareness on behalf of stakeholders of the disparity in academic performance between groups of students along with the unbalanced access to educational opportunities resulting from bilingual education policies. *Marea Verde Madrid*, a platform of collective action against austerity policies in education, brings attention to the segregating consequences of introducing a single district policy in schools. Efforts to create more inclusive and learning environments have also been sought by some schools. As part of the fieldwork conducted by Elisa Hidalgo for the TRANS-CLIL project, one bilingual secondary school has made efforts to mitigate the adverse effects of streaming students in secondary by merging High- and Low-Exposure students in the same content classrooms, thus supporting integration.

While these initiatives are for the most part small-scale, they outline a "politics of location" (hooks, 1989) that opens the door to reflection on the political and social implications of a "global consciousness" (Robertson, 1992). Inspired by the postcolonial scholar Canagarajah and his work Resisting Linguistic Imperialism in English Teaching (1999), we believe that a necessary step forward is not to be "paralyzed by dichotomising perspectives that frame debates around English" (Norton & Kamal, 2003: 310) that overstate the rigid nature of power structures – and hence, arguing in favour and against English – but rather to adopt a "resistance perspective" (Canagarajah) that allows us to think critically about the options available in search for political and ideological alternatives "for personal and collective empowerment" (Canagarajah, 1999: 173). As paths to democratising English, classroom pedagogical practices are no less important. Research carried out in the area of Content and Language Integrated Learning (CLIL) has moved in the direction of incorporating approaches that support content and language learning for all learners in order to promote greater inclusivity (Llinares, Morton & Whittaker, 2012; Llinares, 2015). These are some considerations for future research and action.

Key to transcriptions

/	short pause (0.5 seconds)
//	long pause (0.5–1.5 seconds)
(n")	n seconds pause
<u>word</u>	emphasis on a word or phrase
wo:rd	lengthening of the preceding sound
WORD	talk is louder than that surrounding it
°word°	talk is softer than that surrounding it
>word<	speeding up. This part of speech (one or more words) is produced faster

<word>	slowing down. This part of speech (one or more words)
[ ]	turn overlapping with similarly marked turn
{xxx}	researcher's comments (like laughing etc.)
=	latched utterances
(( ))	non-understandable fragment
((*))	name of school/area

Notes

1 This work is supported by the research Project "TRANS-CLIL: "Integrating and Assessing Content and Language in the Transition from Primary to Secondary Bilingual Education" (Ref. FFI2014-55590-R) funded by the Spanish Ministry of Economy, Science and Competitiveness and the research project "Calidad de la Educación en Iberoamérica: Discursos, políticas y prácticas" (CEAL-AL/2017-12), funded by Universidad Autónoma de Madrid-Santander. This article has also benefitted from academic exchanges conducted within the ISCH COST action IS1306 "New Speakers in a Multilingual Europe: Opportunities and Challenges". We also thank Luisa Martín Rojo and Alfonso del Percio, editors, as well as the reviewers of this volume for their excellent comments and suggestions.

2 We use the term "charter school' (in Spanish, "escuela concertada') to refer to private schools that are financed by the state. In the context of Spain, approximately 30% of students attend to these schools, which are predominantly Catholic.

3 All the participants received a detailed information sheet about the purposes of the research and signed a written consent form.

4 The Common European Framework of Reference for Languages classifies language proficiency in six levels, A2 being one of them.

5 Prior to the introduction of parental choice in 2013, Madrid was divided into school districts and families were able to choose any school within their corresponding zone.

6 From the moment the BP was first launched, it has been optional for schools, and the formula to introduce it has been through a call for projects. This means that the schools interested in taking part in the BP have to elaborate a proposal (e.g. fulfilling certain requirements such as having an adequate number of authorised teaching staff) and apply to become bilingual.

7 In 2017/18, the number of state schools that incorporated the BP in their school offer reached 515 (365 state primary and 150 state secondary).

8 This has been the slogan adopted by the Madrid Region: www.madrid.org/bvirtual/BVCM016309.pdf https://comunidadbilingue.educa2.madrid.org/

9 The Lisbon strategy is the economic agenda adopted by the European Union in 2000 to face the scenario of the global economy.

10 All names of schools and participants are pseudonyms.

11 All interviews were carried out in Spanish and these extracts were translated by the authors for the purposes of the chapter.

12 Access to the Bilingual Section or High-Exposure strand is only granted to students who meet a required level of English proficiency. Students attending a bilingual primary school take a standardised English language test at the end of primary. This test is delivered by an external evaluation institution in charge of issuing certificates that have European validity and recognition.

References

Alegre, M. Á. (2010). Casi-mercados, segregación escolar y desigualdad educativa: una trilogía con final abierto. *Educação & Sociedade*, 31(113), 1157–1178.

Ball, S. J. (2003). The teacher's soul and the terrors of performativity. *Journal of Education Policy*, 18(2), 215–228.

Ball, S. J., & Youdell, D. (2007). *Hidden privatisation in public education*. Brussels: Education International. Retrieved from: www.ei-ie.org/media_gallery/2009-00034-01-E.pdf

Block, D. (2002). Destabilized identities across language and cuptural borders: Japanese and Taiwanese experiences. *Hong Kong Journal of Applied Linguistics*, 7(2), 1–19.

Block, D. (2011). Citizenship, education and global spaces. *Language and Intercultural Communication*, 11(2), 161–169.

Block, D. (2014). *Social class in applied linguistics*. New York: Routledge.

Block, D., Gray, J., & Holborow, M. (2012). *Neoliberalism and applied linguistics*. London: Routledge.

Bourdieu, P., & Passeron, J.-C. (1977). *Reproduction in education, society and culture*. London: Sage.

Bowles, S., & Gintis, H. (1976). *Schooling in capitalist America: Educational reform and the contradictions of economic life*. New York: Basic Books.

Brown, W. (2015/2016). *El pueblo sin atributos*. Barcelona: Malpaso.

Cambridge Tests. (2018). Consejería de Educación e Investigación. Comunidad de Madrid. Retrieved from: www.educa2.madrid.org/web/bilinguismo2/examenes-cambridge

Canagarajah, S. (1999). *Resisting linguistic imperialism in English teaching*. Oxford: Oxford University Press.

Du Bois, J. W. (2007). The stance triangle. In R. Englebretson (Ed.), *Stancetaking in discourse: Subjectivity, evaluation, interaction* (pp. 139–182). Amsterdam: John Benjamins.

Duchêne, A., & Heller, M. (2012). Pride and profit: Changing discourses of language, capital and nation-state. In A. Duchêne & M. Heller (Eds.), *Language in late capitalism: Pride and profit*. New York: Routledge.

Epstein, J. L. (1995). School-family-community partnerships: Caring for the children we share. *Phi Delta Kappan*, 76(9), 701–712.

Fairclough, N. (1993). Critical discourse analysis and the marketization of public discourse: The universities. *Discourse Society*, 4(2), 133–168.

Fairclough, N. (1995). *Critical discourse analysis. The critical study of language*. New York: Longman.

Fairclough, N. (2000). Representaciones del cambio en el discurso neoliberal. *Cuaderno de Relaciones Laborales*, 16, 13–35.

Flubacher, M.-C., & Del Percio, A. (2017). Language, education and neoliberalism. In M. Flubacher & A. Del Percio (Eds.), *Language, education and neoliberalism: Critical studies in sociolinguistics* (pp. 1–18). Bristol: Multilingual Matters.

Foucault, M. (2008). *The birth of biopolitics*. New York: Palgrave Macmillan.

Friedman, M. (1962). *Capitalism and freedom*. Chicago: University of Chicago Press.

Friedman, M., & Friedman, R. (1980). *Free to choose*. 1st ed. London: Secker & Warburg.

Gumperz, J. J. (1982). *Discourse strategies*. Cambridge: Cambridge University Press.

Heller, M. (2008). Why do ethnographies of bilingualism? In L. Wei & M. G. Moyer (Eds.), *The Blackwell guide to research methods in bilingualism and multilingualism* (pp. 249–263). Malden, MA: Blackwell.

Holborow, M. (2015). *Language and neoliberalism*. London: Routledge.

hooks, b. (1989). *Talking black: Thinking feminist, thinking black*. Boston: South End Press.

Jessop, B. (2008). A cultural political economy of competitiveness and its implications for higher education. In B. Jesson, N. Fairclough, & R. Wodak (Eds.), *Education and the knowledge based economy in Europe* (pp. 13–40). Rotterdam: Sense Publisher.

Jódar, F., & Gómez, L. (2007). Educación posdisciplinaria, formación de nuevas subjetividades y gubernamentalidad. Herramientas conceptuales para un análisis del presente. *Revista Mexicana de Investigación educativa, 12*(32), 381–404.

Laclau, E., & Mouffe, C. (1985/2001). *Hegemonía y estrategia socialista*. Madrid: Siglo XXI.

Laval, C., & Dardot, P. (2009/2013). *La nueva razón del mundo*. Barcelona: Gedisa.

Lemke, T. (2001). The birth of bio-politics: Michael Foucault's lectures at the College de France on neo-liberal governmentality. *Economy and Society, 30*(2), 190–207.

Llinares, A. (2015). Integration in CLIL: A proposal to inform research and successful pedagogy. *Language, Culture and Curriculum, 28*(1), 58–73.

Llinares, A., Morton, T., & Whittaker, R. (2012) *The roles of language in CLIL*. Cambridge: Cambridge University Press.

Macedo, D., Dendrinos, B., & Gounari, P. (2003). *The hegemony of English*. Boulder, CO: Paradigm.

Maroy, C. (2008). ¿Por qué y cómo regular el mercado educativo? *Profesorado. Revista de Currículum y Formación de Profesorado, 12*(2), 1–11.

Martín Criado, E. (2014). Mentiras, inconsistencias y ambivalencias. Teoría de la acción y análisis del discurso. *Revista Internacional de Sociología, 72*(1), 115–138.

Martín Rojo, L. (2010) *Constructing inequality in multilingual classrooms*. Berlin: Mouton de Gruyter.

Martín Rojo, L. (2013). (De)capitalising students through linguistic practices. A comparative analyses of new educational programmes in a global era. In A. Duchêne, M. G. Moyer, & C. Roberts (Eds.), *Language, migration and social (in)equality: A critical sociolinguistic perspective on institutions and work* (pp. 118–146). Bristol: Multilingual Matters.

Martín Rojo, L. (2017). Neoliberalism and linguistic governmentality. In J. W. Tollefson and M. Pérez-Milans (Eds.), *Oxford handbook of language policy and planning* (pp. 544–567). Oxford: Oxford University Press.

Martín Rojo, L., & Alcalá, E. (2010, September). *Building migrant identities in interactional practices*. Paper presented at Sociolinguistics Symposium 18, Southampton.

Martín Rojo, L., & Molina, C. (2017). Cosmopolitican stance negotiation in multicultural academic setting. Journal of Sociolinguistics, 21(5), 672–695.

Merchán, F. J. (2012). La introducción en España de la política basada en la gestión empresarial de la escuela: El caso de Andalucía. *Education Policy Analysis. Archives/Archivos Analíticos de Políticas Educativas, 20*(32), 1–24.

Mijares, L., & Relaño Pastor, A. M. (2011). Language programs at Villababel High: Rethinking ideologies of social inclusión. *International Journal of Bilingual Education and Bilingualism, 14*(4), 427–442.

Norton, B., & Kamal, F. (2003). The imagined communities of English language learners in a Pakistani school. *Journal of Language, Identity, and Education, 2*(4), 301–317.

Pérez-Milans, M. (2013). Urban schools and English language education in Late Modern China. New York: Routledge.

Pérez-Milans, M., & Patiño Santos, A. (2014). Language education and institutional change in a Madrid multilingual school. *International Journal of Multilingualism, 11*(4), 449–470.

Polanyi, K. (1957/2016). *The great transformation.* Boston: Beacon Press.

Prieto, M., & Villamor, P. (2012). Libertad de elección, competencia y calidad: las políticas educativas de la Comunidad de Madrid. *Profesorado, 16*(3), 127–144.

Prieto, M., & Villamor, P. (2016). Reformas hacia la privatización de la educación en la Comunidad de Madrid. *Revista de la Asociación de Sociología de la Educación, 9*(2), 265–276.

Relaño Pastor, A. M. (2015). The commodification of English in "Madrid, comunidad bilingüe": Insights from the CLIL classroom. *Language Policy, 14*(2), 131–152.

Rizvi, F., & Lingard, B. (2010/2013). *Políticas educativas en un mundo globalizado.* Madrid: Morata.

Robertson, R. (1992). *Globalization. Social theory and global culture.* London: Sage.

Shore, C., & Wright, S. (2015). Governing by numbers: Audit culture, rankings and the New World Order. *Social Anthropology, 23*(1), 22–28.

Strathern, M. (2000). *Audit cultures: Anthropological studies in accountability, ethics and the academy.* London: Routledge.

Urciuoli, B. (2008). Skills and selves in the new workplace. *American Ethnologist, 35*(2), 211–228.

Wilkins, A. (2015). Professionalizing school governance: The disciplinary effects of school autonomy and inspection on the changing role of school governors. *Journal of Education Policy, 30*(2), 182–200.

Legislative sources and documents

European Commission (n.d.). About Multilingualism Policy. Retrieved from: http://ec.europa.eu/education/policies/multilingualism/about-multilingualism-policy_en

Regional Education Department (2004). Orden 796/2004, de 5 de marzo, de la Consejería de Educación, para la selección de colegios públicos de Educación Infantil y Primaria de la Comunidad de Madrid en los que se llevará a cabo la implementación de la enseñanza bilingüe español-inglés. *Boletín Oficial de la Comunidad de Madrid, 58*, 12–18. Retrieved from: http://w3.bocm.es/boletin/CM_Boletin_BOCM/20040309_B/05800.PDF

Regional Education Department (2010). Orden 5958/2010, de 7 de diciembre, de la Consejería de Educación, por la que se regulan los colegios públicos bilingües de la Comunidad de Madrid. *Boletín Oficial de la Comunidad de Madrid, 17*, 36–66. Retrieved from: http://w3.bocm.es/boletin/CM_Boletin_BOCM/2011/01/21/01700.PDF

Regional Education Department (2013). Decreto 29/2013, de 11 de abril, del Consejo de Gobierno, de libertad de elección de centro escolar en la Comunidad de Madrid. *Boletín Oficial de la Comunidad de Madrid, 86,* 13–21. Retrieved from: www. bocm.es/boletin/CM_Orden_BOCM/2013/04/12/BOCM-20130412-1.PDF

Regional Education Department (2016). Orden 4071/2016, de 28 de diciembre, de la Consejería de Educación, Juventud y Deporte, para la selección de Colegios Públicos de Educación Infantil y Primaria de la Comunidad de Madrid en los que se llevará a cabo la implantación de la enseñanza bilingüe español-inglés en Educación Primaria en el curso 2017–2018. *Boletín Oficial de la Comunidad de Madrid, 1,* 80–92. Retrieved from: www.bocm.es/boletin/CM_Orden_BOCM/2017/01/02/BOCM-20170102-16.PDF

Regional Education Department (2017). Orden 972/2017, de 7 de abril, de la Educación, Juventud y Deporte, por la que se regulan los institutos bilingües español-inglés de la Comunidad de Madrid. *Boletín Oficial de la Comunidad de Madrid, 99,* 102–108. Retrieved from: http://w3.bocm.es/boletin/CM_Orden_BOCM/2017/04/27/BOCM-20170427-11.PDF

5 Leadership communication "skills" and undergraduate neoliberal subjectivity

Bonnie Urciuoli

Introduction

In this chapter, I consider how leadership communication skills are presented to US liberal arts[1] undergraduate students as important for their future. Such skills are heavily promoted in workshops and similar venues, yet workshop guidelines focus more on what such skills accomplish than on how to do them. Nor do students appear to use them except in workshop-type venues. Nor do students seem to internalize the neoliberal subjectivity that inform such skills. Given this volume's theme, the effect of linguistic conduct on subjectivity under neoliberalism, I ask why this inculcation gets so little traction and why, if students internalize neither skills nor their attendant neoliberal subjectivity so prized by the corporate world students will soon enter, it is so important for students to be presented as if they do.

To show how communication skills are imagined as a neoliberal way of speaking, I compare the imagining of leadership communication skills and their users with the imagining of named standardized languages (glottonyms) and their users. I suggest that they parallel as culturally imagined ways of speaking linked to types of social actors. I also suggest that the comparison breaks down because prevalent notions of leadership communication skills emphasize managing outcomes more than specific discursive formats, indicating that "communication skills" exist not as forms but as interactive techniques. To show what students are meant to internalize, I examine a range of paracurricular (Handler, 2008, 2018) leadership training programs, existing outside the academic curriculum. Some are developed by colleges and universities, one is sponsored by the Posse Foundation which partners with colleges and universities that provide scholarships for racially diverse students recruited as future leaders and change-bringers, and one is sponsored by Ashoka U, which partners with colleges and universities to provide fellowships for students to foster social innovation. All these programs displace specific academic content and faculty expertise (Handler, 2018) with generalized communication skills training meant to enhance and standardize students' value as human capital. Finally, drawing from websites, reports, instructional materials, interviews, and a published ethnographic account, I discuss Posse mentoring sessions and a student's report of an Ashoka U social innovation conference to show how students are assumed to perform those "skills", and I address why students generally internalize neither the skills nor their attendant subjectivity.

Dardot and Laval (2014) argue that neoliberalism is productively understood as a rationality of contemporary capitalism and as a governmental rationality in Foucault's sense, integrating techniques of domination over others with those of self. They argue that when market logic becomes a generalized social norm, all institutions play their distinct role in the neoliberal colonizing of social participation and thus of subjectivity. US undergraduate education and the corporate world play conjoined roles by recasting knowledge as hard skills (forms of knowledge with job market value), and social participation as soft skills (forms of sociality with job market value), and students are particularly urged to acquire the "soft skills" of leadership, social innovation, and communication. Corporate-oriented workshops on team and leadership – especially transformational leadership (bringing change to workplaces and workers) – are designed to inculcate these skills. Colleges and universities incorporate similar workshops into paracurricular learning programs described on websites like those examined in the third section of this chapter. Posse incorporates similar training into its mentoring sessions and Ashoka U into its social innovation conference, examined in the fourth section.

Discourses about such skills constitute a folk construction, explained below as a pseudo-register, a way of speaking to which students should aspire. Students give lip service to messages about leadership and transformation but perform those values unevenly. Texts and workshops outline techniques for students to practice but, as is routine for paracurricular programs, specific direction and supervision is left up to administrators or overloaded faculty who are usually little trained in these techniques. Students enact these "skills" in situations where their performance is not assessed. Moreover, while Posse and Ashoka websites seem to imply that students automatically internalize neoliberal values through Posse's mentoring sessions and Ashoka U's conferences and fellowship projects, there is little evidence that students do and more evidence that they do not. What seems most clear is that the image of students doing so matters to organizational and institutional brands.

Since I argue throughout this chapter that students are not actually instructed in formal language techniques, one might ask how "communication skills" are conflated with "language skills". The answer is, communication is consistently conflated with talk, and talk with language. And like referential models of language, Human Communication courses and texts present models of ordinary talk that heavily privilege information transmission and task accomplishment over social uses (Urciuoli, 2008). Such models are the basis for the products of the communication industry which Cameron (2000) characterizes as codifications of techniques for talk, a project with a long history and multiple social and economic roots resulting in the expert-certified production of communication "skills sets" in contemporary enterprise culture. Communication skills thus become the neoliberal workplace model of disciplined and productive ways of speaking, even if the texts that teach that discipline have little linguistic detail.

Producing linguistic forms and engaging in discourse are distinct modes of knowledge, but that distinction fades when both are considered neoliberally instrumental. What makes "knowing a language" and "speaking" equally neoliberal is part of a larger problem of how any knowledge or practice should map how one should be in the world. Forms of knowledge and social practices become neoliberalized when they are imagined as a valued part of oneself as human capital because they maximize one's own market potential or give one's organization a market edge. When people imagine themselves in terms of their capacity to bring value to an organization, whatever they know or do can become neoliberalized. A growing literature shows how named languages can take on neoliberal value; see, for example, Duchêne and Heller (2012) for a general overview on language and neoliberalism, and Flubacher and Del Percio (2017) on language, education and neoliberalism. Knowing a language becomes a value-bringing skill when possessed by an individual, not a group, and used to create a market edge. If knowing a language is a skill, it can be acquired and assessed. Gershon (2017) uses these principles as the basis for her notion of neoliberal agency in which individuals, imagining themselves as bundles of such skills which they are supposed to continually improve, are expected to run themselves like businesses; in this model, failure is an individual shortcoming (lack of flexibility, inadequate skills), not a structural dynamic (certainly not a fault of the larger organization).

Neoliberal agency illustrates Foucault's (1988 and elsewhere) principle that social power is exercised as much through the self as through any other social agency. Martín Rojo (2016) argues that given the Foucauldian dissemination of power through networks of social relations such that its manifestation is not decisive at any one point, it is important for sociolinguists to trace the processes and mechanisms through which this dissemination takes place. Doing so illustrates how semiotic resources remain unequally distributed through discourse formations that institutions reinforce as normative, a power-maintenance technique. Tracing those processes can also demonstrate how communicative practices can tune out structural inequalities (see chapters in this volume by Hidalgo & Fernández, Flores, Martín Rojo, and Pujolar) by showing the technologies of expertise and power maintaining such dynamics while regulating actors' conduct (i.e. governmentality) intertwined with their sense of themselves as subjects (subjectivization). The maintenance of dominant orders is thus reproduced in real time by actors continually internalizing principles of governmentality.[2]

Neoliberal governmentality implies that actors recognize their subjectivity *as workers*, having internalized the idea that their success relies on their capacities to marketize themselves. The value of skills is not decided solely by those "possessing" skills, which is why the concept of *worker* is so salient here. Workers' skills gain value because workers belong to a larger organization which determines the value of their skills (or for the self-employed, success measured against other businesses). Workers always operate in fields of comparison in which the authority to assess success is measured in market or market-congruent terms, an authority readily accepted as normative by all actors. In this regime, market values provide a template for all social values in all organizations (not just businesses): profitability, entrepreneurialism, and flexibility are the overarching values. The "skills" that serve those values are discrete, measurable, transferable, and inculcated through training (Urciuoli, 2008).

Discourse and neoliberal ideology

To understand how "communication skills" give value to workers, let us consider how any set of linguistic practices becomes recognized and gives value to a social group. Silverstein (2003) describes glottonyms (languages as named entities) emerging through processes of *ethnolinguistic recognition*. Forms and patterns become recognized, classified as a discrete entity, named, and associated with a set of users typified as a nation or ethnic group. These connections are reinforced by the publication and sale of dictionaries, grammars, and other authorized entextualizations that include some forms and patterns and omit others, depending on their perceived value. Historically such value reflected literary and correctness norms. It has expanded to the notion that knowing additional, including minority, languages provides "added value" (Jaffe, 2007). This new way to imagine market possibilities has had interestingly neoliberal consequences for the use of languages not long ago considered marginal, quaint, or dangerous as Urla (2012) demonstrates for Basque or Barakos (2012) for Welsh.

The process of recognition rests on the notion that "a language" is reduceable to a set of forms with rules for correct use. As Bauman and Briggs (2003) argue, thus imagining language apart from speaker interaction is foundational to modernity itself, facilitating the construction and naturalization of inequalities among social groups and nations. Casting the purified version in grammars and dictionaries makes language even more imaginable as a "thing" that can be disciplined. This useful object becomes possessable: one can acquire measurable competence through approved forms of education. Under the neoliberal auspices of contemporary capitalism, this object can be marketed as a hard skill.

Glottonyms are imagined as standard and non-standard, the latter generally disvalued and routinely typified as dialects: words, phrases, and pronunciations associated with types of people imagined "within" the named language but differentiated by region, class, race, ethnic/national background, gender, age, occupation, activity, and so on. In the United

States, and doubtless elsewhere, slight formal differences are cast as sharply distinct varieties. For example, the *Business Insider* webpage "22 Maps That Show How Americans Speak English Totally Differently From One Another"[3] shows 22 examples of vocabulary or pronunciation differences across the United States: how do you pronounce *caramel, been,* or *mayonnaise*; is it *pop* or *soda, crayfish, crawfish,* or *crawdad, slaw* or *coleslaw*? These familiar variations are hardly irreparable divides but it is striking that, even jokingly, they can typify "totally different" varieties. This rhetoric of difference is reinforced by what Silverstein (1996) calls the American monoglot standard, the ideology that formal differences "get in the way" of meaning. Hence, the American "common sense" belief that too much deviation from an (imagined) standard is transgressive, inhibiting "effective communication" (see the chapter by Kraft in this volume). Imagining language as instrumental in achieving specific ends makes it possible to criticize on the same basis the "jargon" of professionals, the "bad grammar" and "accents" of African-Americans, and the "deficient communication skills"[4] of millennials who use *like* too often and incorrectly,[5] or exhibit "vocal fry."[6] Thinking about language varieties this way makes it easy to socially order groups in terms of how "effectively" they use language, and even to think about those groups as naturally connected to their discursive habits. It also explains why an imagining of discursive practices designed to facilitate organizational goals, especially in the workplace, becomes a way of thinking about an affiliated set of speakers – workers, leaders, and students as future worker-leaders – as a valued social type.

Speaker groups are routinely typified through folk (or ethno-) metapragmatic statements, as explained by Silverstein (1992, p. 60): metapragmatic as statements of norms for what people should (or should not) do with language; folk (or ethno-) as such statements are based on cultural ideologies of language. Thus, professionals, African-Americans, and millennials are typified by folk metapragmatic statements about "bad" jargon, grammar, or speech habits as impediments to communication. Workers and students are typified by folk metapragmatic statements about "communication skills" that facilitate their performance and organizational contributions, much as Urla and Barakos show for business-oriented users of Basque and Welsh. But professionals, African-Americans, and millennials are metapragmatically typified in terms of forms (pronunciations, grammar, vocabulary) and discursive habits that, however disvalued, are observed in routine use. Workers are typified in terms of discursive habits they are pressured to use (Cameron, 2000), so they use them enough to be observed. Students are typified in terms of habits that they are only observed using (and then sketchily) in training situations.

Let me pause here and summarize some points of comparison. Communication skills, like neoliberally valued glottonyms, are reified as a set of techniques associated with a socially recognized set of users. They have instrumental value, they can be acquired through instruction, and they are characterized by metapragmatic statements about their proper use. It is this latter that most distinguishes glottonyms from skills. The metapragmatics of skills use focus not on the proper forms of skills, but on details (quite heavily entextualized) about what communication skills ideally accomplish.

Folk metapragmatic typifications are linked to ideology-inflected perceptions of register. People participate in registers (the affiliation of discursive practice and social group activity, see, e.g., Agha, 2007) as socially embedded processes of discourse production, enacted in specific activities with specific participant structures. Register participants may be imagined as speaker types but what makes their production – the forms they use, the pragmatic functions served by those forms, the social dynamics indexed – recognizable as a register are not only the forms themselves but the social use patterning that pulls forms together, a patterning continually subject to change. Hence the processual term "enregisterment" for register formation. The forms associated with a cultural type, such as those much-maligned millennials, can be understood as register features but they are understandable as such because of their patterned co-occurrence with other discursive elements when used among certain participants. In other words, that form-speaker association is a manifestation of enregisterment, but enregisterment cannot be reduced to that association. That association is a manifestation of the fact that, as Agha (2007, p. 145) points out, registers serve as "cultural models of action" linking discursive production to "images of person, interpersonal relations, and types of conduct". Enregisterment cannot be disconnected from the formation of social personas and identities: patterns of co-occurring linguistic elements are group-relative processes that carry value for that group.

The association of form and social group without consideration of informing social dynamics can be thought of as a folk notion of register, for example, the *like*-overusing, vocal-frying millennial, the jargon-speaking lawyer. This caricature of an observable register is based on observable forms. When students are typified as communication skill-using innovative leaders, the folk register relies not on what student-leaders are observed to do but on they are ideally imagined to do. And where grammars and dictionaries provide "correct" forms, the texts designed for skills training do not actually specify the form "skills" take. Nor can they: however formulaic "skills" may be made to seem, they do not follow a script. They are techniques for managing tasks and handling situations and are only acquired through long practice. Instead, skill-training texts provide metapragmatic characterizations of what skills are for: through them, leaders find their passion, define their vision, share feelings and thoughts, foster harmony and teamwork, develop strategies, manage tasks, resolve conflict. Leaders are imagined to do all this in their jobs or other real-life contexts and perhaps they do. But students only do them in training sessions. There are no classroom or student life contexts where they apply. Nor, as a couple of supervisors told me, are such training sessions subject to assessment. Hence, the notion of student leadership communication skills as a wished-for but not-really-there folk register based on leadership and social innovation as desired forms of personhood and "communication skills" as what can make that personhood happen.

Speakers of glottonyms are recognized in terms of forms and what speakers should do with those forms to display the valued identity linked to those glottonyms; as Silverstein puts it, "the sociocultural *scheduling of emblematic identity displays*" (2003, p. 538, italics in original), for example, as a political or literary display of identity. Similarly, one can perform one's place in a neoliberal order by deploying glottonymic "hard skills" (e.g. as a name-the-language entrepreneur) to show that one is bringing a market edge. One can also perform one's place in the neoliberal order by deploying communication skills to show that market edge. Thus far, we see a parallel between hard language skills and soft communication skills. Does student skills training activity count as a "scheduled emblematic identity display" of innovative leadership? Yes and no. Yes, insofar as participation in training is imagined as a performance of neoliberal values. No, insofar as it is unclear what exactly is being performed. As I show in the fourth section of this paper, Posse and Ashoka U program personnel appear to attribute such value to whatever students are doing, but the values attach to the Posse sessions and Ashoka U conferences and the fact that students are performing in them, with whatever they perform treated as acceptable.

This is reinforced by the fact that students have been selected for participation in these programs because they are already assumed to be leaders and innovators. While I have certainly encountered students who I think have internalized a neoliberal subjectivity, they were not involved in Posse. The Posse students I spoke with were not particularly neoliberalized about Posse preparing them as leaders to bring value to the school, as we see in the fourth section. Students are selected for Posse and Ashoka U because those selecting them already judge them to be leaders and innovators, confirming that judgment with full scholarships for Posse recruits and grants for Ashoka U fellows. Moreover, Posse students are mostly working-class students of color. They expressed to me some concern about what it meant to be a campus leader but more about the complexities of making it through an elite, largely white college so concerned with its diversity numbers (Urciuoli, 2016, pp. 215–216). The Ashoka U fellow interviewed by LaDousa (2018, pp. 127–128) flat-out rejected the language of neoliberal innovation. As to the sessions and the conference, those are part of the bargain, so students perform what they are required to perform. And if they do perform something that can be formally pointed to as skills, there is no place else in their social or academic lives to repeat that performance.

To repeat a key point, the very notion of "skills" as reified and formulaic is deceptive: what people actually do when they act as leaders and innovators cannot be reduced to a script, as is clear in the instructional materials examined later in this chapter. The ideology of skills makes them seem readily transferable. But as with any learning process, they are only internalized through repeated use, for which students have little opportunity. Nevertheless that ideology exists and allows for the imagining of skills as, like language, a "thing" in and of itself. Stakeholders (note the corporate-friendly term) within and outside higher education (donors, trustees, most parents and future employers) believe that ideology profoundly, and for the rationale that sustains the general communication skills market: good skills get people good jobs (Urciuoli, 2008).

Student leadership as technology of self

The model of leadership associated with the communication skills toward which students are urged is entirely defined in institutional terms as evidenced by websites for student leadership training programs. Using the terms *college student leadership training communication* for internet searches, I found several programs showing consistent features. I chose the four program descriptions examined below (Campus Compact for New Hampshire, California State University Northridge, State University of New York, Alfred University) as useful representatives. These four consistently characterize leadership in terms of taking on a task that forwards the interests of an organization, breaking it into parts, and moving those parts to a conclusion. The communication skills that accomplish this work are listening, explaining, and persuading, all of which can be inculcated through authorized training. Only when enacted within an organization are those discursive elements recognizable as "leadership".[7]

The Campus Compact for New Hampshire, a consortium of 24 schools including Dartmouth and the University of New Hampshire, provides an on-line *Guide to Student Leadership Development Through Service*, designed to train students for service learning leadership roles. The *Guide* directs students to find an affect appropriate for service, share feelings and thoughts, "find their passions", connect with co-workers, and "define a vision".[8] This is done through communication skills:

> **Communication skills.** Effective service leadership relies on the capacity to relate well to others. This attention to relationships requires self confidence and conflict resolution skills that can be learned and practiced.[9]

Students are assumed to acquire them as they carry out exercises labeled "leadership activities" that involve dividing into small groups, completing prescribed tasks of 5–10 minutes each, and then recording their ideas.[10] This is described as a demonstration of teamwork, and the communication through which this is done is assumed to demonstrate leadership skills. Once the tasks are done, students are assumed to have learned leadership communication.

The California State University Northridge *Student Leadership Training Booklet* provides a similar model. Distinguishing "shared" from "top down" leadership, the program espouses a "grass roots" model of shared student leadership in which students work in teams rather than positions of command. Leadership becomes a matter of mutual mentoring to facilitate task assignment, using such skills as serving as spokesperson, developing strategies, fostering harmony and teamwork, recruiting new members, managing tasks, and fostering a positive group atmosphere.[11] Exercises are provided for students to determine whether they have such skills.

The State University of New York (SUNY) Faculty Senate Student Life Committee's report, *Best Practices in Student Leadership Programs* describes several model SUNY programs including the Emerging Leaders program at SUNY New Paltz (for first-years).[12] This highly structured program requires participation in workshops, conferences, and community service activities and is "focused around five core components known as the Five Dimensions of Leadership Development" including "Global/Community Perspectives", "Ethics and Values – Decision Making", "Personal Empowerment", "Interpersonal Skills Component", and "giv[ing] back to communities via opportunities on campus" through service. Attendance at workshops and training is tracked and "giving back" is accounted for through community service forms. More than most, the SUNY New Paltz leadership program specifies what kinds of skills it is designed to inculcate:

> The Interpersonal Skills Component focuses on team dynamics, conflict resolution/mediation, group organization, cooperative learning, communication, listening, delegating, goal setting, leadership styles, and transition.[13]

The Alfred University Leadership Certificate Program has four components: skill building, involvement, commitment, and documentation. Skill building is done through workshop attendance in each of five areas: "Do I have what it takes to be a leader?"; "How do I create a fun and focused team?"; "What is leadership theory and how does it apply to me?"; "I am a leader, now what?" (the only area involving hands-on leadership activities); "Who are leaders?" Each of these involves readings and lectures on task management and assessment techniques; participation is verified through a reflection paper.[14]

In these programs, colleges and universities treat students as both products and consumers. In higher education messaging, students become idealized by administrators of student life, admissions, and institutional advancement as a collection of elements to be assembled and projected to stakeholders outside the institution (Urciuoli, 2014, 2018), parents, alumni, trustees, funding organizations, and potential employers, all imagining students as future employees. The marketing image of the ideal student stresses a clear, continuous transition from undergraduate to work life, featuring students showing themselves to be productive, co-operative, organization-oriented, and task-focused, all of which are seen as (very marketable) leadership qualities.

The idealized and standardized behaviors that constitute these future employee-leaders are constituted as *skills* (*communication skills, listening skills, conflict resolution*, etc.) insofar as *skill* signifies a behavior aimed unambiguously toward an outcome productive for an organization.[15] *Skills* are imagined to be the outcome of student participation in these programs. They indicate the cultivation of neoliberal agency, of running oneself like a business, a model which, as Gershon (2017, p. 235ff) points out, works largely to the advantage of the corporate world, particularly since it leaves no room to argue for a living wage (2017, p. 248). It is no accident that the "skills" driving this construction of self are "soft", segmenting and classifying social behaviors in terms of their job market value and potential organizational contribution. Leadership thus conceived exemplifies Foucault's notion of technology of self whereby social actors "… effect by their own means or with the help of others a certain number of operations on their own bodies and souls, thoughts, conduct, and way of being" (Foucault, 1988, p. 18) that fashion subjectivity in ways congruent with, in this instance, the goals of contemporary capitalism. These technologies are worked into the higher education trend described by Handler (2008, 2018) as paracurricular, parallel to but outside the academic curriculum and displacing discipline-based knowledge by content-interchangeable "skills" that can be overseen by administrators who are less expensive than faculty, in programs in which institutional values readily displace academic values because they are so much more marketable. What is marketed may be thin on specific content, but the promise of the neoliberally governed student is product enough.

Colleges and universities advertise programs based on various configurations of these elements of approved sociality which form templates for what amount to market-driven technologies of self. For example, leadership training is often configured with service learning (as per the Campus Compact for New Hampshire and SUNY New Paltz, above), first year experience (SUNY New Paltz, Indiana University,[16] University of Louisville[17]), experiential learning (Rutgers University[18]), and diversity and inclusion (University of California at Davis,[19] Fordham[20]). Among these configurations is the combination of leadership, communication, and social entrepreneurship (or social innovation or changemaking) as offered, for example, by the *Stanford Social Innovation Review* "informing and inspiring leaders of social change".[21] In the next section, I examine this configuration as ethnographically as possible (admittedly limited) in relation to the pseudo-register problem outlined above.

The degree to which skills should be understood as interactive techniques not reduceable to verbal formulae is made clear in textbooks such as *Leadership Communication* (Barrett, 2014), which is pretty standard for the industry. Author Barrett defines leadership communication as "the controlled purposeful transfer of meaning" by which speakers exert influence, connecting positively with audiences, and eliminating interference (Barrett, 2014, pp. 6–7). Leaders need to take audiences into account, develop strategies, be emotionally intelligent, and understand and value diversity (2014, pp. 8–9). Leaders must understand what Barrett calls the rhetorical situation. Effective leaders may be political or corporate: Martin Luther King, Mahatma Gandhi, Nelson Mandela, Bill Gates, Warren Buffett, Jeff Bezos, Steve Jobs. Barrett discusses ethical leadership and provides case studies and self-assessment exercises. Barrett uses the same basic concepts and organizing assumptions as most leadership communication textbooks: leaders create visions, align people to those visions through effective strategies, and bring about change. Communication skills are "soft" or "human" skills, productive activities that facilitate such outcomes (persuasive skills, organization skills, listening skills, public speaking skills). Good leaders have them. Bad leaders lack them.

Talking like a leader-entrepreneur, maybe

How should student-leaders or student-leader-entrepreneurs acquire their skills? In this section, I examine the mentoring sessions conducted by the Posse Foundation and the fellowship program sponsored by Ashoka U, both in partnership with colleges and university. I describe team-leadership communication exercises for students with Posse scholarships, and student participation in an innovation conference partnered with Ashoka U.

Founded in 1989 and sustained by corporate donations,[22] the Posse Foundation secures full tuition scholarships from colleges and universities for cohorts of ten or so racially diverse undergraduates selected for their leadership and change-making potential to move together through their provider institutions from acceptance to graduation. The model is "rooted in the belief that a small, diverse group of talented students – a Posse – carefully selected and trained, can serve as a catalyst for increased individual and community development".[23] Starting months before they first matriculate, students attend workshops to learn "team building and group support; cross-cultural communication; leadership and becoming an active agent of change on campus; and academic excellence".[24]

Ashoka U is one of several initiatives of Ashoka, founded in 1980 as an international non-profit organization that promotes social entrepreneurship.[25] Ashoka U "collaborate[s] with colleges and universities to break down barriers to institutional change and foster a campus-wide culture of social innovation"[26] through its "Changemaker Campus" initiative established in 2008. For institutions participating in this program, Ashoka U promotes projects in which students learn to act as "social innovators" or "changemakers".[27]

Posse students are required to attend leadership training and mentoring activities in formats designed by Posse's main office and set forth in the Posse *Mentor Manual*. This calls for weekly two-hour long mentoring sessions in which first and second year students share experiences and support, stay current on campus resources, opportunities, and events, discuss successes and challenges, and "continue to develop their skills as leaders" (Posse Foundation, 2014, p. 35). Mentors are urged to document student attendance and lateness, group progress, and individual highlights. Mentors are also urged to facilitate student discussion of specific experiences. The focus is on individual perceptions and feelings, for example, "what was X like", "how do you feel about X", "what was hard (or easy)", "what surprised you". As a current Posse mentor told me, it is largely up to the mentor to work out the application of these principles, which are metapragmatically speci-fied in the following terms: one person talks at a time; one attacks the idea not the person; one makes active responses to demonstrate active listening. As the mentor told me, not all students respond to the format, which is a polite way of saying they are not performing these communication skills. Posse training also calls for corporate team-building exercises, such as ropes courses to instill trust and balancing exercises for teamwork, some of which are carried out in a retreat organized by Posse administrators near their main office.[28] The mentor pointed out to me that it is never quite clear how such exercises relate to what students are supposed to take away from these sessions.[29] He also noted a clear disconnection between what students do in these Posse sessions and what they do outside. He told me that when he asked Posse main office trainers what he should do with his students at the retreat, they said to "go with the flow", "don't overthink", and focus on "process".

The same dynamic was observed at the on-campus PossePlus retreat held yearly, to which faculty and non-Posse students are invited. This takes place Friday night through Sunday, for 40–60 Posse scholars plus their guests. Posse trainers from the main office organize the retreat as team and leader-ship exercises. I attended twice. One retreat focused on the role of students in forming a college identity. One exercise, again patterned after corporate team-oriented exercises, had students address a series of pre-set questions about what helps or hinders formation of their identity with the college, ending with "what is something you're passionate about that people don't know about you?" Again, emphasis was on the expression of feeling as a communication skill. In their "small group discussion" responses, students were urged to focus on individual – not collective – experience. They were also not supposed to raise questions about the procedures themselves. When some students noted that group leaders seemed to repeat the same questions, and began to ignore the scripted "prompts" in favor of their own conclusions, or asked each other unscripted questions, they were gently reprimanded by trainers intermittently monitoring the discussion; trainers also urged group members to take each activity to the full time allotted but not take too long. The small group discussion was followed by general discussion in which the trainers, after again reminding us of the importance of sticking to the rules, asked questions focused on individuals' direct effect on other individuals, or on the "community" as an aggregate of individuals. (See Urciuoli, 2016 for extended discussion.)

Focus on one's individual feelings is consistent with the leadership training prescribed by the Campus Compact of New Hampshire which stresses articulation of feeling, that is, "finding (one's) passions", in the development of communicative connections. Why these associations work – how students learn leadership by talking about individual perceptions, feelings, and visions – are not addressed in the instructional literature. Talking about feelings in mentoring sessions could also backfire, the mentor told me, when one or two of the cohort would dominate the session with such talk to the visible irritation of other mentees. Nor could the mentor imagine where, other than mentoring or training spaces, students would talk to each other in this manner.

In these exercises, as in the literature reviewed in the previous section, *leadership* and *team* are imagined entirely as roles serving an institution, and the routines that students are asked to rehearse appear designed to demonstrate an alignment with their institution that foreshadows future corporate roles. In such leadership training, stress is placed on following the prescribed format, as can be seen in program materials, mentoring sessions, and the PossePlus retreat. Yet as the Posse mentor points out, the rules are not easily enforced: students routinely ignore them. Nor is there any correlation between the degree to which students stick to the rules and the degree to which students are assessed as successful leaders. Indeed, there seems to be no real assessment at any level of student performance. What appears to be an audit process is unenforced, leaving a pseudo-audit, parallel to the pseudo-register.

As to internalizing a neoliberal model of transformative leadership, Posse students with whom I spoke (see Urciuoli, 2016, pp. 215–216) found those roles complicated by racial realities of life on an elite, largely white campus. The few white Posse scholars distanced themselves from the Posse students of color, and rivalries were imposed with students of color recruited through the Opportunity Programs (OP) which also emphasized leadership roles. These rivalries usually became alliances. Several Posse (and OP) students said that alliances mattered more than leadership, an un-neoliberal expression of collective subjectivity. To summarize the most salient points from a longer interview by one Posse scholar, Jared (a pseudonym):

> It was kind of that everything was presented to us with a silver ribbon on it, they made it seem like the school was just the perfect place … but when we got here we just had each other so we weren't really concerned with the campus as a whole… it's like, what are you OP or Posse? So then it's hard for you to even want to contribute to the campus when you don't even feel worthy … It devalues your worth here … because then it feels like you're just helping the college fulfill what they need to do for a quota, or to make their campus more diverse… You're helping the college but the college is not really helping you.

The Ashoka U-partnered social innovation program is even less scripted than Posse. LaDousa (2018) describes one such "social innovation" partnership with a college that began when its public affairs Tower Center had the college designated a "Changemaker Campus".[30] Several faculty and students attended Ashoka U's annual conference to bring change-making ideas back to campus and establish a social innovation fellowship program at the Center. Student-fellows successfully submit a proposal addressing a solution to a social problem and then attend a two-week program (one week on campus, one in Washington, DC) to develop "transformational leadership skills such as global orientation, self-knowledge, ethical behaviors, and regard for the public good" (cited from the Center's website).

LaDousa analyzes a narrative by one student, Shane (a pseudonym), about his social innovation project, an "innovation lab" consisting of a whiteboard-painted room in the Tower Center where students could brainstorm and write out innovative ideas. Shane plays out the stance of the social innovator for which he considers himself a "poster child", speaking "as if he understands the very stakes of the college's survival" (2018, p. 120). Shane talks about applying learning in the "real" world, which in this interview excerpt he contrasts with the campus and classroom "bubble":

> You know, we do function in this little bubble and we don't often get to employ learning in the classroom so I think a lot of people are drawn during the summers [i.e. Tower Center summer research projects] at least to be like, "okay how the fuck do I apply all this stuff and how do I do something real?"
>
> (LaDousa, 2018, p. 125)

Shane makes it clear that "doing something real" specifically means not using discourse forms that match either Ashoka U's or his college's ways of talking about innovation, nor does he see such language as instantiating his status as an innovator. He makes it clear in the interview that his presence at the conference validates his status as an innovator. He specifically criticizes the conference "jargon", including the terms *social entrepreneurship* and *social innovation*. When LaDousa asks Shane whether such jargon signifies the conference organizers' interest in developing language associated with their aims, Shane responds that such language shows their lack of touch with the "real world". He believes that it discourages other students from participating in projects like his, and is thus responsible for students' "failure" to use his social innovation lab. In short, the very language that should mark Shane's neoliberal subjectivity makes the enterprise generating that language problematic (LaDousa, 2018, pp. 127–128).

Shane's social innovation performance is even less monitored and scripted than the performances ostensibly required of Posse students. He aligns himself with the institution not in placing their interests above his, but in seeing the institution's support of his "desire to reform campus and its practices such that the disjunction between campus and elsewhere can be remedied" (LaDousa, 2018, p. 132). He sees no reason to demonstrate that through use of their discourse.

Conclusion

I conclude by asking how it is that Posse scholars or Ashoka U fellows interviewed above show as little investment as they do in the forms of neo-liberal subjectivity connected to the leadership and social innovation communication skills training that define their respective programs.

To begin with, there is the pseudo-register itself and its lack of content. Any discursive techniques that facilitate leadership and social innovation must be acquired through systematic practice which does not happen in these programs, none of which invest in systematic training. Students receive instruction from available personnel who draw on instructional guides, a cost-cutting strategy common to paracurricular programs. Nor are there contexts outside these programs in which students operate as leaders or innovators. With so little practical opportunity, students are unlikely to internalize much neoliberal "skills" subjectivity.

Nor do students invest in these programs to become leaders or innovators: they do them for the scholarships and grants. Students getting tuition scholarships through Posse must already be considered leaders, and students receiving Ashoka U fellowships must already be considered innovators. Mentoring sessions and conference attendance are done in return for scholarships and fellowships. Having said that, we saw in the previous section that Posse mentoring sessions and, especially, retreat participation is more monitored than Ashoka U participation and not surprisingly. As Cameron (2000) observed regarding communication skills training for workers, the lower the status, the more scripted and monitored the performance; the more elite the status, the less monitored the performance and the looser the script. While they are not workers and they all attend elite schools, most Posse scholars are students of color, often from working class backgrounds, whereas the Ashoka U social innovation fellows are from elite white backgrounds (see also Del Percio, this volume). Furthermore, as the Posse website suggests,[31] the presence of Posse cohorts in a college or university is performative, equally enhancing an institution's "diversity" efforts and Posse's brand, a function which probably makes Posse students even more subject to monitoring (they cannot *not* participate in mentoring sessions and retreats).

Do students internalize any neoliberal subjectivity? Probably, but it is hard to know how consistently and from what exactly. Students that I have known over years of teaching have spoken of imagining themselves as "skills bundles" when facing a job market (Urciuoli, 2008). And, again based on personal conversations over the years, students are also likely to see themselves as products, especially when they critically examine higher education marketing. But from skills training? Probably not. Student internalization of neoliberal subjectivity may not even be the main reason why this pseudo-register exists. The pseudo-register clearly plays a central role in branding programs like Posse, Ashoka U, and the leadership programs advertised on school websites. All such paracurricular programs are consistent with the communication skills literature in the design of techniques and the metapragmatic description of outcomes. They create commensurability across institutions, all addressing the same presumed market need for a certain kind of student. "Transformation" is part of the sell, an assurance that students will fit a certain corporate expectation ("bringing change"). The very existence of leadership and social innovation programs and their pseudo-register indexes this market commensurability, pointing to schools meeting stakeholder expectations. Stakeholders invest in the idea of student neoliberal subjectivity, and college and university administrators meet stakeholder expectations.

Under these circumstances, what really counts is that students perform something approximating that discourse to meet such expectations. Students may be imagined as future workers, but they are not yet workers. When worker performance is directly connected to corporate productivity, where, as Cameron shows, there really is pressure to comply, we expect to find actual performance and serious monitoring. But students only need to act their part to provide an image of institutional or program effectiveness for a website or an annual report.

Acknowledgements

This chapter was originally presented in the panel: *Multilingüismo y Neolibolralismo* (*Multilingualism and Neoliberalism*) organized by Luisa Martín Rojo and Alfonso del Percio, at the Symposium EDiSo 2017 (Asociación de Estudios sobre Discurso y Sociedad) at the Universitat Pompeu Fabra, Barcelona, June 28–29, 2017. Many thanks to Chaise LaDousa for his insightful feedback on the arguments developed here, to my two reviewers for their excellent comments, and to Luisa and Alfonso for including me in this project.

Notes

1 US liberal arts undergraduate education, dating from the eighteenth century, exists as university programs and as four-year undergraduate colleges, and is often identified with elite education.
2 Note the strong coherence among Dardot's and Laval's formulation of neoliberalism, Gershon's notion of neoliberal agency, and Martín Rojo's notion of subjectivization.
3 www.businessinsider.com/22-maps-that-show-the-deepest-linguistic-conflicts-in-america-2013–6 (accessed 7-23-18).

4 www.forbes.com/sites/brianrashid/2017/05/04/two-reasons-millennials-leaders-struggle-with-communication-and-how-to-help-them/#4a9d40c6c671 (accessed 7-23-18).
5 www.wikihow.com/Stop-Saying-the-Word-%22Like%22 (accessed 7-23-18).
6 www.ohniww.org/katy-perry-voice-vocal-fry/ (accessed 7-23-18).
7 Communication skills training as described here expanded sharply as an industry in the 1990s though it had been around for some decades. See Urciuoli, 2008 for more details.
8 www.compactnh.org/downloads/StudentLeaders.pdf, p. 10 (accessed 7-23-18).
9 www.compactnh.org/downloads/StudentLeaders.pdf, p. 10 (accessed 7-23-18).
10 www.compactnh.org/downloads/StudentLeaders.pdf, p. 17 (accessed 7-23-18).
11 www.csun.edu/sites/default/files/leadership_booklet.pdf, p. 12 (accessed 7-23-18).
12 http://system.suny.edu/media/suny/content-assets/documents/faculty-senate/Best practicesstudentleadershipfinal.pdf, pp. 2–3 (accessed 7-23-18).
13 http://system.suny.edu/media/suny/content-assets/documents/faculty-senate/Best practicesstudentleadershipfinal.pdf, p. 3 (accessed 7-23-18).
14 http://system.suny.edu/media/suny/content-assets/documents/faculty-senate/Best practicesstudentleadershipfinal.pdf, pp. 5–6 (accessed 7-23-18). Documentation of participation includes a meeting with a career advisor "to find out how to market their leadership skills on resumes and in interviews," receipt of the certificate, and "a distinctive pin."
15 This use of skill is indexical in that it allies the term's user with a set of values and social orientations, a function I have described elsewhere (Urciuoli, 2008) as a "strategically deployable shifter".
16 https://studentaffairs.indiana.edu/student-life-learning/leadership/hoosier-leadership-program/leadership-orientation.shtml (accessed 7-23-18).
17 https://louisville.edu/studentactivities/leadership-opportunities/first-year (accessed 7-23-18).
18 http://leadership.rutgers.edu/first-year-fellowship/ (accessed 7-23-18).
19 http://cll.ucdavis.edu/local_resources/docs/program_flyers/DLDPelectronic.pdf (accessed 7-23-18).
20 www.fordham.edu/info/20911/diversity_peer_leaders (accessed 7-23-18).
21 https://ssir.org/ (accessed 7-23-18).
22 www.possefoundation.org/uploads/reports/Annual-Report-2015_WEB.pdf (accessed 7-23-18).
23 www.possefoundation.org/shaping-the-future/mission-history (accessed 7-23-18).
24 www.possefoundation.org/supporting-scholars/pre-collegiate-training   Part of that "change' is to make schools "more welcoming institutions" (http://www.possefoundation.org/) which should be the paid job of institutional administrators, not the unpaid job of its students of color (accessed 7-23-18).
25 www.ashoka.org/sites/www.ashoka.org/files/Ashoka-Annual-Report-FY12.pdf (accessed 7-23-18).
26 http://ashokau.org/about/what-we-do/ (accessed 7-23-18).
27 Ashoka U's provision to participating schools by way of tangible support toward these goals is unclear.
28 Given the Posse Foundation's focus on how many of their graduates are placed in corporate jobs, and their many corporate sponsors, this is no accident. The stress on individuals in the Posse exercises certainly seems positioned to reinforce naturalization of a governmentality principle that

masks institutional and social inequalities, leaving "changemaking" up to the well-trained individual.

29 One wonders if these exercises even primarily address students; see LaDousa, 2014 for a comparable problem of how to figure out the addressee from instructional language.

30 Being so designated has a pricetag: http://ashokau.org/changemakercampus/process/ (accessed 7-23-18).

31 www.possefoundation.org/ (accessed 7-23-18).

References

Agha, A. (2007). *Language and Social Relations*. New York: Cambridge University Press.

Barakos, E. (2012). Language policy and planning in urban professional settings: Bilingualism in Cardiff business. *Current Issues in Language Planning*, 13(3), 167–186.

Barrett, D. (2014). *Leadership Communication*, 4th edition. New York: McGraw Hill.

Bauman, R., & Briggs, C. (2003). *Voices of Modernity: Language Ideologies and the Politics of Inequality*. Cambridge: Cambridge University Press.

Cameron, D. (2000). *Good to Talk? Living and Working in a Communication Culture*. London: Sage.

Dardot, P., & Laval, C. (2014). *The New Way of the World: On Neoliberal Society*. London: Verso.

Duchêne, A., & Heller, M. (Eds.). (2012). *Language in Late Capitalism: Pride and Profit*. London: Routledge.

Flubacher, M., & Del Percio, A. (Eds.). (2017). *Language, Education, and Neoliberalism: Critical Studies in Sociolinguistics*. Bristol, UK: Multilingual Matters.

Foucault, M. (1988). Technologies of the self. In L. Martin, H. Gutman, & P. Hutton (dir.), *Technologies of the Self: A Seminar with Michel Foucault* (pp. 16–49). Amherst: University of Massachusetts Press.

Gershon, I. (2017). *Down and Out in the New Economy*. Chicago: University of Chicago Press.

Handler, R. (2008). Corporatization and phantom innovation in university marketing strategies. *Anthropology News*, 49(1), 6–7.

Handler, R. (2018). Undergraduate research in Veblen's vision: Idle curiosity, bureaucratic accountancy and pecuniary emulation in contemporary higher education. In B. Urciuoli (Ed.), *The Experience of Neoliberal Education* (pp. 32–55). New York: Berghahn.

Jaffe, A. (2007). Minority language movements. In M. Heller (Ed.), *Bilingualism: A Social Approach* (pp. 50–70). New York: Palgrave Macmillan.

LaDousa, C. (2014). Subject to address in a digital literacy initiative: Neoliberal agency and the promises and predicaments of participation. *Signs and Society*, 2(2), 203–229.

LaDousa, C. (2018). From service learning to social innovation: The development of the neoliberal in experiential learning. In B. Urciuoli (Ed.), *The Experience of Neoliberal Education* (pp. 112–136). New York: Berghahn.

Martín Rojo, L. (2016). Language and power. In O. Garcia, N. Flores, & M. Spotti (Eds.), *The Oxford Handbook of Language and Society* (pp. 77–102). New York: Oxford University Press.

Posse Foundation. (2014). *The Mentor Manual*. New York: Posse Foundation.

Silverstein, M. (1992). The indeterminacy of contextualization: When is enough enough? In P. Auer & A. Di Luzio (Eds.), *The Contextualization of Language* (pp. 55–75). Philadelphia and Amsterdam: John Benjamins.

Silverstein, M. (1996). Monoglot "standard" in America: Standardization and metaphors of linguistic hegemony. In D. Brenneis & R. Macaulay (Eds.), *The Matrix of Language: Contemporary Linguistic Anthropology* (pp. 284–305). Boulder, CO: Westview.

Silverstein, M. (2003). The whens and wheres – as well as hows – of ethnolinguistic recognition. *Public Culture*, 15(3), 531–557

Urciuoli, B. (2008). Skills and selves in the new work place. *American Ethnologist*, 35, 211–228.

Urciuoli, B. (2014). The semiotic production of the good student. *Signs and Society*, 2(1), 56–83.

Urciuoli, B. (2016). Neoliberalizing markedness: The interpellation of "diverse" college students. *HAU: Journal of Ethnographic Theory*, 6(3), 201–221.

Urciuoli, B. (Ed.) (2018). *The Experience of Neoliberal Education*. New York: Berghahn.

Urla, J. (2012). *Reclaiming Basque: Language, Nation, and Cultural Activism*. Reno: University of Nevada Press.

Part II

Language and the neoliberal subject

6 Linguistic entrepreneurship
Neoliberalism, language learning, and class[1]

Joan Pujolar

Introduction

From the bilingualism of Roman elites in Latin and Greek to the contemporary enthusiasm of the middle classes for bilingual or immersion education, learning languages has been an important component of class differentiation. This chapter asks how multilingualism features in contemporary processes of class differentiation, and I use life trajectory narratives as the data source. The questions are who learns languages, how and why, and how learning and using new languages features in people's social standing.

When addressing people's experience in the present, we need to engage with neoliberalism, a set of ideas and practices that has become hegemonic in contemporary politics and economic thought. Neoliberalism provides a narrative to understand how contemporary society works, including a model of person-hood often expressed by the term "entrepreneurial self" (Burchell, Gordon, and Miller 1991). From this perspective, my aim is to assess to what extent people are becoming "linguistic entrepreneurs", that is, whether they engage with language learning in ways that draw from neoliberal principles (or not), and how this is conditioned by inherited differences of access to wealth and social standing.

The analysis is built upon a set of biographical narratives gathered amongst new speakers of Catalan, a sample of 37 people who (mostly) learned and started speaking Catalan during their adult life. These narratives were collected through interviews in which people recounted their decisions, plans and experiences in relation to the learning and using of new languages.

"Agency" will be a key concept in my analysis. Specific ideas about agency and individual freedom are presented as the fundamental tenets of neoliberalism, as the conditions for emancipation and prosperity. This also means that neoliberalism places all its onus on individuals in terms of how to make sense of their life conditions and how to undertake projects to obtain and accumulate resources. Thus I will look into how people make sense of the things they can or cannot do, the persons they can or cannot be, and I will show how different social positions and dispositions provide or withdraw the means and legitimacy that people need to pursue their life projects.

The text is organized as follows. I first provide a socio-political history of the Catalan context. After this I discuss what I understand by constructs such as "agency", and the "neoliberal" or the "entrepreneurial" subject. The next two sections analyse the biographical narratives. What I try to argue is that linguistic entrepreneurship is primarily found amongst people whose social backgrounds are prosperous, which shows that contemporary multilingualism participates in the reproduction of class difference. However, I also find reason to doubt that individual entrepreneurship is necessarily invested with neoliberal ideologies. It seems rather that what we find are contentions over the ideological appropriation of individual and collective initiative.

Language, identity and (post)nationalism in Catalonia

Catalonia is the scenario in which our research participants articulated the meanings of learning and speaking new languages. Most newcomers to Catalonia learn Spanish first rather than the local language (Catalan), and this adds to the anxieties of governmental officials and grass-roots activists about the future of the language. In a context of increasing mobility and multilingualism, abundant resources (both symbolic and economic) have been put in place to make learning and using Catalan both imaginable, feasible, and profitable for outsiders. The Catalan government created in the 1980s the *Consorci per a la Normalització Lingüística* (CPNL), a network of 22 centres funded by 135 bodies amongst municipalities, counties, provinces and the government. In 2017 the CPNL offered more than 3500 language courses, most of them free of charge, and had nearly 77,000 (mostly foreign) students (Consorci per a la Normalització Lingüística 2017).

I would argue that this makes a good context to assess the extent to which people invest in multilingualism as one aspect of their "skills bundle" (Gershon 2011) to compete in the neoliberal marketplace, or whether more varied and complex positionings are at play. To understand the conditions in which people make their decisions, a brief political economic history is necessary.

Of all Catalan-speaking territories in the Western Mediterranean, Catalonia (in Spain's north-eastern border with France) has traditionally provided the focus for a classical nationalist project opposed to that of Spanish nationalism. Language was at the centre of twentieth-century conflicts between Catalonia and Spain. The dictatorship of general Franco (1939–1978) insistently persecuted the public uses of Catalan, which became an almost exclusively oral language. When Woolard (1989) did her first ethnography in the late 1970s, Catalan was only spoken by people born locally. The uses of Catalan and Spanish delimited distinct ethnicities in people's minds. In 1982, however, a new autonomous Catalan government started to implement a linguistic "normalization". Catalan became the predominant language of education and was learned by all. Its ethnocultural and political connotations were gradually eroded (Woolard 2016; Gonzàlez et al. 2014). The efforts to "de-ethnicize" Catalan in public life are also important to understand how the possibility of learning Catalan is made ideologically available to newcomers. Woolard (2016) argues that Catalan nationalism is seeking to develop a form of "rooted cosmopolitanism" that is critical of ethnic nationalism but also of the typical "banal nationalism" (Billig 1995) of state citizenship.

It is also important to understand that Catalan nationalism was always fuelled by the economic drive of Barcelona and its surrounding network of industrial cities and towns. During the boom of the 1960s, a substantial section of the Catalan working-class invested in small and medium business initiatives, gained access to property, education and specialized employment. Economic expansion and social mobility attracted migration from the Catalan countryside and from the much larger rural regions of Spain, thus creating a sizeable Spanish-speaking population in working-class neighbourhoods around the industrial centres. Upward social mobility was common at this time and, for Spanish-speaking families of migrant origin, economic progress was characteristically associated with learning and using Catalan (Woolard 1989).

This is the background of most traditional "new speakers" of Catalan, to which more recently new migrants from all parts of the world have joined, mostly between 1993 and 2008. The resulting demographic make-up of the country is important: of a total 7.5 million people, only 36% declare Catalan to be the language they use most socially, despite the fact that it is used by 65% of those locally born (Idescat 2014). In fact, 36% of the population was born outside Catalonia, half of it abroad (Idescat 2018). Catalan is the language most used only by 14% of those coming from the rest of Spain, and by 8% of those foreign born (Idescat 2014).

The political restitution of Catalan, like the articulation of a classical welfare state in Spain as a whole, took place during the 1980s, that is, just after the oil crisis that eventually triggered (or helped consolidate) the neoliberal turn. Even as the Catalan government was investing in a new public television channel, the Spanish government liberalized broadcasting, effectively surrendering the sector to private ventures. Even as the Catalan government was ensuring that public utilities abided by public sector linguistic regulations, the Spanish government privatized its telecommunications, oil and other monopolies to turn them into multinational companies set to "reconquer" Latin American markets. Despite this neoliberal economic restructuring, the Spanish government continued its interventionist linguistic policies, basically by making Spanish mandatory through sectoral laws and regulations and by using the Constitutional Court to block the Catalan government's attempts to do likewise (Plataforma per la Llengua 2018). For instance, since 2015, applicants for Spanish nationality must present an A2 level certificate of Spanish, while the equivalent Catalan certificates are not valid (Ley 19/2015 de medidas de reforma administrativa 2015). In contrast, after entering the Common European Market in 1986, the Catalan economy gradually loosened its reliance on Spanish markets, such that in 2017 it exported 39% of its GDP. In this context, the Catalan language, despite its weak legal protection, retains significant strength in the job market, which still encourages many people to learn it (Pujolar and Puigdevall 2015).

What are, or who are, the neoliberal subjects?

Foucault and his associates detected in the 1980s an important transformation of ideas about governance and social engineering (Gordon 1991). "Governmentality" was the term coined to cover the wide range of discourses and practices aimed at intervening, or at finding ways not to intervene, in society and the economy. Foucault argued that texts (and textbooks) on liberalism, or dubbed as such, did not necessarily identify how governments operated from the nineteenth century, neither how they changed their modes of operation, for instance, up to the present. The key was how institutions and intellectuals deployed strategies to understand how society operated (knowledge) and what forms of intervention might ensure their stability or progress (the so-called principle of "security").

Inscribed in all the debates was a specific conception of "man" (or the citizen) in terms of what moved or motivated "him". Adam Smith's original idea, whereby each individual contributes to the public good by following his own self-interest, can here be presented as the canonical view of the individual as social actor, a conception that abandoned enlightenment visions of society as founded upon a contract between individuals or between individuals and the state. Civil society, according to the contemporary Physiocrats, generates its own order spontaneously.

The innovation that Foucault perceived in his time was that the "enterprise" was increasingly being presented as a model for all forms of organization and social relations, such that "man" could be seen (or should be seen) as an "entrepreneur of himself" (Gordon 1991: 44; see also Fraser 2003; Foucault 1991; Martín Rojo, this volume).

Later authors have developed the notion of the entrepreneurial self by building on the experience of the new forms of corporate management that have become increasingly common. Laval and Dardot (2013) provide an overview by drawing as sources the works of classical liberals of the Austrian school such as Ludwig von Mises, Friedrich Hayek and Israel Kirzner. "Competition" is here added to the notion of the entrepreneurial self as a principle that informs neoliberalism as a model not just for the economy but for social relations as a whole. A further characterization is that neoliberalism overrules the separation between different spheres of life (the private and the public, religion), such that everything becomes an entrepreneurial exploit: work, consumption, leisure, and so on.

Sociolinguists and applied linguists have produced a number of case studies on how these ideas have played out on the ground, mainly in educational contexts (Block, Gray, and Holborow 2012; Martín Rojo 2010, 2018; Shin and Park 2015). These studies, however, focus mainly on institutional practice in education institutions, i.e. the ways in which schools or universities market themselves or the ideas that they seek to inculcate students (or their parents) about what language is and how language competence figures in people's employment and economic prospects. Thus, Urciuoli (2008) and Park (2016) argue that presenting language as an abstract, disembodied or de-contextualized professional skill is one of the key tenets of neoliberalism. Urciuoli (2010) also argues that such a view is repeatedly inculcated to students by career officers at universities. She also points out that corporate discourses perform specific appropriations of typically progressive value/ keywords such as "diversity" (of race, gender, class, sexuality). What we don't know, however, is how much or how little people (clients, students, citizens) participate in these ideological constructions across different social spaces. Urciuoli acknowledges that the simple use of the vocabulary by people is not evidence enough, as the meanings of these terms (what she calls "shifters") varies in different contexts (Urciuoli 2003). An earlier study by Park and Abelmann (2004) and Martín Rojo (this volume) provide evidence of how students and families engage with the learning of English and other international languages as a form of class marking and in order to be more competitive in future international markets. From this viewpoint, learning English is presented as the development of a discrete skill that the worker can eventually wield to be more competitive in the employment market, a decision that according to Gershon (2011) characterizes how agency is constructed from a neoliberal perspective.

When I engaged with my data analysis, I found that the current ideas about neoliberal subjectivity were too narrow to take account of the complex ways in which people narrate their experiences. So I have tried to build a wider framework. Holborow (2012) argues that the debates on neoliberalism often cause a great deal of confusion, as authors often use the term neoliberalism to refer to (a) particular canonical texts, (b) policies, or (c) descriptions of the contemporary world synonymous with "globalization", the "information age", or "Late Capitalism". It is certainly important to disentangle the uses of the notion as an "ideal", as a "practice" and as a "topos". I refer to neoliberalism primarily as a specific set of modalities in the practice of governance (of both public and private organizations), such as privatization or the creation of market-like conditions. I use the term "neoliberal subject" as the abstract model or target characterized out of the "classical literature" (self-entrepreneur, individualistic, competitive across life spheres). And I treat as "neoliberal discourses" the texts and statements associated with these models of governance and of the self, including ideas of language learning as an abstract and disembodied skill.

To refer to current socio-economic conditions, I use the term Late Capitalism, which to me includes neoliberalism, but also two other aspects. First is the *tertiarization* of the economy, whereby most activity relies on the provision of services, and hence generates forms of employment that rely heavily on the mobilization of linguistic and interactional skills. The centrality of interaction as part of the production process, or as product in itself, is arguably one important aspect of how the economy may get inscribed in people's bodies and their anticipation of returns (Bourdieu 1982) for language learning. Second is *globalization*, which (beyond the obvious multiplication of international contact and exchange) is described by Harvey (1989) as a process of *time-space compression*. For Harvey, time-space compression crucially involves production cycles. As the drive for profit requires the production of goods and services to be designed, manufactured and marketed ever faster, and as the global saturation of supply brings markets to push consumers to recurrently buy new products (through seasonal fashion, planned obsolescence, lifestyle and niche marketing), what we get is a structural unpredictability that affects the investors and the workforce. Added to this we have, of course, the implications of ever shrinking distances, which transform how cultures and economies traditionally relied on territorial and geographic conditions.

Neoliberalism may arguably be one specific response to these tensions that focuses on restricting worker rights and welfare provision, and which entails specific models of person-hood as described above. However, to broaden the purview of contemporary subjectivities I have incorporated additional ideas. Bauman (2000), for instance, argues that in this "liquid modernity", the structures of socialization such as the "nation-state", the church, welfare services, family and community, or the job for life, lose their former consistency. Deprived of these old forms of collective solidarity, individuals rely on consumption to fulfil their desires of identification. Giddens (1991) highlights the role of technologies (such as contraception or in vitro fertilization) and experts (such as psychotherapists), in producing new scenarios of possibility and hence of decision. As old identity categories and practices become obsolete, he argues that contemporary experience revolves around "reflexive projects of the self", the investment in "lifestyles" constructed out of new forms of socialization and consumption. The narratives of Harvey, Bauman and Giddens propose explanations of why old identity categories are in crisis so that people and institutions must face choices whether they subscribe or not to entrepreneurial conceptions of the self. From this viewpoint, neoliberalism is an option, and not an explanatory framework to account for the economy and individual consciousness.

However, one aspect that these contemporary debates often lack (at least at the top of the academic food chain) is attention to class or to the unequal access to resources (Atkinson 2008; Block 2015). Given the profound transformation experienced by both industrial and post-colonial societies in the twentieth century, particularly with the formation of a mass middle-class in the West, it is not surprising that analysts have found the category problematic as compared with earlier times. In this study I reinterpret class in Bourdieu's (1979) terms as "the objective social space of objective positions distributed relationally according to the volume and composition of [economic or symbolic] capital" (the phrasing is from Atkinson 2008: 11).

Here is where agency, as the "socioculturally mediated capacity to act" (Ahearn 2001: 112), comes in. My approach to class relies centrally on the idea of agency. Given that learning and speaking a language requires the development of specific dispositions and of the legitimacy to mobilize them in interactions charged with power relations, to me the key question is who has the resources and conditions to access the new linguistic competence as well as the recognition or authorization to enact it. After all, the whole idea of the neoliberal subject as an entrepreneur is all about an agent supposedly capable of realizing her own potential(s) by transforming herself and the conditions around her. So, we need to know how such agency is socially distributed when it comes to individuals engaging in specific projects of language learning.

Learning languages in late capitalism

In this section I bring up an overview of the different profiles of speakers in my data based on the accounts provided in interviews. The question is to what extent people from different contexts and identity ascriptions have incorporated neoliberal tenets in the way they plan their lives and decide what languages to learn and use. Given that neoliberal subjects are said to be embodied by the figure of the self-entrepreneur, what I have done is to construct different groups of informants according to how the styled themselves as active, that is, agentive, in the process of appropriating languages. For economy of presentation, I will focus on the most and least agentive of informants, and I will finally note how class background played an important role, whereas the connection between agentivity – entrepreneurship – and neoliberalism was not so clear.

The sample of interviewees sought as much diversity as possible in the profiles of new speakers without striving for any numerical proportionality. I will have to be somewhat oblique with the data presentation as more detail could easily lead to identify participants. All interviewees attested to uses of at least three languages; but the processes whereby they came to learn them and use them were markedly different. There were 15 men and 22 women. Five were Catalan born, 8 from other areas of Spain, 10 from elsewhere in Europe (Eastern and Western), 5 from Asia (from Syria to China), 2 from Africa, 7 from America (North and South). Seventeen lived in Barcelona and 5 in surrounding towns with predominantly Spanish speaking populations, while 11 lived in the Catalan-speaking hinterland and 3 either in the rest of Spain or abroad. It was difficult to obtain participants that we could clearly classify as "lower class", which I defined by combining data on level of education and employment of the interviewees and their parents. Eight persons were initially identified as having a modest family background plus an educational capital that seemed arguably narrowed their employment possibilities (mostly with incomplete secondary schooling). To have parents of modest means was more common, which speaks of the chances afforded during the twentieth century to those who invested in education: an additional 12 people fell under this category.

One first group of 9 people could be portrayed as the most entrepreneurial language learners. For 8 of them, their parents were professional people or successful entrepreneurs, whilst the parents of the last one had been industrial labourers and had grown up in socialist Eastern Europe. The five women in this group had carried out language degrees and their attitude towards Catalan (or other minority languages) had been mediated by the contents of the sociolinguistics courses now present in all these study programmes (except for an Italian who had initially constructed Catalan as a "dialect"). Two of them were specifically driven by the idea of pursuing graduate studies in multilingualism, of which one showed impressive resourcefulness when it came to finding activities to practice or pushing her acquaintances to speak her target languages. Two men were young central European postgraduates intent on pursuing academic careers who had already learned good English (one Latin too) at school and took pleasure in learning other languages, although they had developed tactics to learn informally through ordinary talk, reading and other means. One very multilingual craftworker worked in theatre scenography between Ljubljana and Barcelona. The last person was a French man and more of a typical entrepreneur with a family tradition of cultural activism for whom learning and speaking languages expressed both a sense of (European) cosmopolitanism and the opportunity to complexify his business connections.

These "first degree" language learners shared not only a family background slightly above their generation's average. They were both successful school performers and creative language learners in their everyday lives. They had also moved to different places before establishing themselves in Catalonia, and they did not exclude the possibility to move further. In fact, three of them were living and working in two countries at once. One other feature they shared was that they appeared very much in control of their lives, with a clear sense of how they wished to lead it. In this plan, languages were central: their present family was multilingual (sometimes their parents were too), and their professional practice required the use of three or more languages.

Multilingualism was inscribed in their career prospects or economic projects in different ways. Some of the Frenchman's business initiatives relied on the contemporary trend for the *"produits du terroir"*, which in Catalonia (both North and South of the French border) involves the recruitment of language and cultural symbology to market food linked to the territory. One woman's plan required to add two languages to her CV to apply for a specific grant. The Italian woman expressed ambivalent feelings about the use of Catalan for business and complained that the Catalan version of her website had very few hits for its cost. These were the three single occurrences of material that could arguably relate to the literature on neo-liberalism in one way or another: the first would be language as a component of a commodity, the second as a skill, and the third as a cost-benefit issue in a commercial context. However, the commitment to language learning of this group as a whole was primarily presented in terms of personal choices inscribed in their life experiences: connecting with their parents' cultural origin, investing in specific relationships, expanding the purview of their social horizon (e.g. getting to know local people better), or displaying their political commitment to the Catalans as a subaltern community (half of this group was very explicit about this). The production of discourses on linguistic commodification, or on languages as separate skills, was restricted.

When addressing issues of entrepreneurship and language, a mention must be made of those whose profession is directly connected with the materiality of language. Most members of this first group were in that category: translators, journalists, teachers, academics, communications officers. One should almost expect that such profiles may be more creative than others in the ways of learning language; but I separated a group of six whose approach seemed more classical. For these, language learning was primarily achieved through formal study and the obtention of accreditations. So this second group might be said to present ways of constructing language more in tune with the "skills" discourses mentioned in the literature on neoliberalism. Additionally, they also treated languages as immanent entities, countable and subject to regulations, a position that Park (2016) associates with neoliberalism; but not exclusively so. The family backgrounds of this group were more mixed than the first, with three members' parents being industrial or agricultural labourers. The main difference with group one, however, was in the display of initiative regarding mobility and language learning. Their accounts were presented as stages from education to professionalization, with a short stay abroad in one case and a long one in another (a short stay in England that ended up lasting several years). The learning of languages was presented as something requiring hard and constant work.

A third group of five people gathers those who came to Barcelona with training and experience in a profession. They all had skilled jobs: an architect, a doctor, a nurse, an accountant, a computer programmer. On moving to Catalonia, they had been able to get new employment without any knowledge of Catalan; although the medical professionals had had to learn it on the job. They did not show the enthusiasm for moving and learning languages of group one. Although they agreed that they did not need much Catalan for their everyday work, they argued that speaking it made them feel more "integrated" (their term) in the workplace. This group presented patterns of professional mobility consistent with neoliberal ideas of flexible labour, although only one had been moved to Barcelona by her company. They were certainly very attentive to the qualifications connected to their profession. In any case, their choice to learn Catalan, while somewhat convenient to navigate professional and personal contexts smoothly, was primarily constructed in terms of social and cultural interest.

The fourth group of six people, was composed by those who had come to Catalonia to start a new life. Most were women who had met a Catalan man at home and had moved to Catalonia to start a family. They had all attended Catalan classes. The Catalan-speaking relatives and social networks appeared as an important factor to provide the context to speak Catalan socially, and often to help finding employment. In fact, except for Virginia, who came from Argentina, the rest were more fluent in Catalan than in Spanish. Four people of this profile came from very modest families, half of which were arguably in the process of improving socially: they were first generation university graduates. Those who were employed were working as an accountant, a cook, and an all-purpose business owner in residence.

Neoliberal discourses were not really present amongst this group of people whose trajectories did not really follow a logic of strategizing to compete in markets. For them, family and social connections were clearly more productive than collecting skills and sending out CVs. However, Virginia had already been in Catalonia for a long while, and by the time she divorced she had plenty of contacts with different networks speaking in Spanish, Catalan or English. It is particularly relevant to the discussion on neoliberalism that, in her narrative, she constantly presented non-economic motives for learning, from her early curiosity to learn the language of her new boyfriend in Buenos Aires, to her justification for relearning English later in Barcelona:

Extract 1: Virginia

> Virginia: iii · vaig fer · fins alll- · · · al ferst · · però no em vaig presentar a l'examen / perquè jo el que volia era · entendre saps[?] · per comunicar-me · per parlaar · per legir per- · no sé perquè penso que les llengües són com- · bueno és que és part de la cultura · i quan tu pots entendre · · la llengua · d'aquesta cultura és como que estàs més introduïda a la cultura no[?] · perquè · quan tradueixes perds

> Virginia: *Aaand · I studied · up tooo- · · · up to the first [Certificate level] · · but I did not take the exam / Because what I was after was · to understand you know[?] · to communicate · to talk · to read to- · I don't know because I believe that languages are like- · Well it's that it is part of the culture · and when you are able to understand · · the language · of this culture it's as if you are more into the culture right[?]· because · when you translate you lose out*

It seems to come by chance that English became later important for her job, to the extent of speaking it daily. However, during the interview, she kept digressing from my questions about work to underline the many other activities that she carried out: (a) to travel a lot, through couch surfing, at least once a month around Europe, (b) to meet many new people from all over the world as a result, (c) to volunteer to help adults with reading problems, (d) to tend abandoned animals, (e) to work for an Italian NGO in Argentina, (f) to collect typical Catalan idiomatic phrases in a notebook, (g) to participate in a gospel choir, (h) to read fiction, poetry, and history, (i) to listen to Latin American folk music, and (j) to set up and manage a Facebook group for Catalan learners.

Thus, like the people in the first group, Virginia projected a life project in which language learning and mobility (more through new forms of tourism rather than changes of residence) were key components. The project was supported by a stable job; but it was clear that the job played a comparatively small role in her self-definition. Rather, her self-definition pivoted on activities geared towards the accumulation of cultural capital, an orientation traditionally associated with the sections with higher income.

In the sample, there was an exceptional profile. Lin, the youngest interviewee (18), was Chinese and was doing his pre-university studies. His father had sent him to study "in Europe"; and had chosen Spain because he had access to a work permit there. The current popularity of international schools suggests that there may well be a growing population of students like him who are sent to English or Spanish-dominant schools.

The fifth and final group provides a contrast that is important for the overall argument of this chapter. Mario, Teresa, María and José came from modest families and did not present significant improvements in symbolic and economic terms. They also shared a difficult relationship with the learning of languages.

Mario, for instance, was Puerto Rican and had started high school at home, where English was very present, and it was at least the language of his schoolbooks. However, he claimed not to be able to speak or understand English at all. If this had to do with a stance of resistance to anglicization, he gave no hint of it. His sudden move to a Catalan secondary school during early adolescence was also experienced as difficult, partly due to the language question, so much so that he dropped out of his program and signed up in a school of professional training, where he also dropped after a few months against the advice of his teachers who saw potential in him. Since then, he had started and never ceased working in manual jobs. He started speaking Catalan a while after he met who was going to be his wife and started getting pressure from his in-laws.

Maria had moved from Spain after marrying a Spanish-speaking Catalan. Since her marriage she had been essentially unemployed, and her account indicated that she had some difficulties of socialization. She had taken a variety of training courses for the unemployed, including Catalan, which she had learned up to C level, meaning that she was in theory fluent. However, despite living in a very predominantly Catalan-speaking area, she only spoke it with a person who refused to speak Spanish.

José, a French worker of Spanish descent who had moved to a very Catalan-speaking area, learnt Spanish first because their work colleagues decided to help him with it. José claimed not to have made any conscious decision "from today on to speak Catalan" and did not like to feel pushed to speak it. He had learned it by slowly picking up the language outside home and work. In extract 2 we can appreciate how aspects of the process are presented as devoid of intent:

Extract 2: José

MAITE: com és que et vas decidir per apuntar-te · a l'escola d'adults i
          aprendre · català / bueno d'una manera-
JOSÉ: no me'n recordo el porqué [tots dos riuen] noo · (què va)
[... José es planteja diversos escenaris que el podrien haver motivat]
JOSÉ: o alg- potser que algu m'ha dit por qué · no fas · un curs dee ·
          l'escola ii · di- vale · ja m'hi apunto o potser · em sembla que ·
          aquest cas ara que m'ho dius · hi haa · potser hi havia un amic
          ·· un company que era deee- ··· de galícia que · tambíén iba
          al- · al- al saló d'esport i se apuntava i he dit (jo) ja me apunto
          també · algo així
MAITE: *How is it that you decided to sign in · at the adult school to*
          learn · Catalan? / Well, in a way-
JOSÉ: *I can't remember the reason* [they both laugh]. *Noo · (at all)*
          [... José ponders scenarios which could have motivated him to sign in]
JOSÉ: *or someon- maybe someone asked me "why · not do · a course*
          at · the school" aand · sa- "Well · OK I sign in" or maybe ·
          I think that · in this case now that you mention it · there iis
          · maybe there was a friend ·· a guy who was froom ··· Galicia
          who · also went to- · to- to the gym and he was signing in and
          I said "(I) sign in too" · something of the sort

José attended these Catalan classes eight years after he had moved to Catalonia, and this happened because he was encouraged by a friend to sign up. He also pointed out that he had to go abroad often because he repaired the machines sold by his company; but that doing the repair did not require him to learn or speak any languages. He was doing the necessary training courses to keep up to date in his profession and was hoping to eventually find a better job; but he did not seem to be actively searching or taking any specific training to enhance his options.

Teresa was born in Barcelona in Franco's time and never learned and scarcely heard any Catalan at school. She was already in her 50s when she decided to take a course. She claimed to have a hearing problem and that she had always felt insecure about getting along speaking another language. She once witnessed someone who had recently moved from Spain and obtained the linguistic qualifications to work in the public service. This encouraged her to try. When learning about her intention, a work colleague commented that the idea made no sense "at her age", implying that no further career changes were to be expected. Another (male) friend had told her that it was "about time for her to do something profitable". She interpreted the comment as sarcastic. She claimed that this slight was instrumental in getting her to focus on her objective, as she was very mindful of her self-esteem.

Except for Teresa, this group displayed a significant amount of translanguaging in the interview. They also reported doing "*barreja*", 'speaking mixed'. This phenomenon was also common with other people, mainly of lower class origin; but the other examples took place with more recent learners and with people in predominantly Spanish-speaking areas whose opportunities to use Catalan were more restricted. Mario, Maria and José had been around for a while in an area where opportunities to speak Catalan were plentiful and even difficult to avoid. The "mix" consisted of inserting Spanish articles, pronouns, terms and phrases, and switches to Spanish for quotations which, eventually, could lead them to conduct a few turns in Spanish. The switches were often clearly motivated by knowledge gaps or for not having routinized Catalan constructions; but some were also expressive and dramatic, and the boundaries between the two were not always clear. In any case, there was no evidence that these translanguaging phenomena contained any perceivable intention of performing alternative normativities. Maria, for instance, began the interview in Catalan and ended it speaking almost exclusively in Spanish. Thus, her translanguaging practices operated as a means to unobtrusively return to her position of comfort. Mario also reported that he was not able to manage the accurate organized code-switching that local Catalans usually display as they switch languages back and forth with different interlocutors. So, he ended up speaking Catalan to his mother because his sisters spoke always in Catalan, and he was not able to speak Spanish consistently to his children. Teresa was, from this perspective, an exception in this group. She would stop her talk and ask me for words that she did not remember.

One further aspect points to the specific linguistic hierarchies that characterize the contemporary world. Except perhaps for Mario, English was a language either well known for most participants or being permanently learned by a few. Comments that implicitly constructed the different languages as unequal were plentiful, even when qualified, lamented, or self-contested. English was treated as a kind of categorical imperative, a requirement the validity of which was beyond discussion. Parents would talk in it to the children, set up their TVs so that the language was learned by watching cartoons, arrange stays abroad, and so on. Catalan, in turn, was not as important as Spanish. Even when circumstances led some respondents to be more proficient in Catalan, they had a mind to learn Spanish; which does not always happen in the reverse conditions. In fact, group six's reluctant or belated learning process was arguably imaginable in a context in which (Spanish) nation-state ideology made (in theory) the "global" language mandatory, the state language (mostly) necessary and the "local" one a matter of choice.

There is no evidence, however, that this linguistic hierarchy was constructed as part of any neoliberal outlook. When asked about linguistic policies, for instance, virtually all respondents assumed that it was the state's responsibility (in this case, the Catalan state, particularly through education) to manage the need for at least the three languages to be learned. Only one of the most entrepreneurial interviewees criticized some forms of interventions in the so-called (private) economic sector. At the time of the interviews, there was considerable pressure from right wing Spanish parties (*Partido Popular* and *Ciudadanos*) to intervene in Catalan education through the courts or through the central government. Although these parties often used neoliberal ideas (not consistently) such as "freedom of choice", many interviewees dismissed these debates as "political", by which they meant that they pursued to feed the common bickering and arguing of daily party politics.

The class distribution of (linguistic) agency

What the subtle gradation between the groupings above show is that those coming from more capitalized backgrounds, in economic and symbolic terms, tended to engage in language learning in an eminently active and creative way, congruent with how they articulated their life projects in relation to work, family, mobility or leisure. The first and last groups were the most contrasted, with the latter presenting their course of life and language learning more as something *happening* to them rather than something *sought after*. The contrast also emerged in terms of attention to linguistic correctness and boundary keeping, which was a concern for most participants, but which the latter group left in a blurry boundary between inability and disinterest.

Language learning was experienced and addressed differently by people of different class profiles. In group one I found the most successful and active learners, not just for Catalan, but for the four of five languages of their repertoire, and it was in this group where the children of university graduates and professionals clustered. There were also quick and successful learners in other groups, though not always so imaginative and not displaying themselves so much in charge of their life projects in the same way. Amongst these successful learners, there was sensitivity to linguistic correctness and to the boundaries between languages; but their stories engaged with language learning as a process owned by themselves, a process in which formal learning often played just a collateral or minor role (or none at all).

It was in group two of language professionals that I found the "good learners" of the language classroom, devoted to hard work, the attainment of the different levels, the patient collection of educational credit. Overall, within groups two, three and four, there were the trajectories of upward social mobility achieved through a combination of educational qualifications and better employment than their parents' generation.

Group five appeared in stark contrast with the rest. It was a group where people did not express a sense of direction in the interviews, and they showed no specific desires or needs to learn languages in general, or Catalan in particular. I felt that it was the insistent presence and injunctions of Catalan speakers that brought these four people to learn. In other areas where Catalan speakers are not so numerous, people of this profile simply don't learn it. I did not find either an interest in correctness or in keeping the two languages separate. So far, there was no hint of any intended political or linguistic deconstructivism in these practices. For Mario, in fact, this was experienced a problem when it came to organizing his language use in his family life. The accounts were noticeably formulated in ways that expressed lack of agency or of guiding control of decisions and practices. In the formulation of the interview narratives, it was typical in this group to insert themselves as recipients rather than as agents of processes.

Teresa's narrative provided additional elements to understanding what was going on in group six. In constructing her account, she gave an important role to people in her entourage who were disparaging her projects. At another juncture she acknowledged that she had not spoken Catalan most of her life because she felt "*vergonya*", "shyness/insecurity". *Vergonya* (or related concepts) is very often signalled as an important affect that prevents people from projecting their knowledge of Catalan in social life (Gonzàlez et al. 2014; Pujolar 2001). In addition to Bourdieu's (1982) "anticipation of profits" regarding the use of specific linguistic registers, *vergonya* points to the anticipation of *losses*. As Callero (2014) points out in his analysis of Goffman's (1967) reflections on the self, events (or, I would ad, fears) of *loss of face* have a direct connection with processes of reproduction of unequal social structures. Teresa's account finally ended with an experience that represented her *fighting back and winning*, which seemed to be about fighting back as much the negative injunctions of her entourage as her own insecurities. The scene was set in a tourism trip abroad, where she decided to visit a site on her own:

Extract 3: Teresa

> TERESA: anar sola sense parlar una mica d'anglès · una mica però · re ···
> molt- · molt- ·· molt <u>chapurreado</u> · no[?] / jo- vull dir / però · també · és
> que · em passa ·· saps[?] · sempre · l'amor propi em fa · a vegades · fer
> coses que- · dic pos · me'n vaig · ii vaig buscar la informació ho tenia
> molt bé vaig agafar el tren ·· ja sabia on tenia de- on havia de baixar
> ·· però clar · quan- després a l'arribar ·· va haver u- una cosa que-
> que em- ·· el- el autobús ·· que em portava · a Ma[u]thausen · no em

deixava · a Ma[u]thausen ·· em deixava · a la- un parell de quilòmetres ·· i clar ·· jo li vaig preguntar al conductor · en anglès · clar · en anglès ·· em va fer gràcia perquè a mi la gent m'entenia ·· i jo pensava · no ho- no ho parlaré tan malament · la gent em- m'entenia a mi però a mi em costava molt d'entendre la gent el que em deien ·· [...] i · nada en aquest viatge sí que vaig fer això · no[?] · de anar de atrever-me aaa anar a un lloc ·· parlar una mica d'anglès · però ·· no em vaig perdre ·· vaig arribar ·· més o menys bé · i no m'arrep- no · m'arrepenteixo

TERESA: *to go on my own without speaking- just some English · some but · it was nothing. ··· Ver- · Ver- ·· Very* mishmash *· right? / I- I mean / but · it also · happens · to me ·· you know · I always- · my self-esteem makes me · sometimes· do things that- · I say · "I just · go." · And I looked for the information, I had noted down every- thing well, I took the train. ·· I knew where I had to- where I was to step down. ·· But, of course, · when- after arrival · there was a- something th- that- ·· the- the bus · to Mauthausen · was not dropping me · in Mauthausen ·· it dropped people · at the- a couple of kilometres away. ·· And of course, · I ask the driver · in English · of course · in English. ·· I was thrilled because people did understand me. ·· And I was thinking · "I can- I can't be speaking it so badly". · People di- did understand me but it was hard for me to understand what people were saying to me. [...] And · that was all, · in this trip I did do that, · right? · Go, dare to go tooo a place · speak a little English: · but ·· I did not get lost. ·· I got there ·· fairly well and · I don't regr- I don't · regret it.*

What transpires of Teresa's account is how much our capacities are subject to social evaluation in a way that bears on our own perceptions of our own capacity to act. Her narrative was marked by her responses to these negative evaluations, uttered by men (according to her examples), which led to an interesting denouement in an episode in which, while doing tourism abroad with friends, she proved to herself that she could achieve something that disproved these sceptical attributions. In a way, her choice to learn Catalan, obtain the certificates, and display such a process in an interview was one more confirmation of the capacity to act that she was striving to develop, and was largely unrelated to any project of career development.

Conclusion: Entrepreneurship, class, agency

What this collection of narratives suggests is that linguistic entrepreneurship, the disposition to creatively engage in learning and using new languages, is associated with a more general entrepreneurial disposition to practice mobility, accumulate educational qualifications and aim at specialized employment. As such, these are dispositions closely associated with the exer- cise of agency towards the accumulation of material and symbolic resources.

The question is, however, if this entrepreneurship should be taken as evidence that neoliberalism is saturating people's consciousness or becoming hegemonic. The answer is inconclusive.

Most participants engaged in narratives in which they presented themselves as the main actors of their lives, so that the interview genre itself favoured agentive self-representations, if only on grammatical grounds. From this perspective, they all presented themselves as self-entrepreneurial. However, if I ask myself what types of *projects of the self* emerged in their narratives, there was a clear contrast between groups one and five, while the rest of the groups turned this contrast into a continuum. Group one presented the most resourceful and successful language learners clustered amongst people whose socioeconomic background had assured them a good and long education, mostly with both parents having professional or specialized employment. These people's employment, mobility, skills and qualifications – included linguistic ones – were presented as choices they had made, and with which they had succeeded.

For most other participants, groups two to four, qualifications and skills had been obtained more through hard work in conventional education, while employment or mobility were often the result of chance events or of taking advantage of opportunities that came up at specific moments. Profiles of upward social mobility, from low to middle-class positions, abounded in these groups. Finally, those who had invested minimally in educational capital, and mostly came from the low or low-middle classes did not seem to have an agenda, professionally or personally, and language learning seemed more like something that they were being dragged into.

Overall, an entrepreneurial disposition was unequally distributed along class lines; but participants of all profiles drew upon neoliberal discourses very moderately when making sense of their life trajectories. Only group two contained material in which language learning was central to the practice of specific professions, and where the attainment of linguistic qualifications or the maintenance of language skills was important. Other than this, I found isolated examples of an entrepreneur who mobilized language in the commodification of niche products, of a specialized worker worried about the cost-effectiveness of having the Catalan version of a website, or of a student sent by his parents to socialize in a "European" school.

People's attitudes towards English provided an argument that connects economic calculation and linguistic dispositions. English as a "global" language was increasingly used in the workplace together with other less valuable geographically-bounded codes – Spanish and Catalan in this case – and other varieties whose status was ambivalent. The diverse strategies and projects of parents to ensure that their children would learn English admittedly reflected the consolidation of people's orientation to spaces of communication that transcend the regional or the national. In any case, these strategies did not present themselves like the language shifts experienced in Europe or the Americas in previous generations. Parents expected their children to learn *all* the languages, that is, to be multilingual, and hence to keep their choices open for the future. There was evidence of a significant sociolinguistic change here, although it is unclear whether it should necessarily be taken as evidence of a neoliberal approach to languages or multilingualism.

A further aspect to consider is the fact that neoliberal dispositions are said to operate across all domains of life, from public to private, from professional to intimate. In the linguistic biographies studied, learning and using new languages was associated to important life changes in participants' professional and private lives. They could be the *consequence* of mobility, as when people learned Catalan and/or Spanish because they wished to work and live in Catalonia. But they could also be the *cause* of mobility, as when people travelled because of their interest to learn languages and ended up settling in Catalonia or keeping close relations with Catalans. Whatever the case, the languages learned affected people's employment options, their social networks and their leisure practices in multiple ways.

This could provide one reason why it may have been difficult for people to develop discourses that presented languages as exclusively or primarily economic assets. Indeed, the notion that the main value of languages is "cultural" was still much more present. Virginia's comment in extract 1 seems to constitute a response to this, by arguing that her decision to study English followed a "cultural" motivation. The act of not taking the accreditation exam served to symbolically divide what was done for personal reasons from what was done for professional grounds. The idea of taking up language courses (or sometimes acquiring qualifications too) as a form of self-accomplishment came up in a few other interviews. The accumulation of skills and qualifications was reportedly something that had a value in itself, irrespective of its bearing on career prospects. Put this way, this could be regarded as a new disposition in which a neoliberal habitus at once incorporates and mystifies the contemporary processes of symbolic capital accumulation. The accumulation of symbolic credit for the workplace, therefore, colonizes leisure through specific projects of the self.

There is the final question of whether participants constructed languages as immanent structures whose internal rules and boundaries must be respected. The answer is that most of them did. All participants had attended language courses, and they accepted as valid the need to use languages separately and correctly. However, most of them also shared a practical approach to learning in which language classes made sense to make a start; but language socialization and attention to contextualized sociolinguistic norms were just as important (and often struggled upon, as when they complained that Catalan speakers addressed them in Spanish). In fact, the "linguistic entrepreneurs" of group one had exploited informal ways of language learning the most.

To conclude, there is an argument to make that the times we live in offer individuals many options as to what to study, where to live, how to earn your living and how to engage in relationships. However, the disposition to make the most of this choice is not equally distributed: it is found amongst those born in homes with more resources. Such dispositions can well be called "entrepreneurship" provided that its social determinants are not erased in the process, which is what neoliberalism conventionally does. "Entrepreneurship" is one way of expressing modalities of agency that current conditions present as possible, but which are not equally available. The differences of availability may well have their origin in the possibilities to finance education, or the cost of moving, or to obtain visas and work permits; but they may be encoded and embodied in other ways. Teresa's struggle in extract 3 to display her capability to learn and speak languages reminds us that there are social processes and relationships that mediate our sense of self. Speaking new languages is, from this perspective, a good example of a disposition that profoundly implicates one's bodily hexis as it projects itself onto social exchanges that require complex processes of identity claims, authorization and contextualized cultural adjustments. Even as the participants of group one could recount how they mobilized their abilities and set up new social relations to access new linguistic competences, Teresa reminded us of those for whom these projects are risky and who seem to live in social environments that expect them to fail.

What is then the place of neoliberalism in this picture? Neoliberalism is one powerful narrative that claims to provide a framework to understand and act in it. It is a set of ideologies and practices of corporate and institutional governance that tries to bind together work and leisure, public and private activities and resources, and present specific forms of social relations and policies as natural and consistent.

However, as Urciuoli (2003) argues in relation to the appropriation of the value of "diversity" by corporate management consultants, the concepts and the phenomena that they signal are not necessarily exclusive "property" of a neoliberal ideological domain. A nuanced analysis of my data shows that participants narrated experiences and used concepts that have been caught and trussed in the spider web of neoliberalism; but what I mostly see are practices and discourses that could potentially be mobilized to make sense of and to enable alternative, more egalitarian, configurations of discourse and action as well. In fact, it was in the socially more privileged group that I found the discourses most critical with economic and linguistic inequalities. This is why I prefer to address many of the issues associated with neoliberalism from the perspective of the wider lens of late capitalism. Notions such as "projects of the self", "choice" or "self-improvement" certainly express dimensions of contemporary life that have been brought about by capitalist relations of production, liberal legal systems and practices of governance, technological innovations, and the emergence of a middle class no longer tied to an economy of subsistence. Ideally, alternative visions of society and governance should aim at incorporating these concepts and their attendant experiences to more egalitarian political projects.

Transcription conventions

Catalan is in normal font and the English version is in italics.

[Contextual information is set between square brackets]
[...]   segment excluded of unspecified length.
[?]   Typical short interrogative intonation contour, particularly in question tags.
aa   Unorthographical duplication of letters indicates lengthening or dragging of sounds.
·   Single dots indicate short but perceptible pauses important for text organization.
··   Additional dots indicate silences of approximately one-second each.
/   Perceivable change of voice, usually through intonation or speed.
Underlined: segments in a different language, manifest borrowings or codeswitches.
(xx)   Two syllables that cannot be retrieved

Note

1 This research was made possible by funding provided by the Spanish Ministerio de Economía y Competitividad. Project: Linguistic "mudes": an ethnographic approach to new speakers in Europe. Ref. FFI2015-67232-C3-1-P. It has also benefitted from academic exchanges conducted within the ISCH COST action IS1306 "New Speakers in a Multilingual Europe: Opportunities and Challenges."

References

Ahearn, Laura M. 2001. "Language and Agency." *Annual Review of Anthropology* 30: 109–37.
Atkinson, Will. 2008. "Not All That Was Solid Has Melted into Air (or Liquid): A Critique of Bauman on Individualization and Class in Liquid Modernity." *Sociological Review* 56(1): 1–17. doi:10.1111/j.1467-954X.2008.00774.x.
Bauman, Zygmunt. 2000. *Liquid Modernity*. 2006th ed., Vol. 1. Cambridge: Polity Press.
Block, David. 2015. "Social Class in Applied Linguistics." *Annual Review of Applied Linguistics* 35: 1–19. doi:10.1017/S0267190514000221.
Block, David, John Gray, and Marnie Holborow. 2012. *Neoliberalism and Applied Linguistics*. London: Routledge.
Bourdieu, Pierre. 1979. *La Distinction: Critique Sociale Du Jugement*. Paris: Éditions de Minuit.
———. 1982. *Ce Que Parler Veut Dire*. Paris: Fayard.
Burchell, Graham, Colin Gordon, and Peter Miller. 1991. *The Foucault Effect: Studies in Governmentality*. Vol. 1. Chicago: University of Chicago Press.
Callero, Peter L. 2014. "Self, Identity, and Social Inequality." In *Handbook of the Social Psychology of Inequality*, 273–94. Dordrech: Springer.
Consorci per a la Normalització Lingüística. 2017. "Memòria 2017 – Resum." Barcelona. https://arxius.cpnl.cat/arxius/memories/Memoria 2017-resum.pdf. (Accessed 03/05/2019.)

Foucault, Michel. 1991. "Governmentality." In *The Foucault Effect: Studies in Governmentaly* (Vol 1), edited by Graham Burchell, Colin Gordon, and Peter Miller, 87–104. Chicago: University of Chicago Press.

Fraser, Nancy. 2003. "From Discipline to Flexibilization? Rereading Foucault in the Shadow of Globalization." *Constellations* 10(2): 160–71. doi:10.1111/1467–8675.00321.

Gershon, Ilana. 2011. "Neoliberal Agency." *Current Anthropology* 52(4): 537–55. doi:10.1086/660866.

Giddens, Anthony. 1991. *Modernity and Self-Identity: Self and Society in the Late Modern Age.* Stanford: Stanford University Press.

Goffman, Erving. 1967. *Interaction Ritual: Essays in Face-to-Face Interaction.* Chicago: Aldine.

Gonzàlez, Isaac, Joan Pujolar, Anna Font, and Roger Martínez. 2014. *Llengua i Joves. Usos i Percepcions Lingüístics de La Joventut Catalana.* Estudis Barcelona: Generalitat de Catalunya. www.20.gencat.cat/docs/Joventut/Observatori Català de la Joventut/documents/arxiu/Publicacions/Coleccio_Estudis/Estudis30.pdf. (Accessed 03/05/2019.)

Gordon, Colin. 1991. "Governmental Rationality: An Introduction." In *The Foucault Effect: Studies in Governmentality*, edited by Graham Burchell, Colin Gordon, and Peter Miller, 1–52. Chicago: University of Chicago Press.

Harvey, David. 1989. *The Condition of Postmodernity: An Enquiry into the Origins of Cultural Change.* Oxford: Wiley-Blackwell.

Holborow, Marnie. 2012. "What Is Neoliberalism? Discourse, Ideology and the Real World." In *Neoliberalism and Applied Linguistics*, edited by David Block, John Gray, and Marnie Holborow, 14–31. London/New York: Routledge.

Idescat. 2014. "Ús i Coneixement Del Català 2013." 17. Dossiers Idescat. 2013–3898. Barcelona: Institut d'Estadística de Catalunya. www.idescat.cat/cat/idescat/publicacions/cataleg/pdfdocs/dossier17.pdf.

———. 2018. "Població Empadronada. Per Lloc de Naixement. Comarques i Aran, Àmbits i Províncies." *Anuari Estadístic de Catalunya.* https://www.idescat.cat/pub/?id=aec&n=257. (Accessed 03/05/2019.)

Laval, Christian, and Pierre Dardot. 2013. *The New Way of the World: On Neoliberal Society.* London: Verso. doi:10.1017/CBO9781107415324.004.

Ley 19/2015 de medidas de reforma administrativa. 2015. "Ley 19/2015, de 13 de julio, de medidas de reforma administrativa en el ámbito de la Administración de Justicia y del Registro Civil." Boletín Oficial del Estado (BOE) no. 167, from 14/07/2015. Kingdom of Spain.

Martín Rojo, Luisa. 2010. *Constructing Inequality in Multilingual Classrooms.* Berlin: Mouton de Gruyter.

———. 2018. "Neoliberalism and Linguistic Governmentality." In *The Oxford Handbook of Language Policy and Planning*, edited by James W. Tollefson and Miguel Pérez-Milans (pp. 544–67). Oxford: Oxford University Press. doi:10.1093/oxfordhb/9780190458898.001.0001.

Park, Joseph Sung Yul. 2016. "Language as Pure Potential." *Journal of Multilingual and Multicultural Development* 37(5): 453–66. doi:10.1080/01434632.2015.1071824.

Park, Joseph Sung Yul, and Nancy Abelmann. 2004. "Class and Cosmopolitan Striving: Mothers' Management of English Education in South Korea." *Anthropological Quarterly* 77(4): 645–72. doi:10.1353/anq.2004.0063.

Plataforma per la Llengua. 2018. "Novetats Legislatives En Matèria Lingüística Aprovades El 2017." Barcelona. www.plataforma-llengua.cat/media/upload/pdf/report-sobre-les-novetats-legislatives-en-materia-linguistica-aprovades-el-2017_1528193285.pdf.

Pujolar, Joan. 2001. *Gender, Heteroglossia, and Power: A Sociolinguistic Study of Youth Culture*. Berlin: Walter de Gruyter.

Pujolar, Joan, and Maite Puigdevall. 2015. "Linguistic Mudes: How to Become a New Speaker in Catalonia." *International Journal of the Sociology of Language* 2015(231): 167–87. doi:10.1515/ijsl-2014-0037.

Shin, Hyunjung, and Joseph Sung-Yul Park. 2015. "Researching Language and Neoliberalism." *Journal of Multilingual and Multicultural Development* 37(5): 443–52. doi:10.1080/01434632.2015.1071823.

Urciuoli, Bonnie. 2003. "Excellence, Leadership, Skills, Diversity: Marketing Liberal Arts Education." *Language and Communication* 23(3–4): 385–408. doi:10.1016/S0271-5309(03)00014-4.

———. 2008. "Skills and Selves in the New Workplace." *American Ethnologist* 35(2): 211–28.

———. 2010. "Neoliberal Education." In *Ethnographies of Neoliberalism*, edited by Carol J. Greenhouse, 162–76. Philadelphia: University of Pennsylvania Press.

Woolard, Kathryn A. 1989. *Doubletalk: Bilingualism and the Politics of Ethnicity in Catalonia*. Stanford: Stanford University Press.

———. 2016. *Singular and Plural: Ideologies of Linguistic Authority in 21st Century Catalonia*. Oxford: Oxford University Press.

7 Fabricating neoliberal subjects through the International Baccalaureate Diploma Programme

Andrea Sunyol and Eva Codó

Introduction

Uncertainty is the word that describes best the contemporary phase of capitalism (Sennet, 1998), also known as neoliberalised modernity. Uncertainty is associated to instability, intensified insecurity and rapid change. Insecurity and the rhetoric of insecurity have become powerful instruments of social control, because they create a societal mood defined by fear, anxiety and even helplessness (Anderson, 2016). These neoliberal affective dispositions compel all of us to work towards making our lives more secure, less unstable, more certain. This is how neoliberalism governs our conduct, that is, by appealing to the disciplined, self-responsible citizens to act upon themselves in a specific direction: "managing their own human capital to maximal effect" (Fraser, 2003, p. 168). This is the contemporary "care of the self" that Foucault identified as normative to neoliberalism. The self-responsible individual is not only acutely aware of the need to produce value (Gordon, 1991), but s/he is also morally obliged to be "perpetually responsive to modifications in his/her environment" (p. 43). This is why "*homo economicus* is *manipulable man*" (Gordon, 1991, p. 43, italics in the original).

The defining feature of uncertainty is precisely that we do not know exactly the direction in which things will evolve. Therefore, our present courses of action toward tackling uncertainty can, at best, be more or less informed guesses. Yet there is a sense in which we all feel obliged to act upon those guesses, to be prepared (Gao & Park, 2015). In keeping with the culture of financialisation, neoliberal self-capitalisation is speculative (Tabiola & Lorente, 2017): one can never be completely sure of the future appreciation of capitals; there is always risk involved. What is certain, however, is that it is the practice of self-capitalisation itself, as a disciplined act of neoliberal self-governance, that will be valued (Codó & Sunyol, 2019).

Drawing on the concept of neoliberal governmentality (Foucault, 1991; Gordon, 1991; Fraser, 2003; Rabinow & Rose, 2003; Martín Rojo, 2018), this chapter dissects the logics and practices of self-capitalisation of a group of students following the International Baccalaureate Diploma Programme (henceforth IBDP) in a private school located near Barcelona, in the northeast of Spain, during the academic year 2016/17. These students enrol in the IBDP "to be prepared" for their future (this is the actual school motto); in fact, they want to be more prepared than the rest. They decide to take the IDBP, alongside the national baccalaureate, to be maximally efficient (see also Martín Rojo, this volume). When they finish, they will have obtained two educational credentials – unlike most of their classmates. But beyond qualifications, their IB experience will transform them into perfect neoliberal subjects; we will see how and in what direction this transformation takes place and with what effects. We will also discuss what possibilities of resistance there are. We will argue that the IBDP, run by the Swiss International Baccalaureate Organisation (henceforth IBO), is a perfect illustration of how neoliberal governmentality operates: it is dispersed and multi-level, that is, it governs populations "through flexible, fluctuating networks that transcend structured institutional sites" (Fraser, 2003, p. 168); it is driven by market competition; and it is segmented, that is, it aims to create a "hypercompetitive" elite that "coexists with a marginal section of low-achievers" (p. 169).

This chapter will contribute significant insights to ethnographic studies of neoliberal governmentality; it will also throw new light onto processes of commodification of educational programmes and pedagogies (Soto & Pérez-Milans, 2018); finally, it will add to the scarce critical literature on the IB programme (Bunnell, 2008) by examining its localisation in a specific school, Forum International School (henceforth FIS). We shall begin by providing a historicising account of the IB in order to understand when, why and how the programme appeared; what its initial pedagogical bases were and why; and in what ways and to what extent it has changed over the last 50 years.

The International Baccalaureate: A historical perspective

The International Baccalaureate (known as IB or IBDP) is a two-year internationally-recognised university-entrance diploma offered in over 140 countries. Created in 1968 by educators linked to the International School of Geneva, its global popularity has rocketed over the last two decades. There are currently over 3,104 schools in 147 countries offering the IBDP (as compared to 500 in 1994), according to data in Bunnell (2016). The universe of school types offering IB programmes has completely changed in recent decades, from the elite international school profile of the early adopters (100%) to the growing presence of non-international state-funded schools of recent years (56% according to IBO, 2017a). In fact, attracting state schools has been a concerted strategy of the IBO to counter criticisms of elitism and facilitate expansion (Resnik, 2015). Some schools offer only IB programmes, while others combine the national curricula with IB education (as is the case of the institution analysed).

The IB emerged to fulfil a concrete practical need: facilitate home-country university access for expatriate children. It geographical origins (in French-speaking Geneva), first director (Petterson, a British educator) and pedagogical philosophy (with a strong Anglo-American bias, according to Tarc, 2009) defined the initial linguistic make-up of the programme, with French and English chosen as the only vehicular languages. Over time, further educational programmes for younger ages based on the same ideas and values as the IBDP were developed in what became the "IB continuum" (Hallinger, Lee & Walker, 2011). Yet, the IBDP is still viewed as the "flagship" (Tarc, 2009) of the non-for-profit IBO.[1]

The IB philosophy and curriculum: Continuities and ruptures over 50 years

The IB has a highly adaptable curriculum that fits different educational contexts and institutional configurations. It presents itself as a progressive and forward-looking type of education against the background of traditional (national) schooling that is slow to innovate. It is sold as the ideal type of education for a globally-circulating and post-nationally-oriented elite. This is no longer understood as the super rich (Weenink, 2005; Ball & Nikkita, 2014), but increasingly includes professional customer-families whose parenting style is defined by the strategically-planned nurturing of their children's capitals (see also Hidalgo & Fernández, this volume) to make sure that, as adults, they will be able to realise their full potential (Park, 2016).

As we mentioned, IB beginnings were defined by a concrete practical goal: creating an internationally-recognised university-entrance credential for expatriate school leavers. Yet, its promoters were also imbued with ideals of pedagogical and social reform. Their aim was not to create a programme for the elites but for everyone, with the aim of bettering the world (yet, the elitist tension has always been there linked to the programme's elite origins and partially elitist philosophy –despite efforts of the organisation to present the IB as non-elitist). The IB first director was, as mentioned, A. Petterson, a British school teacher and headmaster, who combined a career in education with a career in the military. Petterson, the soul of the IB in its initial years and still a revered figure, was a strong defender of humanist-liberal types of education against what he saw as the over-specialisation of the British pre-university system. In line with Petterson's ideas, the IB aimed to educate "the whole person" to create "well-rounded individuals" that is, not only focus on students' academic performance, but also on the moral and aesthetic dimensions. The philosophy of the IB combined traditional humanist views of education for the elites (Williams, 1961), aimed at character-building, and cultivating taste and moral virtues, with progressive versions of humanism, centred on creativity, democratic citizenship and developing students' inner potential. As Hickox and Moore (1995) argue, these two trends do not encapsulate radically opposed views, but rather, they form two alternative poles of humanist-liberal education.

The IB curriculum tried to achieve "breadth and depth" of education (Tarc, 2009). In other words, it shied away from a narrow and specialist/ technical training, and gave philosophy, literature and the arts a significant place (this is "breadth", but also a way of cultivating the aesthetic and the moral), while at the same time guaranteeing academic rigour and high standards ("depth"). Depth was also achieved through fostering conceptual learning (rather than facts and figures), transversal thinking and criticality. Pedagogically, the programme was defined by student-centred methodologies, experiential learning and a focus on learning how to think (later transformed to learning how to learn). Socially, inspired by the UNESCO policy discourse of intercultural understanding for world peace, the IB intended to advance ideas of internationality and cosmopolitanism in search for a better world. At the time, advancing these ideas was not straightforward, as many governments saw the IB (and international education more generally) as treading on one of the state's key policy terrains, and even as challenging their sovereignty (Tarc, 2009).

Today, the IB curriculum still follows the founding principle of providing students with a "general education". All IB students take nine subjects throughout their two years of study. Most IB courses can be taken at two levels of expertise: standard or higher. Students need to take a minimum of three (and maximum of four) courses at higher level, which means that they receive more hours of instruction and cover additional topics. This allows them to specialise in a few subject areas (usually required by university entrance examinations), and at the same time, become acquainted with other disciplines that will expand their cultural capital. Out of the nine courses students must follow (of which they have a choice),[2] there are three *core* compulsory subjects, that is, Theory of Knowledge, the Extended Essay and Creativity, Action and Service. These three courses encapsulate the transdisciplinary goal of the programme, and its search for a well-rounded individual who commits part of his/her time to creative, physical and social service activities.

The flexibility and adaptability of the IB curriculum have been indispensable for the global success of the programme, even though the current corporatisation and branding strategy of the IBO (Tarc, 2009) require strong regulation and normativisation. In order to meet the company's growth plans, the DP curriculum has had to incorporate local realities into its globalist outlook. Making programmes available in more languages – such as Spanish (1983) – and adapting exam dates to match the southern hemisphere school calendar were strategic steps towards expansion in the Latin American and Asian markets. The determination to adapt to the local is also reflected in how course programmes can be tailored to meet the requirements of each national education system, and to the practicalities of implementation in each school (i.e., availability of resources, as we shall see later in the case of FIS). Courses allow for a certain degree of freedom for schools – even individual teachers – to decide on the actual content. One of the areas where this is more visible, history and geography aside, are the studies in language and literature. Language A courses examine the literary production and linguistic features of the students' "best language" (IBO, 2017b). The IB makes these available in 55 languages (Language A: literature) and 17 languages (Language A: language and literature), including a non-state language such as Catalan.

On the whole, the current structure of the IB curriculum and its general philosophy (both ideological and methodological) are fairly similar to the initial years. The rhetoric also continues to be one of tolerance and world peace (with the recent addition of the environmental discourse, as IB students are presented as "guardians of the planet"). However, in the last decades there has been a key shift, which we argue aligns the programme with the neoliberal rationality. If previously, the emphasis was on the type of education the IB aimed to advance (sold as progressive despite its elite influences), now the focus is on the standard commodity the programme claims to produce: a type of student – imagined as a neoliberal protoworker (see also Urciuoli, this volume), as we will dissect later. Thus, the current IB mission statement devotes two (out of three) goals to describe the aspired characteristics of IB graduates (inquiring, knowledgeable, caring, respectful, tolerant, active, compassionate and life-long learners) while specifying nothing of the programme's pedagogical approach or view of education, except that is a "challenging programme" with "rigorous assessment" – see IBO (2014a). In addition, we have observed the discursive (and practical) centrality of the learner profile, which we shall analyse later, a ubiquitous promotional document containing the 10 traits defining the standard IB person produced by the programme. For example, in the publication entitled *What is an IB education?*, the learner profile is presented on page 2, right after the mission statement just referred to. The neoliberal rationality of the learner profile and the ways in which students are made to conform to it will be discussed later. Let us now turn to a brief overview of the current appeal of the IB in Catalonia and Spain.

Evolution of the IB in Catalonia and Spain

In Spain, the growth of the IB in recent years has been significant. According to Resnik (2015), there were 49 schools offering the IB in 2009. In 2017, there were 108 (IB website). In Catalonia, where Forum International School is located, there are currently 21 schools offering the Diploma, four of which are state-funded. Although it was first offered in 1986, 66% of all Catalan schools implementing the DP have adopted it after 2010, due to the feelings of economic insecurity caused by the global economic crisis, which hit Spain in particularly acute ways (see also Hidalgo & Fernández, and Martín Rojo, this volume). Emigrating to more prosperous economies was seen by many as the only way of finding a job or maintaining class status, and obtaining an "international" type of education, as the ideal way to self-capitalise. At the same time, this process has constituted internationality as one of the main axes of distinction in the Catalan education system at present.

The 17 private schools that teach the IB in Catalonia at the moment of writing this paper are of different types: some are international/European schools; some others follow a foreign national curriculum (American or British); and some others are just private schools without an international profile. (All of the latter are religious.) Most schools offer the programme in Spanish. The IB taps on the discourse of excellence and innovation, and construes itself as fostering reflection and original thinking skills against what is regularly presented as a banking, teacher-centred, rote learning form of education (Barnés, 2016). Resnik (2015) attributes the success of the IB in Spain to its "international aura", its focus on English (although, as we have mentioned, the programme is mostly taught in Spanish) and its promise of an easier access to the global work and educational marketplace. She also points out that the discredit of the system that began when compulsory education until age 16 was introduced (due to perceptions of lowering standards linked to the presence of demotivated and disruptive students) may have played a role. The arrival of large-scale economic migrants in the early 2000s (most of whom were schooled in the state system, see Martín Rojo, 2010), and the significant budget cuts on education during the economic crisis contributed to worsening the reputation of the system.

IB localisation: An ethnographic case study

In this section, we ethnographically analyse the process of localisation of the IBDP in a school located in greater Barcelona: Forum International School (FIS).[3] FIS is a rather large school (it hosts approx. 1500 students) that was founded in 1989. The school's fairly high fees, as well as its tradition of educating privileged families, engagement with excellence, extensive curricula, geographical location and outstanding facilities define an elite profile. FIS offers all educational stages, from nursery to baccalaureate and vocational training. In 2008, following school property changes, it became "international". This re-orientation and re-branding process (explained in more detail in Sunyol, 2017) entailed, among others, a change in language policy (Spanish and English became "official" languages alongside Catalan, until then the school's preferred vehicular language), a reworking of the language programme (a non-European language such as Mandarin Chinese, which was already offered, gained curricular importance, see Codó & Sunyol, 2019, for further information), and a "restructuring" of the teaching staff. In some cases, this meant downgrading long-standing coordinators and form teachers; in some others, replacing older Catalan-speaking teachers by younger ones who had studied abroad and were proficient in English. In 2012, a new international feature was added: the IBDP (shortened to IB in the school). The idea of the school was to try out the IB to later expand the offer to other IB pogrammes for earlier stages.

The introduction of the IB at FIS was part of the school's marketisation strategy; it was a process of external validation that legitimated the school's educational project, both academically, as the IB was presented as a marker of educational excellence, and in relation to its internationality. This was happening in two ways: first, through the adoption of an internationally-valued and internationally-oriented curriculum, and second, through the capacity to attract the children of transnationally mobile families. This was desperately needed by the school in order to create a "truly international" atmosphere (constantly under scrutiny by parents, students and even teachers, as some of them thought the school used the word "international" as a mere branding strategy). In sum, the IB was and is a tool by the school to further capitalise itself, both symbolically and practically, in order to deepen its distinctive and elite profile in the competitive local school market (no other school offers the IB in this (upper)-middle class area) and increase enrolment rates (see Codó & Sunyol, 2019 for a more elaborate account of how FIS tried to distinguish itself from other schools, both private and public, in the area).

Implementing the IB at FIS

We followed the IB programme closely from December 2016 until June 2017 (as part of a two-year broader sociolinguistic ethnography of FIS).[4] The data we draw on for this chapter consists of ethnographic observations of classes and events (such as Christmas shows, Model United Nations conferences or language credential award ceremonies) carried out during this period. We also conducted individual and focus group interviews with 13 IB students, 4 educators (1 Spanish, 2 Catalan and 1 English language teachers), the IB coordinator and the school's headmaster. As part of our ethnographic endeavour we have also examined textbooks, student diary entries, student Instagram posts, IB policy documents, the school's website, and visual material from the school's landscapes.

FIS students can choose among two IB itineraries, that is, science, or individuals and societies. As the DP is offered as part of a double degree with the national baccalaureate (referred to as LOMCE in the school),[5] and in order to maximise time and teaching resources, some subjects are shared. In practice, this means that some subject content is adapted or overlaps, and students do not have to fully complete both programmes. The IBO retains control over the curricular content, methodology and evaluation of the DP. It also offers training to teachers and administrative staff, and conducts periodical inspections. The school assigns the best teaching resources to the programme: the most committed and well-reputed teachers.

At FIS the IB is implemented in Spanish. However, the linguistic regime is flexibilised depending on the social composition of classes, and teacher preferences. When there are non-local students, classes are taught in Spanish. Otherwise, they are unofficially taught in Catalan because it is the habitual language of use among the student population at baccalaureate level (they were schooled before the internationalisation process began), although evaluation items (papers, exams, etc.) are always written in Spanish.

Doing a double degree comes at an extra cost for families (an additional 100€ monthly) and time investment for students. IB students spend four extra weekly hours at school, and have to manage a greater workload. Unlike their LOMCE schoolmates, their weekly schedule includes afternoon sessions in which they have lab sessions or extra classes for some of the subjects. This creates a general feeling of having very little or no free time, as we shall see later.

Despite that, in its five years of implementation the number of students has increased from 13 (2012) to 53 (2017). In 2017 almost 25% of all baccalaureate students took the double degree option. The school has increasingly hired teachers with previous IB experience – as both teachers and examiners – and with the changing demographics of IB students, that is, as there are more non-local students with transnationally mobile trajectories, the school has widened its linguistic offer. English A (as a first language) and Spanish B (as a second language) are now being offered.

Not all students can access the programme, and there are different access procedures for FIS and non-FIS students. FIS students are guided (or not) towards the IB at the age of 14–15 when they are on their third year of compulsory secondary education. Teachers recommend the IB to those students they think are motivated/curious to learn and mature enough (and in so doing make it difficult for parents not to follow the school's recommendation to enhance their children's potential). Selected students then enrol in a pre-IB course which is construed as a test to see if they are responsible and hard-working, by which they mean checking whether they are self-sacrificing enough to be able to complete both IB and LOMCE. Those who are new to the school, and who mostly join FIS to do the IB, must have a personal interview with the IB coordinator. In general, they are students who are academically-oriented and value education. In addition to considering their academic file, the coordinator takes into account maturity, attitude and motivation. However, to our knowledge, no one has ever been rejected. The entry requirements and selection process are symbolic gatekeeping mechanisms to advance the idea of an elite community being created within the (elite) school, as we shall discuss in the following sections.

Transforming students into ideal neoliberal subjects

The aim of this section is to, first, discuss IB rationality through the analysis of the currently most emblematic and widely-reproduced discursive artefact of the programme, the IB learner profile. This will be followed by the examination, through ethnographic data, of the disciplinary techniques put into practice by the school to (self-)transform IB students into desirable neo-liberal subjects.

IB neoliberal rationality: The "IB learner profile"

In 2006 the IBO launched the "IB Learner Profile". This was part of the organisation's branding strategy and was accompanied by, among others, the development of a new corporate logo. The creation of the IB profile sought to enhance coherence across IB schools through standardisation (Bunnell, 2010). The learner profile is presented as the unpacking of the mission statement goal of creating "active, compassionate and lifelong learners" (IBO, 2017a). It is one among a vast range of "communication (see promotional) materials" (posters, flyers, booklets, etc.) containing the IB selling lines that the IBO offers to schools in order to "marketise themselves" (IB website). The profile is, thus, clearly and primarily a school marketisation instrument intended to sell the standard commodity produced by the IB: a specific type of person. Below are the key traits that define an "IB person".

Extract 1

IB Learner Profile
The aim of all IB programmes is to develop internationally-minded people who, recognizing their common humanity and shared guardian-ship of the planet, help to create a better and more peaceful word.
As IB learners we strive to be:

INQUIRERS
We nurture our curiosity, developing skills for inquiry and research. We know how to learn independently and with others. We learn with enthu-siasm and sustain our love of learning throughout life.

KNOWLEDGEABLE
We develop and use conceptual understanding, exploring knowledge across a range of disciplines. We engage with issues and ideas that have local and global significance.

THINKERS
We use critical and creative thinking skills to analyse and take respon-sible action on complex problems. We exercise initiative in making reasoned, ethical decisions.

COMMUNICATORS
We express ourselves confidently and creatively in more than one lan-guage and in many ways. We collaborate effectively, listening carefully to the perspectives of other individuals and groups.

PRINCIPLED

We act with integrity and honesty, with a strong sense of fairness and justice, and with respect for the dignity and rights of people everywhere. We take responsibility for our actions and their consequences.

OPEN-MINDED

We critically appreciate our own cultures and personal histories, as well as the values and traditions of others. We seek and evaluate a range of points of view, and we are willing to grow from the experience.

CARING

We show empathy, compassion and respect. We have a commitment to service, and we act to make a positive difference in the lives of others and in the world around us.

RISK-TAKERS

We approach uncertainty with forethought and determination; we work independently and cooperatively to explore new ideas and innovative strategies. We are resourceful and resilient in the face of challenges and change.

BALANCED

We understand the importance of balancing different aspects of our lives –intellectual, physical and emotional – to achieve well-being for ourselves and others. We recognize our interdependence with other people and with the world in which we live.

REFLECTIVE

We thoughtfully consider the world and our own ideas and experience. We work to understand our strengths and weaknesses in order to support our learning and personal development.

The IB learner profile represents 10 attributes valued by IB World Schools. We believe these attributes, and others like them, can help individuals become responsible members of local, national and global communities.

(Extract taken from IB learner profile: www.ibo.org.)

As we can see, the profile consists of 10 features that "go beyond academic success" (IB website) aimed to develop "internationally minded people who [...] help to create a better and more peaceful world", as stated in the profile. How these attributes contribute to creating "internationally minded people" is not apparent in the profile, which only contains passing mentions to "issues and ideas that have local and global significance" and to appreciating "the values and traditions of others". In *The History of the IB* (IBO, 2017a) this international perspective is simplified to the IB offering "multiple perspectives" instead of a "national perspective", but the concept is not elaborated further either. This is in continuity with the traditional underspecification of how international-mindedness was to develop in the IB: as deriving from the general education/humanist perspective, rather than through the inclusion of specific content.

Although the profile is a *learner* profile (our italics), the relationship between adjusting to the profile and obtaining the diploma is left unspecified; this proves that the learner profile is not aimed at improving academic performance but at ensuring that students know what is expected of them: to rethink themselves along IB lines, assess their degree of fit (note that each attribute contains a number of assessable action-oriented descriptors), and self-transform (the use of first-person plural "we" instead of third-person "they" is a rhetorical appeal to self-commitment). The profile is, thus, a technology of the self (Foucault, 1988), an explicit, normative exhortation to students to act upon themselves. The stated goal is "to help individuals and groups become responsible members of local, national and global communities". In fact, being a good IB student is equated with being a good citizen. In that sense, it is more than a technology of the self; it is a technology of citizenship (Rose, 1996), aimed to create a specific type of citizen: one which has a global orientation but is firmly grounded on the national. For Tarc (2009), this is related to IB's initial tensions with states (mentioned in an earlier section), which derived "in a version of internationalism that does not challenge the existing state-centered order" (p. 243). In that sense, it fits well with the (cultural) nationalist outlook of neoliberalism (Harvey, 2005).

But what is the nature of the profile 10 attributes? There are various visual representations of the profile, but for the purposes of this chapter, we shall discuss one that we find particularly illuminating (see Figure 7.1 next page).

Both the round shape and the jigsaw are recurrent tropes for visually displaying the profile. While the round shape reminds us of the globe (the IB aspirational spatial context) and of a holistic type of education, the jigsaw describes a person made up of separate (and separable) parts that, together, make a coherent whole. These separate parts, the IB aspirational personality traits, are, in fact, skills, defined by Urciuoli (2008, p. 212) as "a disparate set of practices, knowledge, and ways of acting and being". Most of the aspirational student attributes in the profile (inquirers, risk-takers, open-minded, reflective) are in fact "soft skills", that is, forms of sociality (see Urciuoli, this volume) or "aspects of personhood with exchange value" (p. 211). As we shall see later, that is in fact how students are asked to self-imagine, that is, as sets of (soft) skills that are distinct, measurable and subject to improvement. Interestingly, in the figure under analysis, binding all these traits-skills together, is the key soft skill of the contemporary workplace: communication (interestingly translated into Spanish as "*good* communication"). Without communication, the IB subject falls apart, ceases to exist. But the centrality of communication is not a mere representational issue; we observed how communicating adequately and regularly was one

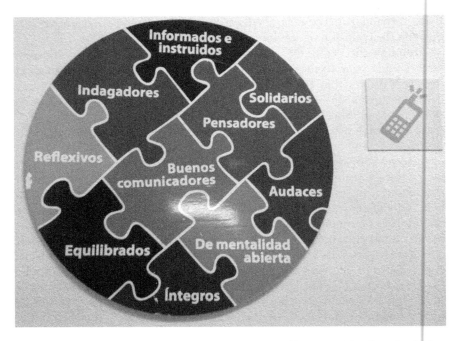

Figure 7.1 Visual representation of the IB learner profile in Spanish. Photo by Andrea Sunyol. An English version of this image can be found, among others, on www.nordagliaeducation.com.

of the defining criteria for students to be classified as "IB" (or "non-IB") at FIS. This will be further discussed in the following section.

So, what we have seen is that the humanist idea of educating the whole individual, defining the IB since its beginnings, has easily enabled a neo-liberal co-optation of the programme. However, the well-rounded IB individual is no longer one who develops aesthetically, physically and morally, but one which moulds him/herself to advance a series of traits/dispositions that are "sellable" parts of themselves. As Urciuoli (this volume) also discusses, IB students are conceptualised as simultaneously customers and products. In the next section we will discuss how the neoliberal rationality of the IB in general, and of the learner profile more specifically, is inculcated into students.

Transforming IB students

As we have said, the IB is not just an academic training scheme; it is a disciplinary apparatus aimed to transform not only students but the whole school community ("they [the human capacities described by the profile] imply a commitment to help all members of the school community...", reads the

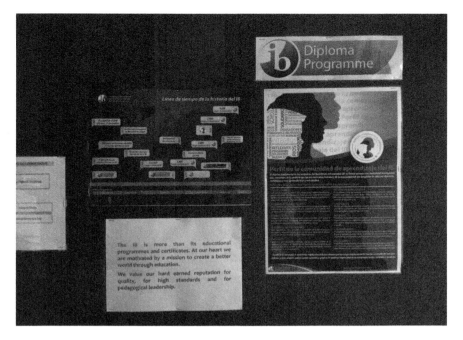

Figure 7.2 IB learner profile posted on the stair walls. Photo by Andrea Sunyol.

Figure 7.3 Dining room decorations based on the learner profile attributes in English, Spanish and Catalan. Photo by Andrea Sunyol.

preamble to the learner profile contained on the IB website). In line with this objective, the IB learner profile was visually very salient at FIS. The school had it posted in full colours in the IB corridors and in every classroom; it was also on the opening page of every IB textbook. In fact, the 10 traits of the profile had transcended the programme's physical spaces: posters strategically hung all over the school, most visibly in key areas such as the reception hall, or there was a word cloud in the general dining room (see Figures 7.2 and 7.3 above), for everyone to see. The profile clearly sought to transform, not just IB students and educators, but the whole school by constantly reminding each of its members of the goals that they should work at and work for.

In the extract below, we see how acutely aware students were of the transformational impact their participation in the programme was having on them, while at the same time displaying that transformation by telling themselves as reflective individuals (remember that reflective is one of the profile attributes).

Extract 2[6]

Participants: M (Martí), L (Laura), Al (Alexia), all students.

```
01  M:   I/ (.) I remember/ I remember a le::sson/ from last year\ that I think
02       that:/ we had no tea:cher/
03  L:   =yes:::\
04  M:   =and we were/ all\
05  Al:  =all\
06  M:   =sitting/
07  Al:  =working [(    ) of work/
08  M:              [wo::rking/ and then/ suddenly\ I get up and say\ (.) [does
09       anybody see
10  L:                                                                   [what's
11       with us/
12  M:   what's going on/ [I mean\
13  L:                    [what's going on with us/ guys\
14  Al:  ((laughs))
15  M:   two years [earlier/
16  L:             [they were all sitting [in si::lence/
17  M:                                    [we wouldn't have ima::gined this/
```

Martí, in lines 8–12, is struck by the silent atmosphere in his class, and prompts his classmates to notice their out-of-ordinary and exemplary behaviour. Asked about what makes the IB different from the national baccalaureate, Martí chooses to tell us this circulating anecdote that has become a sort of shared, group-defining identity story. Martí narrates how despite the teacher's absence, the class of 16-year-olds were all sat, working silently and focusing on their tasks; they knew it was their responsibility to finish the work assigned to them. He points out how unthinkable this behaviour would have been only two years earlier, when they were still in compulsory secondary education. As they are co-telling the story, Laura and Martí summarise the morale of the story in two slightly but significantly different ways. Martí's "what is going on" (*què està passant* in Catalan) becomes Laura's "what is going on with **us**, guys?" (*què **ens** està passant, nois*). Laura's reformulation points to the sharp realisation that something within them has changed: they have become different people. The IB programme has turned them into self-responsible, hard-working and self-sacrificing individuals, but also individuals always ready to reflect on and discuss their transformation. Two years earlier they would have preferred to chat among themselves or rest, unaware of their conduct. They would have needed to be externally guided, supervised, policed. This is not necessary anymore; they have become reflexive self-governing individuals focused on being efficient (through good time management skills) in order to "be prepared" for their future.

However, self-transformation is not easy; it requires effort. The word "strive" in the profile indexes this. Becoming this new person is a fight to better oneself. But that effort is worth it; it is the key to becoming a "developed" person. In the highly moralised discursive regime of the IB, adjusting to the normative IB subject is equated with "developing as a human being" and "developing positive traits within oneself" (website testimonials). These key ideas were appropriated and retold by FIS students whenever we asked them what the IB did for them. "It helps you develop as a person", said Alexia, another IB student. These students seem thus to imagine themselves not only as positively transformed but as having actually been "saved" from remaining "underdeveloped" by the IB (note that this echoes the pastoral logic of governmentality, discussed by Foucault, oriented to the "salvation" of individuals, Rabinow & Rose, 2003, p. 132). It is in and through the repetition of these key phrases that they embodied being good students and indexed their total alignment with the IB philosophy.

But who were the "underdeveloped" students? If we recall Fraser's words (2003, p. 168), neoliberal governmentality is segmented, that is, unlike fordist regulation, it does not "aspire to universality" (see also Pujolar, this volume). Instead, it aims to discipline only those that are worth investing on. "Working largely through population profiling, it separates and tracks individuals for the sake of efficiency and risk prevention" (p.169). This is exactly what happened at FIS. "Ideal" IB students, meaning motivated and hard-working ones, were advised to opt for the IB-LOMCE combination rather than just follow LOMCE. Martí, featured in Extract 2, was one of the chosen few. After selection, he joined the preparatory pre-IB group, but when it was time to finally decide (at age 16), he enrolled in the national programme. After a week, he requested to go back to the IB. He missed his friends from the previous year, but allegedly, he was also feeling out of place, as he longed for the "better" working atmosphere of the IB and its charismatic teachers.

Going back to the LOMCE programme had somehow been "a step back-ward" that he wanted to undo. So, what we are trying to say with Martí's example is that at FIS the implementation of the IB did not simply mean a broadening of the educational offer; it meant altering the socio-discursive order of the school. It became a tool for streamlining students (and teachers), and creating and naturalising hierarchies based on programme choice.

A great deal of discursive effort was put into positivising not only the IB programme, but basically, IB students, while negativising their LOMCE counterparts to the point of *othering* them. Indeed, the latter were system-atically stereotyped as lazy, weak, unruly and non-motivated (and imagined to remain as such), whereas the former were hard-working, well-behaved, norm-abiding and extremely motivated (and constantly working at self-betterment). In such a discursive regime, IB students could not possibly cease to improve themselves to (IB) perfection. To act otherwise would have turned them into students unfitting for the programme, that is, non-IB. IB was, in fact, regularly employed as an identity label. Students, teachers but also comments or jokes could be *very* IB, IB, or simply not IB. Marta (one of our focal student participants) and her classmates labelled conversation topics as "very IB" when they required them to think and inquire, or to elaborate complex arguments, linking "being IB" to intellectual challenge. However, being in the IB programme did not necessarily grant IB status. In one of the interviews, Marta explained how she did not like her language A teacher because "he is not IB enough". His teaching style resembled that of the national baccalaureate. Lessons were teacher-centred and based on memorising concepts, and he was always late for class. He was not identified as the self-bettering, self-sacrificed, creative and up-to-date worker that the IB coordinator defines as "the prototypical IB teacher".

This moralised dichotomy (IB *vs* non-IB) was precisely one of the key dis-ciplinary techniques employed by the IB teachers, who, not surprisingly, sys-tematically referred to the ways of behaving they were intent on eradicating as "non-IB". This placed IB students under constant (self-) surveillance. What were these key IB traits? We shall focus on the three student dispositions that we ethnographically identified as distinguishing IB from non-IB students, and which to us, encapsulate IB rationality, as it was implemented at FIS: commu-nication; open-mindedness; and respect and compassion.

Communicating "adequately" was central to IB life. This was particu-larly salient to us (and the students) because such a strong emphasis on oral communication is unusual in Catalan/Spanish schooling. When students contributed to lessons (which they were always encouraged to do), teachers paid special attention to form; content corrections were rare. Students were expected to structure their contributions well – contextualise their ideas and provide coherent arguments – and employ precise vocabulary and a formal register. One Language A exercise, for example, consisted in the discussion of a literary work. One student presented on the piece, and the class engaged in a critical evaluation of it. In their contributions, students were asked to refer to excerpts, make quotations explicit, polish their vocabulary and provide a logical reasoning for their thoughts. What mattered seemed to be inculcating in students the value of effective/adequate communication, as a central IB soft skill, as we have seen, but also a distinctive capital in the local marketplace. Martí, one of the students, mentioned "learning how to talk" as one of the advantages of following the IB. Interestingly enough, "appropriate" communication skills were not associated with a given language. In fact, FIS students made a point of emphasising that the IB was not taught in English, an assumption that, allegedly, many of them had had to counter when talking to friends and relatives about the IB. Although the reasons why the IB at FIS was taught in Spanish were pragmatic and economic, that is to ensure higher marks for students and increase enrolment rates, it is true that the IB language policy at FIS somewhat challenged the hegemonic linking of innovative, quality education and English so prevalent in the Catalan/ Spanish public discourse (see also Hidalgo & Fernández, this volume). Yet, at the same time, it reinforced the idea that modern, internationally-minded education was incompatible with Catalan, the local minority language in which the national baccalaureate was taught.

Apart from their communicative abilities, IB students were regularly flagged as being open-minded. This meant nurturing superficial cosmopolitan dispositions à la Hannerz (1996), that is, appreciating and being positively pre-disposed towards everything foreign. Alexia, one IB student, summarised the international distinctiveness of the programme as "teaching you about the good things that there're abroad".[7] Open-mindedness meant developing and displaying a genuine interest in the world. In one of the classes we observed, Judit, the English teacher, urged students "not be oblivious to what is happening in the world anymore (class observations, 9/12/2016.)". "As IB students you have no excuse", she continued. "You have to know what's happening, be smart". Being smart meant, to Judit, "making intelligent decisions, based on facts, things that you know, things that you read, and then making your own choices", as, for example, when casting their votes. In order to become engaged adult citizens, IB students were expected to read the news, travel, and learn about everything, "history, geography, politics, religion and gastronomy", in Judit's words. As IB students, they could not afford to act otherwise.

Finally, the third attribute (by which we mean one of three, not ranked third) that was foregrounded was respect. Respect was mostly (though not completely) articulated around good manners: teachers insisted that IB students should say please and thank you (as one trilingual poster hanging on the walls had it), and be poised and well-behaved with their teachers, classmates and parents. In the words of Pere, the Catalan language teacher, "they [IB students] don't make you tense or nervous […] I even rest when I teach them". Yet, there was more to "respect" than good manners. In the poster we just mentioned, students were also expected to apologise to one another – if necessary – (also a form of regulation of communicative conduct) and be happy (*somos felices*, in Spanish); in sum, create a positive and "caring" atmosphere (recall that "caring" is one of the IB learner profile attributes). Their normative relationship was referred to in the same poster as that of "one big family". As part of a "family", we observed how students regularly engaged in a great deal of affective labour with everyone, including the researchers. They explicitly showed concern for others' well-being and were always supportive and understanding towards one another (also towards their teachers, as the IB coordinator made a point of emphasising in the interview). Given the amount of extra work the DP meant and how stressful the situation was for some, students regularly organised informal group therapy sessions in which they discussed their worries and anxieties, and comforted their tearful classmates by expressing their shared suffering. These compassionate selves echo the normative moral subjects identified by Muehlebach (2013) in neoliberal Italy. She claims that,

> The science of *homo oeconomicus* has begun to include the science of *homo relationalis*: of humans who relate to one another not through self-interest but through dispositions –moral styles- that are, to return to Putnam et al. based on trust and reciprocity. It is not just material wealth but vibrant social relationships and even happiness (Wali 2012) that are now considered key to the wealth of nations. The post-Washington consensus, although firmly wedded to methodological individualism and rational choice, nevertheless exhibits a tendency that attempts to capture and harness the powers of the relational and the interpersonal.
>
> (p. 461, italics in the original)

This moral neoliberal (compassionate and loving) is, according to Muehlebach, not a way of compensating for the excesses of neoliberalism or challenging neoliberalism's structural features, but a changing type (and ethics) of neoliberalism, what she calls "'benign' third way neoliberalisms" (p. 460). This "warmer" version of neoliberalism or "Catholicized neoliberalism" (as opposed to "cold" Lutheran neoliberalism based solely on profit and market logics), is a more robust version of neoliberalism because it "weds markets to a specific moral form" (p. 456) and produces "the disembedded individual and the embedded person at once" (p. 461). This combination of market and morals, calculation and care, is exactly the kind of neoliberal we saw being created at FIS. Let us now turn to one of the key spaces through which IB neoliberal governmentality was enforced, that is, the Creativity, Action and Service course.

The Creativity, Action and Service subject: Developing self-expertise to become balanced individuals

Creativity, Action and Service (CAS) is one of the singularities of the IBDP. It is one of the three core subjects that all students must take. The IBO refers to CAS as the course more clearly cultivating IB learner profile attributes, as being "at the heart of the DP" (IBO, 2015); FIS students and educators systematically employed CAS to illustrate *how* the DP was different. CAS encapsulated the idea that the IB was a programme of "general education" aimed to educate "whole individuals".

The course is structured in three strands: *Creativity*, *Action* and *Service*. For two years, students must undertake weekly or one-off activities related to at least one of these three areas, and write a final reflection paper. Engaging in these activities should contribute to the creation of a well-rounded individual, one who can "think out of the box," according to Judit, the English teacher.

The expected learning outcomes of CAS (IBO, 2015) reflect the skillified personhoods we discussed in relation to the profile and focus exclusively on students' personal gains. They include "identify own strengths and develop areas for growth", "demonstrate that challenges have been undertaken, developing new skills in the process", "show perseverance and commitment" and "recognize and consider the ethics of choices and actions". In sum, reflexivity, perseverance and self-expertise for self-betterment. This is what CAS aims at. Let us now turn to the examination of how this specifically happens, in what directions CAS disciplines students, and what its effects are.

The case of Alexia, an IB student, is particularly illuminating. The first semester in the IB was chaos for Alexia. She could not manage to combine studying with ballet and the intensive rehearsals for the Christmas show that she starred (both activities part of CAS). She used to get home at 10 pm, and still had her homework to do. She felt stressed out and under a lot of pressure. In the second semester, she pulled herself together and decided to bring change to her life. From this moment on, even if she did not have specific tasks due the following day, she habituated herself to advance work every afternoon to avoid it snowballing. She learned how to manage time adequately to be able to cope with IB work pressure, which in fact meant disciplining herself to work all the time. In fact, time management skills have become one of the IBO newly incorporated selling points, as they prepare DP students for "further education and the working world" (IBO, 2014b). What seems clear from this story is that CAS led Alexia to personal growth: she self-reflected, got to know herself better, and took action to improve her time management skills. In sum, she transformed herself through self-discipline.

Claudia, in turn, praised the "obligation" she had to do sport under CAS because it made her "unwind" and "feel happier". "If it weren't for action I wouldn't do sport because we have so many things to do but since it's compulsory it's actually good that they oblige you because you need to do sport", she stated in the interview. What we see is a student who has normalised (academic) productivity and hard work, but who has to continue self-sacrificing to adjust other parts of herself to become the *balanced* IB student of the profile, one for whom well-being is (another) "obligation" to be internalised (Del Percio & Flubacher, 2017). This echoes contemporary corporate interest in enhancing employees' well-being (through, for example, coaching sessions or courses on mindfulness) to make them more productive. The balanced individual that was the ideal of the humanist-liberal education of the early days has become a product attractive to the corporate world, and a self-branding strategy for IB graduates in the labour market. As balanced individuals, Claudia, like Alexia in the previous vignette, will make better, that is, more productive, workers. Marta, another IB student, actually drew on this self-branding discourse when she stated that the IB made them more "complete" because "hobbies count" and that is "something valued when applying for higher education abroad (unlike in Spain)". She conceptualised CAS as a tool for converting hobbies and pastimes into quantifiable – and certifiable – assets, and her becoming self as more attractive and sellable thanks to CAS.

When discussing CAS, most students foregrounded the *Service* strand, because it encouraged them to step out of their "bubble" and see harsher realities (social diners, nursing homes, etc.). Despite a seeming concern with social inequality, the way students talked about *Service* revealed that they conceptualised it as a tool for self-improvement. *Service* helped them be more adaptable in heterogeneous social spaces. Alfred, one of the students, described the benefits of *Service* as "enabling me to be creative and contribute things to people". Rather than a focus on the community, what we see is a focus on himself. Through *Service*, Alfred was developing his creativity and his ability to identify how *he* could become an asset for others. In broader social terms, CAS also worked to normalise a neoliberal perspective on social welfare, which rather than address the causes of social injustice, commodified volunteer work. In fact, in line with observations by Windle and Stratton (2013), we see CAS as yet another strategy of marketisation and legitimisation by IB schools. The *Service* in CAS enables IB schools to appear as more "socially-minded" than the rest, something certain middle-class families may be on the lookout for, to counter what for some may be an excessive emphasis on success, self-interest and competition in elite schooling. But this was delusional since, as we have seen, *Service* was conceptualised as yet another tool for neoliberal self-governance.

Resisting IB transformation (or maybe not?)

Despite the multiple micro-techniques of power (Foucault, 1977) put into place to transform the IB elite, some students reported resisting these forms of subjection (Foucault, 1982). In extract 3, from the focus group discussion, Martí summarises his more laid-back attitude as "not fighting like the rest" (line 07), his word choice underscoring the extent to which the IB was constructed as a race to become the most self-sacrificing, and thus, the "best" IB person. Not studying "a little bit more" to reach perfection – a 10 – is "his problem" (line 04).

Extract 3

Participants: M (Martí), Al (Alexia), R (Roger), I (Irene), students; An (Andrea), researcher.

```
01   M:    =er:::/ (.) you can study::/ just enough/ to pass::/ and you can get a
02         good gra:de\ if on top of that you have/ (.) the capacity\ (.) but\ then if
03         you study just enough\ and a little bit more::/ in order to\ for example\
04         if you have an eight\ (.) to reach a ten:::/ I:::\ I don't do this\ [and I think
05         this is my problem\
06   Al:                                                              [((laughs))
07   An:   =okay\
08   M:    =I don't::\ I don't fight li:ke/ like the rest\
09   R:    there's people:::/ also\ who::/ (.) me for example: / (.) well\ and::/
10         (.) that is\ who/ devote a lot of time to the IB:: but:::\ we also have a
11         life outside::\ and::/ (.) we also like to enjoy life\
12   M:    =I mean\ it's not/ [we are not saying/ that people who devote a lot of
13         time to it\
14   An:                     [I see::
15         do not have a life::/ (.) but::\ we::/ (.) it seems like like:/
16   I:    =but it depends on the day:/
17   M:    =yes::\ of course::/ we [are not\ we are not as well organised\ probably\
18   R:                            [well\
19   I:    =no::\
20   M:    =because we could organise ourselves better\ and have::/ both things::/
21   R:    =but in my case for example::/
22   M:    =but::\ we prefer to waste our time\
```

Martí and Roger feel the need to justify their non-fighting attitude, and though initially they say it is because they also want to "have a life" (line 13), they end up converging to the IB discourse that it all boils down to having good time management skills. They have not undergone Alexia's transformation to make both compatible; they prefer to "waste their time" (line 24). Wasting their time, in Martí's case, means, as he clarifies later, being on the computer, on his phone or watching TV. He then goes on to explain that these activities are a waste of time because "they do not count". What we clearly see is how, despite Martí's confessed partial mis-alignment with IB values, he has also interiorised the commodifying and calculative neoliberal logic of the programme institutionalised by CAS. In fact, afterwards, he retraces his words and proudly tells his classmates how his English grades have improved because he watches series and films in English; he has turned his hobby into educational capital. So, even though he is resisting IB governmentality by refusing to work to the limit, he is aware that he is swimming against the current, and that sooner than later he will "give in" (a bit later in the interview he uses the adverbial "yet" to indicate that this is just a matter of time). The IB logic has permeated the whole of these students' lives. Ultimately, this extract is an exercise in self-reflexivity in which both Martí and Roger analyse their behaviour and talk about it as *experts,* identifying their *weaknesses* and how they should "strengthen themselves in order to survive competition" (Martín Rojo, 2018, p. 550).

Conclusions

Just as neoliberalism is constantly reinventing itself (Anderson, 2016), so is the IB programme. What was initially a curriculum designed for and aimed to attract a specific population (i.e. the children of expatriate families) has, over time, become a much-desired educational credential for post-nationally-oriented national elites (Resnik, 2012) In a context where consumption practices – including educational ones – have become increasingly status-oriented, the IB is regarded as a "positional good" (Bunnell, 2010, p. 167) and IB credentials as convertible into the types of economic and cultural capital that grant students better positions in their never-ending race for brilliant futures.

The selling line of the IB (and what most families look for) is for IB students to receive the type of training that will ease their circulation in global spaces, be they educational or work spaces. This is allegedly facilitated both practically/bureaucratically, through IBO agreements with universities and national education systems that have centralised regulations for university access, and educationally, through the inculcation of desirable ways of learning, and of doing being (good) students. Yet, as we have seen, IB governance goes far beyond that. The IB humanist-liberal goal of educating the "whole person" (and not just students' intellects) has been the ideal breeding ground for the gradual metamorphosing of the programme into a neoliberal technology of citizenship aimed at subjectifying students to embody neoliberal selves. Essentially, what this boils down to is the creation of citizen-workers always anxious to outperform in all aspects, to become not just "A students" but "A people", brilliant academically but also excellent self-carers and disciplined affective selves. The ultimate goal, as we have seen, is for them to become agents of (neoliberal) change, people who can transform places into positive environments in which everybody can feel happy to work more and better, that is, to enhance efficiency and productivity. These individuals are inculcated the values and dispositions of the corporate world; they are encouraged to imagine themselves as separable pieces, as sets of mainly soft skills, which they should "strive" to improve to perfection, no matter what it takes. The IB helps you to "know your limits", as students repeated at FIS. Working "to the limit" was actually what was expected of them; that is why it was important to know one's limits. But also because out of self-knowledge came strategies for self-betterment and for pushing oneself further by taking a step beyond (*"anar més enllà"*, in Catalan), a phrase students employed over and again to express the distinctive identity trait of the IB "elite" (see also Martín Rojo, this volume).

If we go back to Fraser (2003), we can see how in contemporary forms of social regulation, there is no clearly identifiable "governing" source; governmentality agents, such as the IB, are networked, "flexible", "dispersed" and "multi-levelled" (p. 167). In that sense, globalised governmentality is de-statised and profoundly marketised. In fact, we have discussed how the IBO formally sets out to cooperate with national school systems to actually enter into competition with them for students, resources, power and influence. If, previously, schooling was one of the state's key apparatuses for moulding the (national) social body, currently, this role is taken over by different non-state actors, ranging from private and non-profit organisations, like IBO, to contemporary technological forms of governance of the self, such as that exerted by algorithms (Just & Latzer, 2017). Finally, we have seen how globalised governmentality increasingly works through hierarchisation and elitisation, that is, through taking care of and perfecting the "transformable" few and dismissing (and problematising) those that refuse to enter the race.

Communication and discourse are fundamental instruments in effecting all of the above. As a competitive twenty-first-century organisation, the IBO is not only a powerful discursive machine; it is a discursive regime. The IBO aims to "take over", erase, any previous discourse existing in the school. The IB promises a new beginning, a way for schools (as well as for students) to reinvent themselves. The learner profile, with its 10 attributes, is one of the IB's communication totems; as we have seen, it is a key instrument for subjectifying students into the logics of the standardisation of the self and in the specific directions desired and made desirable by the corporate neoliberal regime. We have seen that transforming oneself entails not only communicating adequately with others, but also telling oneself differently. The IB speaking subject is, above all, a reflective self-expert ready to discuss himself/herself with others (see also Martín Rojo, this volume).

Finally, the IB language policy articulates the logic of standardisation with the logic of expansion and pragmatism that is at the core of the IB enterprise. While students' A (best) languages (including Catalan) are made part of the programme and, if different from French, English or Spanish, enable students to obtain a bilingual mention on their diploma, only one of the three languages mentioned above can officially be medium of instruction (and assessment) in the rest of the subjects. The reason is standardisation of materials, teacher support and assessment. This language policy has proven most successful, because it allows the IBO to handle the tension between a transportable type of education, and situated communicative needs and contexts of learning. At the same time, this language policy naturalises linguistic hierarchies (the inclusion of A languages is limited to one course), and links major European languages to educational quality and modernity. However, our ethnography revealed that the picture was more complex. Despite its global reach, the choice of Spanish in the school investigated (and in many others in Catalonia and Spain) was in tension with the language indexicalities of the word *international* in contemporary Catalonia/Spain, i.e. English-speaking. For this reason, it needed intensive justification, as it questioned the value of the programme in the local educational marketplace. However, the "aura" of the term international, in Resnisk's words (2015), still allured many families, anxious for their children to further self-capitalise by adding (international) "extras" to the official curriculum (another contemporary example is the double French-Spanish baccalaureate, *batxibac*, increasingly popular among Catalan middle-class families). But unlike batxibac, the IB at FIS was not a programme of linguistic training (English language credentials had to be obtained separately). This brought its (trans)formative goals into sharper focus: the fabrication of an elite of globally-minded, outward-looking protoworkers ready for the transnational corporate market.

Transcription conventions

PART: participant name
(.) short pause (0.5 seconds)
(:) long pause (0.5–1.5 seconds)
() incomprehensible fragment
AA loud talking
a:: lengthening of vowel or consonant sound
[] turn overlapping with similarly marked turn

- self interruption
= latching
\ falling intonation
/ rising intonation
(()) non-verbal or paralinguistic
  information

Notes

1 According to the IBO webpage, the fees IBO charges schools are meant to cover its functioning expenses.
2 The rest are grouped under six areas of knowledge: studies in language and literature; language acquisition; individuals and societies; sciences; mathematics; and the arts. Students must choose at least one course from all areas (except arts) and decide which courses to study at standard level of expertise and which ones at higher level.
3 All names appearing in this chapter are pseudonyms to protect the anonymity of informants and of the institution.
4 This research was funded by the Spanish Ministry of Science and Innovation (MICINN) through the APINGLO-Cat research project (ref. FFI2014-54179-C2-1-P, 2015–2018 and by the Secretaria d'Universitats i Recerca of the Catalan Government and the European Social Fund (2016FI_B00753, predoctoral grant). We would like to thank Iris Milán and Daniel Pujol for their help with data transcription. We are also indebted to the two editors of this volume and to two anonymous reviewers for their perceptive feedback. To all of them, and in particular to Luisa Martín Rojo, many thanks. Any remaining flaws are only attributable to us.
5 LOMCE is an acronym which stands for Ley orgánica para la mejora de la calidad educativa (Organic Law for the Improvement of Educational Quality), which is the legal framework regulating the current version of the Spanish baccalaureate.

It was passed in 2013 under conservative PP rule (not without controversy and major opposition from the educational community).
6 All the extracts presented in this chapter were originally in Catalan and have been translated into English by the authors for reasons of space.
7 In fact, Resnik (2012) argues that the current IB discourse in relation to (multi-) cultural issues has moved away from the "civic multiculturalism" of the second half of the twentieth century, aiming for peace and reconciliation after World War II and based on the respect of difference, to become what she calls "corporate multiculturalism", consisting in the commodification of culture to increase productivity and competitiveness.

References

Anderson, B. (2016). Neoliberal affects. *Progress in Human Geography*, 40(6), 734–753.

Ball, S.J., & Nikita, D.P. (2014). The global middle class and school choice: A cosmopolitan sociology. *Zeitschrift Fur Erziehungswissenschaft*, 17, 81–93.

Barnés, H.G. (2016). "Conoce a los 3 jóvenes españoles que han arrasado en el Bachillerato más exigente". *El Confidencial*, 20 July.

Bunnell, T. (2008). The global growth of the International Baccalaureate Diploma Programme over the first 40 years: A critical assessment. *Comparative Education*, 44(4), 409–424.

Bunnell, T. (2010). The International Baccalaureate and a framework for class consciousness: The potential outcomes of a "class-for-itself." *Discourse: Studies in the Cultural Politics of Education*, 31(3), 351–362.

Bunnell, T. (2016). The dearth of International Baccalaureate schools across Africa. *Africa Education Review*, 13(2), 181–195.

Codó, E., & Sunyol, A. (2019). "A plus for our students": The construction of Mandarin Chinese as an elite language in an international school in Barcelona. *Journal of Multilingual and Multicultural Development*, 40(5), 436–452. doi: 10.1080/01434632.2018.1543694.

Del Percio, A., & Flubacher, M. (2017) Language, education and neoliberalism. In M. Flubacher & A. Del Percio (Eds.), *Language, Education and Neoliberalism. Critical Studies in Sociolinguistics* (pp. 1–19) Bristol: Multilingual Matters.

Foucault, M. (1977). *Discipline and Punish: The Birth of the Prison*. New York: Vintage Books.

Foucault, M. (1982). The subject and power. In H. Dreyfus & P. Rabinow (Eds.), *Michael Foucault: Beyond Structuralism and Hermeneutics*. Chicago: University of Chicago Press.

Foucault, M. (1988). *Technologies of the Self: A Seminar with Michel Foucault*. Edited by L. Martin, H. Gutman, & P. Hutton. London: Tavistock.

Foucault, M. (1991). Governmentality. In G. Burchell, C. Gordon, & P. Miller (Eds.), *The Foucault Effect: Studies on Governmentality* (pp. 87–104). Chicago: University of Chicago Press.

Fraser, N. (2003). From discipline to flexibilization: Rereading Foucault in the shadow of globalisation. *Constellations*, 10(2), 160–171.

Gao, S., & Park, J.S.Y. (2015). Space and language learning under the neoliberal economy. *L2 Journal*, 7(3), 78–96.

Gordon, C. (1991). Governmental rationality: An introduction. In G. Burchell, C. Gordon, & P. Miller (Eds.), *The Foucault Effect: Studies on Governmentality* (pp. 1–51). Chicago: University of Chicago Press.

Hallinger, P., Lee, M., & Walker, A. (2011). Program transition challenges in International Baccalaureate schools. *Journal of Research in International Education*, *10*(2), 123–136.

Hannerz, U. (1996) *Transnational Connections: Culture, People, Places*. London: Routledge.

Harvey, D. (2005). *A Brief History of Neoliberalism*. New York: Oxford University Press.

Hickox, M., & Moore, R. (1995). Liberal-humanist education: The vocationalist challenge. *Curriculum Studies*, *3*(1), 45–59.

International Baccalaureate Organisation. (2014a). What is an IB Education? Retrievable from: www.ibo.org/globalassets/digital-tookit/brochures/what-is-an-ib-education-en.pdf (last accessed 30 July 2018).

International Baccalaureate Organisation. (2014b). 10 reasons why the IB Diploma Programme (DP) is ideal preparation for university. Retrievable from: www.ibo.org/globalassets/digital-tookit/posters/dp-10-reasons-poster-en.pdf (last accessed 30 July 2018).

International Baccalaureate Organisation. (2015). International Baccalaureate Diploma Programme subject brief: Creativity, action and service. Retrievable from: www.ibo.org/contentassets/5895a05412144fe890312bad52b17044/cas-2016-english-1st-final-web.pdf (last accessed 30 July 2018).

International Baccalaureate Organisation. (2017a). The history of the IB. Retrievable from: www.ibo.org/globalassets/digital-tookit/presentations/1711-presentation-history-of-the-ib-en.pdf (last accessed 30 July 2018).

International Baccalaureate Organisation. (2017b). Diploma Programme: Learning a language. Retrievable from: www.ibo.org/programmes/diploma-programme/what-is-the-dp/learning-a-language/ (last accessed 30 July 2018).

Just, N., & Latzer, M. (2017). Governance by algorithms: Reality construction by algorithmic selection on the Internet. *Media, Culture and Society*, *39*(2), 238–258.

Martín Rojo, L. (2010). *Constructing Inequality in Multilingual Classrooms*. Berlin: Mouton de Gruyter.

Martín Rojo, L. (2018). Neoliberalism and linguistic governmentality. In J. Tollefson & M. Pérez-Milans (Eds.), *The Oxford Handbook of Language Policy and Planning* (pp. 544–567). Oxford: Oxford University Press.

Muehlebach, A. (2013). The catholicization of neoliberalism: On love and welfare in Lombardy, Italy. *American Anthropologist*, *115*(3), 452–465.

Park, J.S.Y. (2016). Language as pure potential. *Journal of Multilingual and Multicultural Development*, *37*(5), 453–466.

Rabinow, P., & Rose, N. (Eds.) (2003). *The Essential Foucault. Selections from the Essential Works of Foucault, 1954–1984*. New York: New Press.

Resnik, J. (2012). La programme du baccalauréat international et la formation (humaniste?) des élites internationales de demain. In C. Magnin & C.A. Muller (Eds.), *Enseignement secondaire, formation humaniste et société (XVIe-XXIe siècle)* (pp. 253–269). Geneva: Slatkine.

Resnik, J. (2015). The development of the International Baccalaureate in Spanish speaking countries: A global comparative approach. *Globalisation, Societies and Education*, *7724*(September), 1–28.

Rose, N. (1996). Governing "advanced" liberal democracies. In N. Rose, A. Barry & T. Osborne (Eds.), *Foucault and Political Reason* (pp. 37–64). London & Chicago: UCL Press.

Sennet, R. (1998). *The Corrosion of Character: The Personal Consequences of Work in the New Capitalism*. New York: Norton.

Soto, C., & Pérez-Milans, M. (2018). Language, neoliberalism, and the commodification of pedagogy. *Language and Intercultural Communication, 18*(5), 490–506.

Sunyol, A. (2017). Educació multilingüe per a l'era global: el valor de les llengües en una escola internacional. *Treballs de Sociolingüística Catalana, 27*, 269–283.

Tabiola, H.B., & Lorente, B. (2017). Neoliberalism in ELT aid: Interrogating a USAID ELT project in Southern Philippines. In M. Flubacher & A. Del Percio (Eds.), *Language, Education and Neoliberalism: Critical Studies in Sociolinguistics* (pp. 122–139). Bristol: Multilingual Matters.

Tarc, P. (2009). What is the "International" in the International Baccalaureate: Three structuring tensions of the early years (1962–1973). *Journal of Research in International Education, 8*(3), 235–261.

Urciuoli, B. (2008). Skills and selves in the new workplace. *American Ethnologist, 35*(2), 211–228.

Wali, A. (2012). A different measure of well-being. *American Anthropologist 114*(1):12–13.

Weenink, D. (2005). Upper middle-class resources of power in the education arena: Dutch elite schools in an age of globalisation. Unpublished PhD dissertation, University of Amsterdam, Faculty of Social and Behavioural Sciences.

Williams, R. (1961). *The Long Revolution*. Harmondsworth: Pelican.

Windle, J., & Stratton, G. (2013). Equity for sale: Ethical consumption in a school-choice regime. *Discourse: Studies in the Cultural Politics of Education, 34*(2), 202–213.

8 The "self-made speaker"

The neoliberal governance of speakers

Luisa Martín Rojo[1]

How do neoliberal principles reach into the very grain of individuals?

Within a context of neoliberal governance (see Martín Rojo & Del Percio in this volume), language learning and practice play a significant role in the social construction of the "successful" individual and in determining that those subjected to a neoliberal regime must be "managed", "guided", "encouraged", "trained" and "empowered" to achieve their social and/or professional life goals. This fact not only explains why discourses celebrating multilingualism are currently becoming hegemonic; it is also stark evidence of the extent to which, within the neoliberal outlook on world dynamics, economic principles impact on individuals' behaviour and subjectivities, becoming an extended form of governance.[2] However, the mechanism that makes this impact possible remains imperfectly understood. The present chapter addresses this crucial question and proposes some answers.

To explore the role played by language practices in current forms of governance, this chapter focuses on language learning, particularly in educational institutions. Traditionally, schools provide a disciplinary framework in which students are trained to speak in accordance with a template such as the native speaker model, and to adopt the standard language and its associated norms of language behaviour. However, within neoliberal logic, schools shape the conduct of students by creating competition and urging them to become fully competent in at least one "international" language. As I show in this chapter, it is the individual (encouraged by educational institutions) who assumes most of the responsibility, by consenting or resisting to the perceived need to accumulate language competencies, in the understanding that this creates economic value for the person concerned, for employers and for the community.

In this chapter, I try to answer the previous question, focusing on universities. Knowledge and education (often referred to as "human capital") are often treated as productive assets or even as business products, and educational institutions are expected to obtain their own resources and to compete for students. And in the case of Madrid, these institutions have undergone an extensive transformation, within a geographic region seeking to prosper within the global economy. New degrees, tighter requirements for university entry, curriculum and syllabus design in accordance with labour market needs, assessment processes, university rankings, and many aspects of university life all reproduce and contribute to spreading and implementing these neoliberal principles. As the following analysis of students' views and experiences shows, in this context the assumption of the economic value of languages is not only reproduced, but it is adopted and normalised by the institutions and by students.

In my analysis of the personal accounts, students of different origins enrolled at universities in Madrid produced, as part of a series of activities developed within classrooms to increase linguistic awareness and reflexivity, an interesting association between self entrepreneurship and language as a profit discourse becomes apparent (Martín Rojo, 2017). This imbrication has been seen as a force that is intimately linked to the control and management of the population and its conduct, binding individuals to a particular lifestyle and to a given way of managing their languages and language competences (see Urciuoli, 2010; Park, 2011; Martín Rojo, 2017). The present chapter goes a step further in this line, explaining how the above discourse of entrepreneurship reaches individuals and compels them to act in a particular way and to see themselves as entrepreneurs. In order to understand these processes, we need to explore power mechanisms. As we will see in this chapter, the enterprise is at the core of a model of subjectivity, *the entrepreneurial subject*, who administers her/his own assets. It is the existence of a model to be followed that impacts on the subjects' behaviour, revealing the fundamental concept of governmentality, that is, the process of "conducting conduct", a process which is not enforced by violent means, but which often acquires the complicity and even the agency of social actors and institutions, which are in fact the objects of governmentality. Analysis of students' accounts of their participation in tasks designed to increase their linguistic reflexivity shows that this model has a linguistic correlate, which I term the *self-made speaker*, a version for our times of *homo(locutor) œconomicus* (see references below), and one that challenges traditional models of speakerhood such as that of the native speaker. The university students whose voices are presented in this study make reference to this speaker model when they explain their linguistic trajectories in line, offering often little or no resistance to its precepts in this higher educational context. However, this model also mobilises another power mechanism: students adopt this model as a value-given measure when they view understand themselves as subjects. Thus, they consider themselves subjects under construction, responsible for their own transformation, and hence involved, through self care, in a persistent search for personal improvement. As a result, in some cases they achieve compliance with the model, achieving satisfaction and successfully improving themselves, but in others they experience failure and feel excluded or even ashamed. Through the analysis of these power mechanisms we can finally understand how neoliberal principles reach the subject. And we can also see how sociolinguistic process, in which actual linguistic forms are mapped on to social functions and value judgments, has been translated into a form of governmentality at least in flagship degree programmes at Madrid universities that compels speakers to enter into a spiral of language accumulation, (self)training and coaching, in which we recognise the exercise of power and self technologies such as discipline, surveillance, normalisation and self-care, and self-examination (Martín Rojo, 2017). All these techniques are mobilised in both in the regulation of behaviour and in the processes of subjectification. Finally, this chapter shows how the same power techniques can be used to reflect critically upon the power-knowledge relations that constitutes one's subjectivity and to engage in practices of resistance and self-transformation.

In order to investigate the role of language in neoliberal rationality, this chapter first examines how the neoliberal economy has transformed the field of education, with particular respect to universities. This is a key scenario for observing how language commodification intervenes in education policies, and helps institutions cope with the present lack of financial support. Secondly, I discuss how current models of speakerhood mirror and even push beyond the *homo œconomicus* model. I go on to analyse the logic of competition, performance and desire which can be perceived in the words of these Madrid university students when they refer to language management and self mastery. I then consider the techniques of power that are exercised in relation to languages, and show how social differences and understandings emerge. Finally, I present some conclusions and summarise the main features that define neoliberal speakers and the potential resistances they show.

Neoliberalism and the formation of mobile workers in Madrid universities: Field work and case studies

Within the context of neoliberalisation, higher education has become a social field of particular relevance. The "knowledge economy" is a major concept within neoliberal rationality, expressing the fact that knowledge and education (often referred to as "human capital") are often viewed as productive assets or even as business products, in the understanding that innovative intellectual products and services can be exported and high returns thus obtained (Drucker, 1993). Under the label of "autonomy", universities have been confronted with funding cuts and forced to seek other sources of revenue, via external funding, market-applied research and saleable teaching materials (Saunders, 2010). The same logic dictates, in the name of public accountability, that they implement measures centred on a culture of auditing and evaluation (Wilkins & Huisman, 2012). Against this backdrop, entrepreneurial slogans now emphasise competition, efficiency, innovation and flexibility (Wilkins, 2012). In addition to this pervasive pressure to obtain funding, what makes the neoliberal institution's approach unique is that job training and career development explicitly define the development and educational outcomes that students are expected to achieve. Thus, the formerly-hidden curriculum focused on meeting the needs of capital is now voluntarily exposed and embraced (Aronowitz, 2000; Saunders, 2010, p. 61).

The university experience in this setting, in which immaterial goods such as culture and language are increasingly commodified, helps explain why languages have become an important form of symbolic capital. Firstly, linguistic policies aimed at internationalising universities efficiently require an online multilingual projection, translation services, coursework delivered in international languages (mainly English) and a wide-ranging offer of prestigious and economically influential languages in degree programmes (see, among others, Jacobsen, 2015). Secondly, and as various researchers have highlighted, higher education institutions are of fundamental importance in shaping and preparing a future elite workforce for a flexible and delocalised labour market, by equipping students with an international and multilingual orientation (Zimmermann & Flubacher, 2017, p. 207; see also Urciuoli, 2010, and Hidalgo & Fernández, in this volume). Thus, one of the universities' main strategies for meeting the needs of the labour market, and which is contributing to increasing competitiveness, is to purpose-design degree courses to train an mobile and sometimes also an elite corps of workers.

The above-described demands made of language education are of particular significance in the Madrid region (which has considerable autonomy under Spain's decentralised system of government), where since the political transition to democracy[3] a succession of conservative governments have adhered enthusiastically to the neoliberal economy. As part of their strategy to attract investment and to become a venue for major organisations and international institutions, the region has been branded "a bilingual community" (see Hidalgo & Fernández, in this volume, on the importance of education in developing a neoliberal and global economy). The majority of the population subscribe to this ideal of increasing the language training offered in the region, partly in response to the perceived demands of the labour market. However, this global tendency has location-specific features in Spain. Since the end of the political isolation experienced during the Franco dictatorship, and with Spain's membership of the European Union, languages have occupied a significant place in education. EU policies not only consider languages as "essential to ensuring that European citizens can move, work, and learn freely throughout Europe", but also state that improved language skills would contribute "to reinforcing EU integration, boosting jobs and growth, reducing unemployment, increasing living standards and ensuring that language does not restrict participation in society" (see, for example, the EU strategic framework for cooperation on education and training 2020, ET 2020). During the 1980s, language programmes were developed within a social-democrat approach, but more recently, and particularly in the Madrid region, they tend to present the characteristics of a neoliberal frame.

In this setting, Madrid universities have undergone major institutional policy changes. Students are now provided with internationalisation-related resources but are also subjected to access constraints. Furthermore, an exhaustive revision of undergraduate degree programmes has been mandated, modifying both the subjects offered and the languages of instruction (Block, 2011; Starkey, 2011). Thus, in the humanities, new degrees have been designed and implemented, with an unmistakable applied bias, presenting two main traits: a focus on multilingualism and multiculturalism, and an emphasis on meeting the needs of the international labour market.

For example, the information brochure for one of these innovative degrees, Modern Language, Culture and Communication, offered at Madrid Autonomous University, states that:

> Multilingualism keeps diversity alive, enhances intercultural understanding, facilitates international trade and opens doors to new professional horizons. In response to demands for multilingual education, the degree provides solid linguistic and cultural training, to promote fluency in foreign languages, a field that is notoriously difficult for the Spanish, and achieve a profound understanding of communication.

Another of the programmes offered, International Studies, at the same university, is described thus:

> The degree in International Studies incorporates various Social Sciences and Humanities degree subjects to provide students with an education of global scope, equipping them with the basic instruments needed to undertake a career in the international field.

Implemented at a time of economic crisis, these degrees have been welcomed by students anxious about their future. In fact, in January 2018, the youth unemployment rate in Spain was over 36%, and the emigration of highly qualified young people had more than doubled since 2009, to destinations such as France, the United Kingdom, Germany and Argentina (OECD, 2015). This difficult economic situation explains why many young Spanish citizens now see themselves as "workers of the world" (a situation partially equivalent to that experienced in the Philippines; see Lorente, 2012) and why the demand for these university courses is very high and entry requirements so competitive.

Thus, my research question was how students, in these flagship degree programmes at Madrid universities, position themselves towards a neoliberal rationality and agenda. The high position in the international rankings of these universities enhances the prestige of the new degrees offered, and also impacts on students' recruitment. Thus, because of the rigorous entry requirements, only a minority can access the course and thus aspire to be trained on multilingualism, intercultural communication and in international relationships, taking advantage of the global trend that encourages and rewards elite mobility. It is precisely in this respect that higher education plays such a crucial role.

For this research, therefore, I chose to conduct a case study of two recent, innovative degree programmes: International Studies; and Modern Languages, Culture and Communication. Having taught classes in both of these programmes for several years (from 2010 to 2018), I have first-hand knowledge of the students, the teachers, the subjects and the general expectations aroused within the universities in this respect. The International Studies programme is intended for students with an interest in international affairs, political science, international cooperation and diplomacy, while the second programme focuses on languages and social communication. Both were designed with the explicit purpose of comprehensively equipping students to enter an international job market. Further, both programmes have one of the university's highest cut-off entry requirements, and are considered to enrol only the best students. The multilingual and intercultural nature of the programmes also attracts international students and the descendants of migrants. Languages form a highly relevant aspect of both courses. In fact, the International Studies programme was one of the first to be offered entirely in English. Because of my participation in this programme, I realised that several anthropological subjects taught in this degree programme provide students with a critical perspective on colonialism and international relations, which specifically points to how neoliberal rationality has become present in education. Therefore, in a second round, I have incorporated students from the anthropology degree programme into this study. Diversity is a core theme in this programme, and teachers and students often present a critical attitude towards neoliberal logic. Cut-off entry requirements are much lower for the anthropology degree, and the student body includes activists in urban, gender and university movements. The information brochure for this degree course states the following regarding potential students:

> This degree in Social and Cultural Anthropology will appeal to students with a marked critical awareness of the reality that surrounds them, with a keen interest in understanding and intervening in how today's world is being transformed.

This critical position often results in the socio-political engagement of students and teachers. My observation and the data obtained confirmed that these students differ in their expectations, in how they present and understand themselves and in their aims – many have a professional interest in Latin America, NGOs or the welfare services. Thus, by incorporating them into this study, I was able to examine whether this critical positioning had a significant impact on students' trajectories and subjectivities. Adding this programme to the study allowed me to take social class differences into account, although this aspect cannot be fully analysed in the present chapter.

In fact, the number of anthropology degree students who had taken public or private bilingual programmes (English/Spanish or French, Italian, German/Spanish) was lower than in the other degree programmes. As in the other two degree courses, anthropology studies attracts international students and the descendants of migrants.

Applying an action research strategy, I have produced data working with my students in my own courses, whilst simultaneously conducting research. Following a critical pedagogy, I view teaching as an inherently political act, the goal of which is to promote emancipation from oppression through an awakening of the critical consciousness. In the understanding that language is one of the most effective means of domination, I have included a series of tasks designed to highlight students' problems and experiences in relation to language and communication, particularly those related to their current conditions of living (precarity, mobility, work flexibility, etc.). Given that I consider this technique can help to resist the process of internalising the power relation to which we are subjected, these activities were mainly based on self examination, including questions, narratives of experiences, reflections. In later sessions, the anonymous results of these tasks and activities were discussed in the class, highlighting the connections between their experiences related to language and the social contexts in which they are embedded (Freire, 2009). The subjects I taught, Intercultural Communication and Linguistic Anthropology, address crucial issues such as linguistic socialisation, language learning, cultural and linguistic differences and linguistic stereotypes and ideologies. The aim of these activities was that participants should reflect on their own sociolinguistic repertoires (Blommaert, 2010, p. 102ff) and trajectories, and to consider the extent to which these aspects have become increasingly complex. I gave students writing assignments, asking them to describe their linguistic background, including their experiences in everyday life in Madrid. One item asked whether they were learning a new language, and if so, how and why. As discussed in the next section, this question gave rise to discourses on entrepreneurship and language commodification. It was my intention to accompany them for a short time along their educational paths, to learn from their life experiences and insights, and raise awareness of the impact made by entrepreneurial discourses on their subjectivities (see Bucholtz et al., 2016, p. 28). Thus, I also asked the students to report situations experienced in which they felt they had been excluded or had excluded themselves from particular social domains and activities because of their language skills or varieties. Examples of reasons for exclusion were given as linguistic insecurity, social selection, fear of not knowing how to express oneself, or even shame.

I collected more than 200 voluntary and anonymous writing assignments that were in a second phase discussed in class. In a third round of data collection, I explained my students that I was studying bilingual programmes in education and I asked for voluntary collaboration to the students following university degree courses, such as International Studies, taught in English at universities in the Madrid region. In this case, I asked whether participants considered themselves well prepared for this track, whether this had been a personal choice, and what opinions or arguments had influenced their choice. Further questions were about how they believed this linguistic option might benefit or harm them in the present and in the future that students were open to answering, given the positive classroom atmosphere. Finally, discussing all these materials in class, I was able to contrast the data collected with my own observations and with the students' profiles.

In this research, these assignments, as interviews, are understood as social practices (following Talmy, 2010). Consequently, my analysis focuses on students' strategic moves to build a positive social image, and on the incoherencies and contradictions they present in reproducing dominant discourses and, at the same time in presenting what they actually do and think. All the questions were designed to increase their reflection about their own values, and practices, and some were also designed to raise contradictions, taking into account that we are all subject to numerous and often contradictory constrictions, which determine our actions, whatever our beliefs may be. Consequently, in many cases individuals are not coherent: what we do and what we say vary according to the situation, and we arrange our discourses and beliefs in order to save face and justify our behaviour, strategically handling the stock of available cultural resources (Martín Criado, 2014).

From *homo œconomicus* to the *self-made speaker*: A model for "conducting language conduct"

This section explores the extent to which university students have internalised the discourse of language profit, and also considers how a new speaker model is evoked to explain and justify their linguistic trajectories and conduct.

In the discourse samples compiled, the students' comments on whether and why they are currently learning one or more languages evoke a rationality that weighs the value of language competence against its contribution to an individual's life and work objectives. This outlook is particularly apparent among the students on the International Studies degree course. As illustrated in Excerpts 1–3, this requires them to seek to attain specific, predetermined goals to the greatest advantage at the lowest possible cost. In fact, it evokes the *homo œconomicus* model, defined by theorists (Mill, 1874; Pareto, 1906/2014) in which humans are considered to be "rational", self-interested subjects optimising the utility function in their consideration of perceived opportunities.

Excerpt 1

Besides a personal interest, I believe that in the future, knowledge of these languages will allow me to travel and work in different countries in which I would like to live or spend time.

This example also articulates the belief that the languages learnt will enable social and geographic mobility (see also Gao & Park, 2015). The latter, in particular, is believed to be associated with employability. Thus, rational choice presupposes that the more languages are accumulated, the more employable a person will be, as made explicit in Excerpt 2.

Excerpt 2

I believe that knowing as many languages as possible will open up more job opportunities in the future.

Other than the expected benefit from cultivating language learning, these students, whether they take their university degrees in English alone or together with Spanish, also refer to its possible costs, as illustrated in the following statement by a second-year student:

Excerpt 3

I'm continuing to learn English every day through my bilingual degree programme. I know it's quite useful. Moreover, I'm pretty good at it and don't find it difficult.

This kind of logic, in which costs and benefits are weighed up (language learning is considered useful and not difficult) reproduces one of the features traditionally associated with *homo œconomicus*. This is particularly so when it is complemented by the assumption of rational choice and expectations when individuals consider what would be best for their long-term trajectories and labour-related wealth. In this regard, as in the following example, students refer to the value of language, as they would to a fixed and predictable quoted market price.

Excerpt 4

English, in a large part of Europe, Asia and America, and French, in a large part of Africa, will be important to improve communication and understanding.

Students show certainty (e.g. in using a performative future tense) in relation to these predictions, which are formulated beyond the local market, in this case referring to former colonial languages that are now viewed as linguae francae. These commonplace perspectives, referring mostly to English, are often assumed without criticism or counterargument. Universities offering the types of degree programme considered in this chapter, which are viewed by many as the best and hence are in high demand, play a key role in spreading the view that English is a means of acquiring an advantage in the labour market (see next section). Obviously, this view shapes students' opinion that English is necessary for success, and explains how attitudes are adopted and normalised. Certainly, the students who took part in the present research study seem to endorse and have internalised such attitudes, which are not strictly new, or intrinsically linked to neoliberalism:

Excerpt 5

Nowadays, English, obviously, is presented as the basic language of opportunity.

These kinds of prediction are not only present in students' discourses, they are also pervasively reproduced in education, as in universities' own descriptions of their degrees and curricula, and in other social fields – to the point of becoming hegemonic in society (see, for example, Flores, and Hidalgo & Fernández in this volume). Thus, they can be discerned in the assignments conducted, in which we seek to determine predominant social values. In the following excerpts pressurised by their parents:

Excerpt 6

I started studying English privately at age 7 because my parents believed that having more languages was necessary for my future.

Excerpt 7

I studied in a bilingual school where subjects such as mathematics or history were taught in English. At the time, it wasn't my decision, but something encouraged by my parents; in fact, I didn't like English.

In contrast, some significant differences with the logic of *homo œconomicus* can also be detected within the students' discourses, seemingly reflecting a neoliberal shift in this model. In the 1978–1979 Collège de France lectures, Foucault referred to a shift in *homo œconomicus*, from classical economic liberalism to neoliberalism, which leads to the construction of the subject as an entrepreneur of her/himself (Foucault, 2008, pp. 225–226).[4] In this context, the scenario of neoliberal competitiveness is that of global competition, in which students believe they are immersed. The following extracts from the questionnaires show how the terms "language" and "international dimension" are strongly connected.

Excerpts 8

With knowledge of this language [English] you can work abroad, something that many people are doing due to the difficult economic situation in our country!

Nowadays, English, obviously, is presented as a key language and a basic ability for getting by in any setting, above all, internationally.

[English] is the universal language that is spoken in all kinds of business and dealings at an international level, and therefore it is essential for my future career.

As a result of the international dimension assigned to languages, institutions and individuals seek to maximise linguistic competences and capital, an ambition that is reflected in the "CV development" obsession that is pervasive in universities, and exemplified in new courses dedicated to developing students' CV writing skills. In the following example, we see how this improvement is prompted, spurring the individual to accumulate ever-greater language skills:

Excerpt 9

I learn English all the time, from books, films, the news … as well as from the theoretical texts they give us in class.

These examples show how the current model of the neoliberal subject departs from the liberal model of *homo œconomicus*, as observed previously by Dardot and Laval:

> *It is the efficient, competitive individual who seeks to maximize his human capital in all areas, who not only seeks to project himself into the future and calculate his gains and losses like the old economic man, but above all seeks to work on himself so as constantly to transform himself, improve himself, and make himself ever more efficient.*
>
> (2014, p. 295)

It is precisely in this behavioural norm of the enterprise-subject, as the possessor of a "human capital" – one accumulated through enlightened choices arising from the responsible calculation of costs and benefits, that human conduct is shaped and directed. Achievements made in the course of a lifetime result from a series of decisions and efforts that must be correctly managed. The enterprise is promoted to become a model of subjectification: thus, everyone is an enterprise to be managed and a source of capital that must be made to bear fruit. In students' discourses, the mode of governmentality specific to neoliberalism can be identified as a particular way of producing economic subjects, who are structured by specific tendencies, preferences and motivations. This "subjectification"[5] gives rise to the "entrepreneurial" or "neoliberal subject", and the present study identifies its linguistic correlate, the self-made speaker. This subject, as Urciuoli shows, becomes a fragmented self of usable traits (Urciuoli, 2008).

The total self involvement apparent in the students' personal projects of self valorisation seems to assume an equivalence between the market's valorisation of personal endeavour and self valorising. Gao and Park (2015) articulated this idea in stating that developing English competence is an emblematic action, indexing self responsibility and professional worth. Language learning under neoliberalism "comes to represent a dedicated investment in self development, a professional morality, and an ideal subject under neoliberalism, a lack of which would indicate less initiative and commitment and invite questioning, doubt, distrust, or even contempt" (Gao & Park, 2015, p. 87). Examples like Excerpt 10 show that students calculate the necessity of language investments as a means of increasing their competitive edge, and those lacking the resources and time to (self-)invest are aware of their limited possibilities (Park, 2011, p. 453). Nevertheless, the project of asserting one's personal worth is highlighted in our data as a lifelong goal. Examples abound in the data, revealing the ongoing, permanent character of the task of self development and self assertion:

Excerpts 10

I keep on learning and getting better at English.

I learn English all the time, from books, films, the news … as well as from the theoretical texts they give us in class.

Yes, I'm broadening my knowledge of English and French.

I'm getting better […] and it's a lengthy project.

Entrepreneurship often starts in childhood and for many parents it is an educational priority. In fact, as Excerpt 11 shows, the view of language learning as an investment begins early, communicated by parent to their children through.

Excerpts 11

I started studying English privately at age 7 because my parents believed that having more languages was necessary for my future. Now I consider it necessary when travelling abroad and when I need resources that I can't achieve with Spanish alone.

I'm continuing to learn English (by reading and at an academy) since it is a key language in the current global system.

The logic by which competences are accumulated also seems to mean that language is constructed as individually accumulated and accountable asset rather than as a communicative instrument that requires the engagement of others (Blommaert, 2018, p. 36). This view is certainly reproduced in my study data, as shown in Excerpt 2, that is, the more languages are accumulated, the more job opportunities will be obtained. Nevertheless, this view has also been contradicted, for example in Excerpt 12, where the student refers to language as a communicative instrument requiring the engagement of others ("communicate with people from all over the world") and observes that economic logic includes many elements other than job opportunities ("to travel around the world").

Excerpts 12

Knowing different languages makes it much easier to travel around the world, which is one of my goals.

For me, the main reason is to be able to hold my own when travelling to other countries.

I am learning these languages [English and Chinese] because I want to be able to communicate with people from all over the world, whether I'm travelling or at home, whenever I meet people who don't speak Spanish.

In these cases, students figure themselves not only as individualistic economic rational actors but also as cosmopolitan citizens who seek to communicate with cultural others and not simply to accumulate capital. The desire to communicate with people from all over the world motivates students to expand their repertoire of languages, an ambition that is especially pronounced among the anthropology degree students. However, this outcome may also reflect the role of leisure and pleasure within a neoliberal rationality. If the principle of "accumulation and self mastery" shapes students' discourses, that of "pleasure", with respect to communication, also seems to play a role, as I discuss in the next section.

Manufacturing self-made speakers: An apparatus of performance and pleasure

In spite of the fact that all these students mentioned that they were learning languages for work-related reasons, the analysis of the students' discourses not only reveals adhesion to neoliberal principles, and to the discourses that are dominant in this context. Some apparent contradictory discourses emerge by means of which students seem to distance themselves from the economic logic of accumulation in language learning. In that cases, as in the following discourse samples compiled, participants in their answers combine obligation verbs like "have to" or "must" regarding language learning with verbs of aspiration, such as "want", "like", "hope", "aspire to", and even "enjoy".

Excerpts 13

I learn because I enjoy it.

I want to make French a language in which I can communicate fluently.

I want to work in another country.

I'd like to emigrate.

I hope to get involved in an international environment.

These examples show how students reveal these points to inconsistencies in the discourse of economic self-improvement, referring to a more general interest in languages, and also as a hobby and for pleasure.

Excerpts 14

I'm very interested in languages for their own sake and I think it's a challenge.

I am thinking of learning Italian and Portuguese. The reason for this interest is that I feel attracted to cultures that are so close to Spanish, like Italian or Portuguese. But I'd also like to explore Brazil some day.

I enjoy learning languages, it's something I've been doing since I was a child and that I'm proud of.

I find the Italian language really attractive and I've been wanting to study it for several years.

I love languages and I believe that's what I'm best at.

I believe it's important to know other languages. Moreover, I study languages because I enjoy it.

However, the students in the anthropology degree course, who provided the following examples, more frequently chose words and phrases related to pleasure:

Excerpts 15

If I learn any language, if I am interested in it, it is simply because I enjoy it.

The reasons are, essentially, the pleasure of language.

It is certainly true that the languages mentioned by participants in these essays are not those considered to be imperative or an asset towards upward social mobility. Languages such as Italian, Korean and Japanese are associated with leisure and are characterised as hobbies; as one person said: "Learning Korean is just a hobby for me" (note the subordinate value ranking, expressed by "just"). This choice could be reinforced by the official EU language policy, because to some extent it reproduces the "mother-tongue-plus-two" formula with (a) "mother tongue", (b) second language for practical purposes (labour market), (c) a third one for pleasure. According to Moore, in contemporary EU policy discourse, this plan is presented as a familiar:

> kind of "win-win" scenario: universalisation of the trilingual repertoire will primarily serve economic goals by supporting the reskilling of European workers with flexibility to meet the demands of an export-driven Knowledge-Based Economy (KBE), and supporting the overall integration of the EU labour market with social cohesion and better intercultural understanding as added benefits.
>
> (Moore, 2015, p. 28)

However, in order to address the complexity and the apparent contradictions observed in these discourses, it is needed a model of power that combines high demands of "performance" with "pleasure". This combination, as Melman claims, is a key element of the transition from a psychic economy organised by repression to an "economy organised by the exhibition of pleasure" (Melman, 2002, pp. 18–19). As Melman explains:

> it is no longer possible today to open a magazine, to admire characters or heroes from our society without being marked by the specific state of exhibition of enjoyment. This enjoyment creates radically new duties, impossibilities, difficulties and different sufferings to individuals.
>
> (Melman, 2002, p. 19)

Following the same observation, Dardot and Laval proposed that the combination of performance and pleasure produce a power apparatus (Foucault, 1977b)[6] that encompasses various institutional, physical and administrative mechanisms and knowledge structures which enhance and maintain the exercise of power within the social body. Thus:

> far removed from the model of a central power directly controlling subjects, the performance/pleasure apparatus is apportioned into diversified mechanisms of control, evaluation and incentivisation and pertains to all the cogs of production, all modes of consumption, and all forms of social relations.
>
> (Dardot & Laval, 2014, p. 319)

In fact, performance not only underpins speakers' resolve to master language "properly" (see Berlant, 2011 on the role of hoarding in capitalism), but is also a key element in personal branding (Boltanski & Chiapello, 2006; Sennett, 2006). In relation to this self branding, some differences were observed, which seemed to be related to the students' social position: while those in the International Studies degree programme highlighted their skills and had positive expectations, presenting themselves as fully in charge of their success (Zimmermann & Flubacher, 2017, p. 208), some individuals in the anthropology degree programme produced discourses referring to the weaker social position that some of these students had vis a vis the International Studies' students. Statements like the following highlight difficulties and a lack of expectations and the flavour of failure:

Excerpt 16

I am trying to learn English, due to the social and labour market limitations I face in life.

Whether affected by success or failure, these participants indistinctly focus on "me and my skills", "me and my way of behaving", but also on "my desire to improve", "the attraction I feel", the need to be "special", "interesting", "fascinating", and so on. Thus, linguistic performance is bound to speakers' sense of individual agency and their scenario of potential success and self-branding. To some extent, the contradiction between the hedonistic values of enjoying learning and the ascetic values of the entrepreneurial aim of accumulating languages seems to disappear when two kinds of social obligation are established as equivalents, namely, the duty of performing well and the duty of pleasure. The aim of the imperative of producing "ever more" and enjoying "ever more" seems to be "to intensify the effectiveness of every subject in all areas – educational and professional, but also relational, sexual, and so forth" (Dardot & Laval, 2014, pp. 213–214)[7].

It seems that the endless process of learning and of capitalising personal attributes (i.e. self capitalisation) is not just about exertion; rather, it is a process of finding satisfaction in improving oneself, thus self pleasure is achieve through the requisite performance. The self entrepreneur is a being made to "succeed", to "win", and he or she is expected to enjoy it.

Governmental technologies: How to become a self-made speaker

Once we have identified and understood the main features of the models of subjects and models of speakerhood that are at the core of neoliberal rationality, and the complex need of performing well and joyful, we can address the main question of this chapter: by which means the entrepreneurial model and the performance/pleasure apparatus reach individuals and govern their behaviour and shape the understanding of themselves. To answer these questions we need to focus on what I will call governmental technologies, a particular kind of technologies in which power technologies and the technologies of the self interact.[8] And this is precisely here where we detect the main innovation of neoliberal governmentality that consists in directly connecting the way in which subjects are governed from without to how they govern themselves from within. It is precisely the self-made speaker model that articulates the encounter between techniques of power exercised by others and techniques of conducting oneself, in what Foucault calls governmentality (Foucault, 2001, p. 1604; see also Foucault, 2000). This speakerhood model is part of the knowledge that is disseminated by current neoliberal rationality but at the same time, like all models, it compels individuals to behave and examine themselves according to the standard presented. Taking this into consideration, I now analyse some of the power techniques observed in the students' discourses.

Power technologies

In this section, I refer firstly to the technologies of power, which "conduct" the conduct of individuals, such as internalisation, normalisation, self surveillance, external and internal accountability, free choice and self discipline, self training and self capitalisation. Secondly, I examine other technologies of power, those of the self, such as introspection and confession.

Internalisation and normalisation

In the examples cited above, the references to the importance of languages in general, and that of English in particular, as a means of satisfying requirements for increasing performance but also for success in work and in life in general, are pervasive. Accepting the high value of English as axiomatic has a normalising effect, driving the self-improvement logic which launches a disciplinary process. In this respect, Foucault states that "normalising judgment" distinguishes individuals in terms of the overall rule that is "made to function as a minimal threshold, as an average to be respected, or as an optimum toward which one must move" (1977a, p. 197). In the present case, the norm is an entrepreneurial model that also correlates with a process of self constitution, by means of which speakers are considered as enterprises that must ensure their own profitability. Thus, when individuals failed and cannot achieve a high degree of performance, they reproduce the norm and feel ashamed, as in the following example:

Excerpt 17

And even today I still feel inferior when it comes to ordering food in a restaurant because I think I don't know how to pronounce it properly.

Free choice and self discipline: Self training and self capitalisation

Within this frame, information about languages as social and cultural capital and their position in current and future markets is identified as information that speakers require in order to make choices. Once the language expectations (of universities, families, corporations, the media, and so on) are established, they become an information apparatus that transfers the risk associated with a particular linguistic choice to the speaker. Not only do speakers "choose" a particular language; they also take on the responsibility of "choosing" a particular form of training, and of determining other aspects of their future. As indicated in Chapter 1, the new subject of globalised governmentality is an "active responsible agent" (Fraser, 2003, p. 168; see also Gershon, 2011). Accordingly, externally-imposed discipline tends to be replaced by self discipline. It is precisely in relation to discipline that the role of educational institutions has changed within the neoliberal order (Martín Rojo, 2017). Under neoliberal logic, schools are now seen as institutions that evoke competitiveness as the overall value to be achieved, instead of providing training and discipline.

The dynamics that turn market-governing processes into modes of social organisation and of self constitution transfer the process of self capitalisation to subjects who must enhance their productivity by taking their own decisions. The preceding analyses of students' discourses illustrate how the behaviour of individuals, and that of the population in general, is expressed, with the continual use of verb phrases such as "I am working/ studying", or "I am continuing to improve", which presuppose actions in progress.

Excerpts 18

I'm always working on my English in order to get better at it.

I continue to learn English every day through my bilingual degree programme. I know it's something useful. Also, I'm quite good at it and it isn't hard.

I'm improving my English even more.

I'm learning French and improving my understanding of English even more.

I teach English classes, to keep up my own level.

(Bilingual Spanish-English Student)

Training is, in fact, the cornerstone of disciplinary power; however, it also seems to be crucial in relation to governmentality. As soon as individuals start to transform themselves by means of training, the competition is extended to an individual dimension, in which individuals seek to advance themselves and/or their organisations. Surprisingly, these students do not refer to their teachers or to the educational system when it comes to their language learning, unless they are criticising the low level of English in the university's bilingual programmes, which is mentioned as an obstacle. Thus, in all these examples, we not only see how free choice and self discipline produce self training and self capitalisation, but also that these qualities generate considerable introspection, converting governance into governmentality. This tendency is in accordance with self evaluation, as the increasing focus of educational institutions, and it is also related to the following power technique.

Self surveillance and external and internal accountability

"Surveillance" is a mechanism of control, which can be defined as permanent, exhaustive and omnipresent observation, capable of making everything visible, while itself remaining invisible (Foucault, 1977a). In this research, the effects of language observation are similar to those highlighted by Foucault when he explains that the person:

> who is subjected to a field of visibility, and who knows it, assumes responsibility for the constraints of power; he makes them play spontaneously upon himself; he inscribes in himself the power relation in which he simultaneously plays both roles; he becomes the principle of his own subjection.
>
> (Foucault, 1977a, pp. 202–203)

Consequently, surveillance easily becomes self surveillance, in both public and private spheres. Hence, those who seek to learn an international language have to face normalising judgments. In fact, non-native speakers report permanent and exhaustive surveillance of their language practices, which are still shaped by the native speaker model. Self surveillance becomes a means to avoid being caught infringing rules or disappointing expectations (Martín Rojo & Márquez, 2019), and a technology of self knowledge. Thus, self examination is an instrument of self transformation, as the following techniques show.

Technologies of the self

In view of these considerations, what seems to be distinctive of neoliberal governmentality is that not only do power techniques become self exercised, as in the cases of self surveillance and self discipline, but also that the kind of technologies of power presented in these examples are in fact technologies of the self, "which permit individuals to effect by their own means or with the help of others a certain number of operations on their own bodies and souls, thoughts, conduct, and way of being, so as to transform themselves in order to attain a certain state of happiness, purity, wisdom, perfection, or immortality" (Foucault, 1988). In the case I describe, however, the appearance of technologies of the self, such as self examination and confession, cannot be explained solely in terms of neoliberalism. The technologies of self that reproduce and internalise power can also create resistance, if they are reappropriated and utilised for other ends in striving towards "autonomy" (Lilja & Vinthagen, 2014). Furthermore, self examination and the exchange of personal experiences were in this case decisively encouraged by the awareness-raising exercises and the overall context of an exchange of experiences that was established in the classes, as part of a critical pedagogy stance, with the aim to students engage in practices of self-transformation. As a result of this examination this last section takes us into the experiential dimension of trying to be the self made speaker, exposing some of the tensions students face, following this model of speakerhood.

One of the key elements that explains the tensions speakers face is the fact that the self-made speakers are subject to the principle of accountability: speakers feel the need to account for themselves, through self examination and confession, and to be evaluated in accordance with outcomes. In the following excerpts, we see how these speakers are trained to acknowledge and measure their own competences in terms of standardised metrics.

Excerpts 19

I have a medium-high level of English and German, and I try to keep on improving my skills in these languages. I've been studying English since I was at school, although lately I've neglected it a bit. In contrast, I've been studying German since high school and recently I've been strengthening and improving it, as I lived in Germany for six months. I'm hoping for opportunities to use my knowledge of these languages in the future.

Since it's not a compulsory language at university, I'm studying it at a language academy in the afternoons and I'll take exams to get a higher rating.

At this point social differences among students and their access to degrees of greater or lesser prestige become evident, and students may feel frustrated at not having achieved their goals. In some cases frustration arises because they consider their language level to be quite high, until it is put to use and the practical circumstance reveals their limited competence in communicating with fluent speakers of other languages. This problem was especially common among the anthropology degree students, whose course did not give them the same quality of access to English; hence, these students lacked the necessary opportunity both before and during their university studies.

Excerpts 20

I took it for granted that I had a good grounding in English, but when you move outside the academic field, intonation and accent are greater barriers than the language itself.

It was a bit frustrating, as I thought I had a higher level of English.

Consequently, the fear of making a mistake is inhibiting and in many cases leads to self censorship. The statements in the preceding excerpts could be understood as forms of "confession", in Foucault's term (2007; see also

Kunming & Blommaert, 2017), a key veridictional genre that has become extremely widespread and shows the important role played by the well-known technology of self examination, i.e. being critical and having self doubt, in neoliberal governmentality. This was true of the students in all the degree programmes considered who must study and communicate via a language other than their own (usually English). These students' experiences had an evident impact on the process of subjectification, as reflected by their references to themselves as "less competent" or even "inferior", and on extending the care of the self to self training in the following discourse samples compiled:

Excerpts 21

Although we actually liked them, we preferred not to talk to them because, even if we could hold a fluent conversation, they spoke English very well and we were embarrassed about making mistakes when we spoke.

I felt ashamed about having made the mistake.

And even today I still feel inferior when it comes to ordering food in a restaurant because I think I don't know how to pronounce it properly.

In these excerpts, the students relate how they monitor their own accent, highlighting as "mea culpa" their anticipation of the effect if they were to get it wrong. Thus, their language skills, after formal assessment at school, according to norms, have now become internalised as self monitoring, affecting how and when they choose to speak or to remain silent.

We have then finally reach the point were speakers govern themselves from within, taken as a reference external models and norms. We can then see how the performance/pleasure apparatus operationalises governmentality and among its effects we can identify a high subjective "cost". While the "losers" suffer on account of their inadequacies, the "winners" exhibit their superiority. Illusion and hope are easier problematised among those who do not have the same opportunities of mobility and access. By contrast, those who have access to language resources, bilingual degrees and family financial support will tend to assume attitudes of complacency and omnipotence and at the same time extend the already widespread social illusion of total, free mobility, and achievable success.

However, at the same time, the ensuing debates and exchanges of experiences during the classes had also contributed to collectively developing a new way of reading the models, principles, practices. Within these debates, unfortunately not recorded, the feelings of shame and responsibility were collectively challenged, principles such as accumulation were connected to exploitatation. These exchanges show how the proposed critical task allows students to engage in practices of self-transformation. At the same time, the evocation of alternative models of speakers throughout these discussions, such as those represented by representative antocolonial thinkers such as

Gloria Anzaldúa and Fanon, shows how at least incipiently other conducts were examined, with other objectives, or procedures/methods.

Conclusions

Neoliberal rationality is a normative order of reason, which governs without governing, a form of political rationality representing "world-changing, hegemonic orders of normative reason, generative of subjects, markets, states, law, jurisprudence, and their relations" (Brown, 2015, p. 121). Political rationalities are always historically contingent. In the case of Madrid universities, we have seen how this rationality has permeated educational institutions and their participants, in a context of economical neoliberalisation and European language policies, in a region that seeks to enter and be prominent in a global economy. This rationality generates the production of knowledge about language and an emergent form of "self made" speakerhood. This knowledge often governs language conduct and speakers' trajectories as if they were uncontested truths (at least until or unless challenged by another political rationality). As Dardot and Laval explain, this rationality also highlights the unparalleled advantage of linking all power relations in the framework of a single discourse. Discourses – in our case economic, educational, language and speakerhood discourses (e.g.) – intersect in the concepts of "enterprise" and "self enterprise". The new understanding of the social subject effects an unprecedented unification of the plural forms of subjectivity that liberal democracy has allowed to survive and helps maintain. In this respect, the lexicon of enterprise has the potential to connect the goals pursued by institutions, business and governments with every component of social and individual existence.

We have also examined the current model of speakerhood, which seems to be distanced from the traditional *homo œconomicus* model. Today's neo-liberal or entrepreneurial subjects are governed by the demand to improve and leverage their competitive position and to enhance their (monetary and non-monetary) portfolio value across all endeavours. The linguistic correlate of this subject is the "self-made speaker". This chapter discusses the main features of this model of speakerhood (for the differences with the "native speaker", see Martín Rojo, 2016), namely that (i) students may present themselves as socialised in multilingualism and globalisation, having internalised the discourse of languages as capital and the discourse of self entrepreneurship and mobility; (ii) they manage their language capital and competences by calculating profits like the *homo economicus*, supplying accountability, but also mobilising the aspiration of "self realisation", seeking self satisfaction and even pleasure; (iii) with this kind of rationality and the knowledge it provides, power techniques become self ex1ercised, as in the cases of self surveillance and self discipline, and mobilise traditional technologies of the self, such as self examination and confession. Thus, whether language is considered an individual enterprise and singular capital or an instrument of communication geared towards human relations, languages are always framed in a context of social and geographical mobility, inextricably bound to a neoliberal economy and rationality.

The series of tasks that these university students were encouraged to perform, to reflect critically upon the power-knowledge relations that constitutes subjectivity and to engage in practices of self-transformation, reveals the existence of particular forms of subjectification. These forms demand continual self improvement and constant involvement, as an excess of self over self which, in its very regime, is constitutionally aligned with the logic of enterprise and, with the imperatives of the "market". Success and failure are then the exclusive responsibility of the subject. If neoliberalism is viewed as a particular production of subjectivity, then it can be related to the way in which individuals are constituted as subjects of "human capital". Speakers' self investment in their skills or abilities increases their capacity to earn income, to achieve satisfaction and to conform to a model of speakerhood that increases language capital and skills, that is, the investment in human capital. We have seen that in the context of governmentality, "power reaches into the very grain of individuals, touches their bodies and inserts itself into their actions and attitudes, their discourses, learning processes and everyday lives" (Foucault, 1980, p. 39). In this respect, this chapter has gone a step further, showing how the discourse of entrepreneurship is take up by individuals and used as a way of understanding and narrating their experiences and actions. In order to understand these processes, this chapter has considered the technologies of power and how they are applied in relation to language and speakers, and grasped significant transformations related to the way power is exercised. Although students have presented incipient examples of resistance towards the discourses presenting them as self-made speakers and neoliberal subjects, these attempts point nevertheless to two consistent forms of resistance: "counter-conducts" or conducts done differently, by other leaders (conducteurs), with other objectives, or procedures/methods (Foucault, 2007, pp. 194–195), and to the engagement in practices of "self-transformation"; both will be then the object for further research.

Research, accompaniment, and awareness-raising tasks, such as those I described, may curb the infiltration of these neoliberal principles into the subjects and therefore spark resistance. As teachers and students, following a critical pedagogy, we face education as an inherently political act, and as an urgent way to promote emancipation from oppression through the awakening of the critical consciousness of how language is one of the most effective means of domination, which reaches bodies, languages, knowledge, behaviours, duties and even pleasures. This approach could opens up space for resistance to the kind of subjectivity given by power relations and giving place to conducts done differently, with other objectives, models, and or procedures. Resistance, however, cannot be individual, but requires the construction of an alternative discourse and another rationality, of new hegemonies that contribute to create new subjectivities. To do so, new social movements, such as the quiet revolution of the commons, can help advance new models and values, such as those of the cooperative subjects (see Martín Rojo, in preparation).

Finally, with respect to social reproduction, inequality and class, the neo-liberal transformation of education is very efficient in moulding, as well as benefiting, a privileged elite, while others lack access to the global labour market in question. Once again, it can be seen that the way in which linguistic capital is managed in educational programmes contributes to the social reproduction of class inequality in society. This is a very important and socially relevant matter that cannot be fully addressed in a single chapter and requires development in future research.

Notes

1 I would like to thank Jacqueline Urla, Jan Blommaert, Alfonso del Percio, Lara Alonso, Nelson Flores, Yvette Bürki, José del Valle and Mary Bucholtz for their useful comments on earlier versions of this article. I am also grateful to the Madrid universities students who anonymously shared their everyday experiences with me, and to doctoral students at the Graduate Center for their useful comments to this text. This work was supported by the research project, funded by FEDER/Ministerio de Ciencia, Innovación y Universidades – Agencia Estatal de Investigación, *Linguistic superdiversity in peri-urban areas. A scalar analysis of sociolinguistic processes and metalinguistic awareness development in* multilingual classrooms. Ref. ffi 2016-76425-p. I would also like to thank my colleagues Jesús Rodríguez-Velasco and Bernard Harcourt, for organising the seminar series – Foucault 13/13 – at Columbia University, which give me the opportunity to follow up these rich and productive directions for research.

2 "Governance" has often been described as a new way of exercising power, comprising national and international political and legal institutions, associations, churches, enterprises, think tanks, universities, and so forth. Without entering into an examination of the nature of the new global power here, let us note that the new competitive norm has involved the increasing development of multiple forms of concession of authority to private enterprises, to the point where we might speak of public-private coproduction of international norms in many areas (Dardot & Laval, 2014, p. 242).

3 The Spanish transition to democracy (known in Spain as the Transition) is a period of modern Spanish history, that started on 20 November 1975, with the death of Francisco Franco, who had established a military dictatorship after the victory of the Nationalists in the Spanish Civil War.

4 A detailed analysis of these changes is given in Brown, 2015, pp. 79–111.

5 Understood as the process of becoming a subject in an endless power/knowledge/discourse relation.

6 *Dispositif*, translated as apparatus, is a term used by Michel Foucault to refer to the various institutional, physical and administrative mechanisms and knowledge structures which enhance and maintain the exercise of power within the social body (Foucault, 1977b).

7 These authors follow Gilles Deleuze and Félix Guattari, and Deleuze's late work that emphasise the relationship between this liberation of flows of desire, which extend beyond the social and political frameworks in capitalist societies, in

186 *Martín Rojo*

order to reincorporate them into the productive machine and to organise them for the reproduction of the system of production. In the 1970s Deleuze explicitly referred to the relationship between this liberation of flows of desire and the apparatuses for directing flows in the "society of control", by means of a mode of subjectification that stimulates "desire' and at the same time generalises the evaluation of performance (Deleuze, 1995).

8 In 1982, at a talk delivered at Stanford, Foucault distinguishes four types of technologies (Foucault, 1988). Two years late, in an interview he refers to a fifth type, the governmental technologies, by means of which the technologies of the self are freely excised by subjects, but compelled by an external rationality (Fornet-Betancourt, Becker, Gomez-Müller & Gauthier, 1987).

References

Aronowitz, S. (2000). *The knowledge factory: Dismantling the corporate university and creating true higher learning.* Boston: Beacon Press.

Berlant, L.G. (2011). *Cruel optimism.* Durham, NC: Duke University Press.

Block, D. (2011) Citizenship, education and global spaces. *Journal of Language and Intercultural Communication* 11(2), 161–169.

Blommaert, J. (2010). *The sociolinguistics of globalization.* Cambridge: Cambridge University Press.

Blommaert, J. (2018). *Durkheim and the Internet.* London: Bloomsbury.

Boltanski, L., & Eve, C. (2006). *The spirit of new capitalism.* New York: Verso.

Brown, W. (2015). *Undoing the demos: Neoliberalism's stealth revolution.* Cambridge, MA: MIT Press.

Bucholtz, M., Casillas, D.I., & Lee, J.S. (2016). Beyond empowerment: Accompaniment and sociolinguistic justice in a youth research program. In R. Lawson & D. Sayers (Eds.), *Sociolinguistic research: Application and impact* (pp. 25–44). Oxford: Routledge.

Council conclusions of 12 May 2009 on a strategic framework for European cooperation in education and training (ET 2020). *Official Journal C 119, 28.5.2009,* 2–10. https://eur-lex.europa.eu/legal-content/EN/TXT/HTML/?uri=LEGISSUM: ef0016&from=EN

Dardot, P., & Laval, C. (2014). *The new way of the world: On neoliberal society.* London: Verso Books.

Deleuze, G. (1995). Postscript on control societies. In *Negotiations: 1972–1990* (pp. 177–182).

Drucker, P. (1993). From capitalism to knowledge society. In *Post-Capitalism Society* (pp. 15–34). New York: HarperCollins.

Flores, N. (2017). From language as resource to language as struggle: Resisting the coke-ification of bilingual education. In M. C. Flubacher & A. Del Percio (Eds.), *Language, education and neoliberalism: Critical studies in sociolinguistics.* Bristol: Multilingual Matters.

Fornet-Betancourt, R., Becker, H., Gomez-Müller, A., & Gauthier, J.D. (1987). The ethic of care for the self as a practice of freedom: An interview with Michel Foucault on January 20, 1984. *Philosophy & Social Criticism,* 12(2–3), 112–131.

Foucault, M. (1977a). Discipline and punish: The birth of the prison. New York: Vintage.

Foucault, M. (1977b). The confession of the flesh interview. In C. Gordon (Ed.), *Power/knowledge. Selected interviews and other writings* (pp. 194–228). New York: Pantheon Books.

Foucault, M. (1980). *Power/knowledge: Selected interviews and other writings, 1972–1977.* New York: Pantheon Books.

Foucault, M. (1988). *Technologies of the self: A seminar with Michel Foucault.* London: Tavistock.

Foucault, M. (1997). *Ethics: subjectivity and truth*, ed. by Paul Rabinow. New York: New Press.

Foucault, M. (2000). Governmentality. In J. D. Faubion (Ed.), *Essential works of Foucault, Vol. 3:* Power (pp. 201–222). New York: Norton.

Foucault, M. (2001). Les techniques de soi. In Dits et écrits, tome 1: 1954–1975 (1708 p.), tome 2: 1976–1988 (1736 p.). Paris: Gallimard.

Foucault, M. (2007). *Abnormal: Lectures at the Collège de France, 1974–1975.* New York: Picado.

Foucault, M. (2008). *The birth of biopolitics: Lectures at the Collège de France, 1978–1979.* New York: Springer.

Foucault, M. (2009). *Security, territory, population: Lectures at the Collège de France 1977–1978.* New York: Picado.

Foucault, M., & Burchell, G. (2011). *The government of self and others: Lectures at the College de France, 1982–1983* (Vol. 7). New York: Macmillan.

Fraser, N. (2003). From discipline to flexibilization? Rereading Foucault in the shadow of globalization. Constellations, 10(2), 160–171.

Freire, P. (2009). *Pedagogy of the oppressed.* New York: Continuum International.

Gao, S., & Park, J.S.-Y. (2015). Space and language learning under the neoliberal economy. *L2 Journal*, 7(3), 78–96.

Gershon, I. (2011). Neoliberal agency. *Current Anthropology*, 52(4), 537–555.

Godelier, M. (1998). *El enigma del don: Dinero, Regalos, objetos santos.* Barcelona: Paidós Ibérica.

Guilherme, M. (2009). English as a global language and education for cosmopolitan citizenship. *Journal of Language and Intercultural Communication*, 7(1), 72–90.

Henrich, J., et al. (2001). In search of Homo economicus: behavioral experiments in 15 small-scale societies. *American Economic Review*, 92(2), 73–78.

Hirsch, P., Stuart, M., & Ray, F. (1990). Clean models vs. dirty hands: Why economics is different from sociology. In S. Zukin and P. DiMaggio (Eds.), *Structures of capital: The social organization of the economy* (pp. 39–56). Cambridge: Cambridge University Press.

Hong, S., & Allard-Huver, F. (2016). Governing governments? In P. Mcilvenny, J.Z. Klausen, and L.B. Lindeegard (Eds.), *Studies of discourse and governmentality: New perspectives and methods* (pp. 149–178). Amsterdam: John Benjamins.

Jacobsen, U.C. (2015). Cosmopolitan sensitivities, vulnerability, and global Englishes. *Language and Intercultural Communication*, 15(4), 459–474.

Kunming, L., & Blommaert, J. (2017). The care of the selfie: Ludic chronotopes of baifumei in online China. *Tilburg Papers in Culture Studies*, 197 1–22.

Lilja, M., & Vinthagen, S. (2014). Sovereign power, disciplinary power and biopower: Resisting what power with what resistance? *Journal of Political Power*, 7(1), 107–126.

Lorente, B. (2012). The making of "workers of the world': Language and the labor brokerage state. In A. Duchêne and M. Heller (Eds.), *Language in late capitalism* (pp. 183–206). New York: Routledge.

Martín Criado, E. (2014). Mentiras, inconsistencias y ambivalencias. Teoría de la acción y análisis de discurso. *Revista Internacional de Sociología*, 72(1), 115–138.

Martín Rojo, L. (1997). Jargon. In J. Verschueren and J.O. Östman (Eds.), *Handbook of pragmatics*, Vol. 2 (pp. 2–19). [Reprint. In M. Fried, J. O. Östman & J. Verschueren (2010). Variation and change: Pragmatic perspectives (pp. 155–170).] Amsterdam: John Benjamins.

Martín Rojo, L. (2016). Language and power. In O. Garcia, M. Spotti, and N. Flores (Eds.), *The Oxford handbook of language and society* (pp. 77–102). Oxford: Oxford University Press.

Martín Rojo, L. (2017). Neoliberalism and linguistic governmentality. In J.W. Tollefson and M. Pérez-Milans (Eds.), *The Oxford handbook of language policy and planning*, (pp. 544–567). Oxford: Oxford University Press.

Martín Rojo, L.M., Anthonissen, C., García-Sánchez, I., & Unamuno, V. (2017). Recasting diversity in language education in postcolonial, late-capitalist societies. In D. Ikizoglu, J. Wegner, & A. De Fina (Eds.), *Diversity and superdiversity: Sociocultural linguistic perspectives*. Washington, DC: Georgetown University Press.

Martín Rojo, L., & Márquez Reiter, R. (2019). Language surveillance: Pressure to follow local models of speakerhood among Latin students in Madrid. Journal of Sociology of Language, 257(4) 17–48.

Martín Rojo, L. (in preparation). The quiet revolution of the commons: The collective construction of discourses and practices in commoning.

Mauss, M. (1924/2009). *Ensayo sobre el don: forma y función del intercambio en las sociedades arcaicas.* Barcelona: Katz Editores.

McIlvenny, P., Klausen, J.Z., & Lindeergard, L.B. (Eds.) (2016). *Studies of discourse and governmentality: New perspectives and methods.* Amsterdam: John Benjamins.

Melman, C. (2002). *L'homme sans gravité: Entretiens avec Jean-Pierre Lebrun.* Paris: Denoël, p. 96.

Mill, J.St. (1874). On the definition of political economy, and on the method of investigation proper to it, London and Westminster Review, October 1836. In *Essays on Some Unsettled Questions of Political Economy*, 2nd ed (Essay V, paragraphs 38 and 48). London: Longmans, Green, Reader & Dyer. (pp. 86–114)

Moore, R. (2015). From revolutionary monolingualism to reactionary multilingualism: Top-down discourses of linguistic diversity in Europe, 1794-present. *Language & Communication*, 44, 19–30.

OECD (2015). *Connecting with Emigrants: A Global Profile of Diasporas 2015.* Paris: OECD Publishing. https://doi.org/10.1787/9789264239845-en.

Pareto, V. (1906/2014). *Manual of political economy: A critical and variorum edition.* Oxford: Oxford University Press.

Park, J.S. (2010). Naturalization of competence and the neoliberal subject: Success stories of English language learning in the Korean conservative press. *Journal of Linguistic Anthropology*, 20(1), 22–38.

Park, J.S. (2011). The promise of English: Linguistic capital and the neoliberal worker in the South Korean job market. International Journal of Bilingual Education and Bilingualism, 14(4), 443–455.

Persky, J. (1995). Retrospectives: The ethology of *Homo Economicus*. *Journal of Economic Perspectives*, 9(2), 221–231.

Pezet, É. (Ed.) (2007). *Management et conduite de soi. Enquête sur les ascèses de la performance*. Paris: Vuibert.

Polanyi, K. (1989). *La gran transformación*. Madrid: La Piqueta.

Relaño-Pastor, A.M. (2018). Bilingual education policy and neoliberal content and language integrated learning practices. In J.W. Tollefson and M. Pérez-Milans (Eds.), *The Oxford handbook of language policy and planning*, (pp. 505–525). Oxford: Oxford University Press.

Sahlins, M. (1972/2003). The original affluent society. In M. Sahlins (Ed.), *Stone age economics* (pp. 1–40). London: Routledge.

Sharkey, J. (2018). The promising potential role of intercultural citizenship in preparing mainstream teachers for im/migrant populations. *Language Teaching Research*, 22(5), 570–589.

Saunders, D.B. (2010). Neoliberal ideology and public higher education in the United States. *Journal for Critical Education Policy Studies*, 8(1), 41–77.

Sennett, R. (2006). *The culture of new capitalism*. New Haven, CT: Yale University Press.

Starkey, H. (2011). Citizenship, education and global spaces. *Language and Intercultural Communication*, 11(2), 75–79.

Talmy, S. (2010). Qualitative interviews in applied linguistics: From research instrument to social practice. *Annual Review of Applied Linguistics*, 30, 128–148.

Urciuoli, B. (2008). Skills and selves in the new workplace. *American Ethnologist*, 35(2), 211–228.

Urciuoli, B. (2010). Neoliberal education: Preparing the students for the new workplace. In C.J. Greenhouse (Ed.), *Ethnographies of neoliberalism* (pp. 162–176). Philadelphia: University of Pennsylvania Press.

Urla, J. (2012). *Reclaiming Basque: Language, nation, and cultural activism*. Reno: University of Nevada Press.

Von Mises, L. (1960). Remarks of the fundamental problem of the subjective theory of value, homo economicus. In *Epistemological problems of economics: George Reisman* (pp. 177–194). Auburn: Ludwig von Mises Institute.

Wilkins, A. (2012). School choice and the commodification of education: A visual approach to school brochures and websites. *Critical Social Policy*, 32(1), 69–86.

Wilkins, S., & Huisman, J. (2012). The international branch campus as transnational strategy in higher education. *Higher Education*, 64(5), 627–645.

Zimmermann, M., & Flubacher, M.C. (2017). Win-win?! Language regulation for competitiveness in a university context. In M.C. Flubacher and A. Del Percio (Eds.), *Language, education and neoliberalism: Critical studies in sociolinguistics* (pp. 204–229). Bristol: Multilingual Matters.

9 Resetting minds and souls

Language, employability and the making of neoliberal subjects

Alfonso Del Percio and Sze Wan Vivian Wong

Introduction

Scholars of language and power have recently noted that, in many industrialized societies, current social, cultural and economic changes have affected the theories that inform the state management of populations (Heller & McElhinny, 2018). Certainly, the regimentation of society is still mediated by a bureaucratic, patriarchal and patronizing state apparatus which relies on complex systems of classification and knowledge and which disciplines people through coercive techniques of societal control (Duchêne & Humbert, 2017; Vigouroux, 2017). However, commentators argue that the *disciplining society* is gradually being replaced by a neoliberal rationality that governs people through acts of freedom, flexibilization and competitiveness which affects the ways inequality is produced, rationalized, and justified by authorities of all sorts (Dardot and Laval, 2013; Fraser, 2003).

These shifts and continuities in the regulation of populations become particularly clear when we look at the ways welfare states currently govern poverty and unemployment. For example, in the United Kingdom, where Alfonso is currently based, Jobcentres (the government-funded agencies that comprise both the employment services and the social security offices) have historically played a key role in defining and quantifying the "problem" of the "unemployed", and managing and controlling the "poor". Jobcentres are not only places where people get access to labor. Along with older institutions such as the "Workhouse", which between the Middle Ages and the Victorian times provided work and accommodation to the "poor", or the more recent "poor laws" and benefits systems (e.g. the "Beveridge model") managing poverty and unemployment in the United Kingdom, Jobcentres are part of a larger disciplining apparatus that contributes to the normalization of what is often thought of as an unruly, immoral section of the populace, and in certain cases, a latent revolutionary threat to civil society (Kidd, 1999).

The restructuring of the British welfare state since the end of the 1970s has involved a redefinition of the ways state authorities apprehend citizens and unemployed subjects in particular (Harris, 2004). While for many decades access to social benefits was seen as a constitutional right, since the 1970s labor experts (in the service of the Thatcher regime and the governments following Thatcher) have claimed that unemployed subjects should no longer be passive recipients of benefits (Spicker, 2018). The authorities role thus became one of guiding unemployed subjects in the process of actively engaging in a job-hunting practice and showing flexibility in terms of their willingness to take a wider variety of jobs over a greater geographical dispersion (Bristow, 2014). Of course, this was not entirely new: unemployment benefits have never been given for free. Willingness to work has historically been a precondition of receiving benefits. In the early 20th century for example, the "dole", a payment that was made to unemployed workers, was already subjected to rigid means tests and "able" people were ineligible as they could ostensibly take care of themselves (Kidd, 1999). What was changing, however, was how unemployed subjects were expected to understand their selves as well as the forms of expertise that underpinned and regulated the processes informing their (re)integration into work.

One of the implications of these changing theories was, at first, a terminological one. In the early 1980s, the administrative category of "the unemployed" was replaced by the category of "job seekers" – a term which stressed the need for a more active and self-responsible job search on the part of the unemployed individual. Furthermore, these changes affected the spatial configuration of Jobcentres. Counters and queues were replaced by self-service notice boards providing information about employment opportunities and requiring the unemployed to literally *seek* employment by physically moving from board to board, within both the structured space of the self-service section and the wider economic structure of the market (Bristow, 2014). Recently, these changes have also led to the implementation of a series of employability programs asking unemployed individuals to invest in upgrading their human capital through lifelong learning and personal development programs. These employability programs are not necessarily provided by the Jobcentres themselves. Along with current changes in public administration in which models of public-private partnerships dominate the provision of public welfare, employability programs nowadays in the United Kingdom are outsourced to local charities and social organizations.

In this chapter, we present an ethnographic documentation of an employment program provided by *Connections*, a charity located in East London that targets young people considered at risk of poverty and delinquency. We take this employability program as a starting point to generate a critical understanding of the ways in which these programs operate on the ground and thus contribute to the governmentality of poverty and unemployed subjects in London. Our analysis will draw on ethnographic data jointly collected by Alfonso and Vivian between Spring and Fall 2017 during a research project on language and employability conducted in Newham, East London. This ethnographic data set includes observational data of training activities as well as observations of practices that occur outside the framework of the employability program. It also involves formal and informal conversations with unemployed trainings participants, program coaches, trainers and counselors, as well as program funders.

The ethnographic account put forward in this chapter claims that the management of populations by all sorts of authorities cannot be theorized without a consideration of the ways in which governmentality is *done* on the ground and how it has real-time effects for people (Rose, 1999). We particularly assume that an ethnographic documentation of the communicative practices observed during the training activities enables us to study government not as an institution, nor as a mode of reasoning, but rather as a set of activities operating at the intersection between what Michel Foucault calls "technologies of power which determine the conduct of individuals and submit them to certain ends and domination", and

> "technologies of the self which permit individuals to effect by their own means or with the help of others a certain number of operations on their own bodies and souls, thoughts conduct and way of being so as to transform their selves in order to attain a certain state of happiness, purity, wisdom, perfection and immortality".
>
> (Foucault 1988a, p. 18)

Drawing on these assumptions, this paper then argues that the investigated employability program strives to disrupt poverty and unemployment through a set of disciplining techniques that target the individuals' minds and their understanding of their selves. We will show that, while these techniques are anchored, both institutionally and ideologically, in larger histories of knowledge about, and discipline of, "poverty" and the "poor", the type of self that training participants are asked to become is informed by a neoliberal rationality that extends market principles to every domain of social life. We will particularly show that the investigated program is emblematic for a form of neoliberal governmentality that asks the participating subject to engage in a never-ending practice of self-improvement, self-management and self-monitoring, which requires them to understand their selves in terms of quality, competitiveness and freedom. At the same time, we will argue that, far from being a closed, totalizing, functional theory determining the actions of individuals and their understanding of their selves, the complex set of ideas informing this training program do not determine the actions or thinking of the participating subjects. This neoliberal rational is rather mobilized, rationalized and dialectically engaged with on the ground by (some of) the unemployed subject who problematize and challenge the program and contest its inability to promote their access to jobs and socio-economic inclusion.

Based on our findings, and inspired by current scholarship on language and governmentality (Dlaske et al. 2016; Martin-Rojo, 2018; Urla, 2012), we will further show that language plays a key role for the everyday *doing* of the type of neoliberal governmentality documented in this paper. We will demonstrate that *language* is the medium through which a neoliberal rationality is circulated by different sorts of individuals and actors, which penetrates and colonializes every sphere of social life and interpellates individuals as neoliberal subjects. Secondly, we will explain that it is through language, that is, practices of reflexivity and introspection mediated through writing, speaking and thinking about oneself, that individuals come to understand themselves as specific self-projects that need to be constantly monitored, analyzed and managed. Thirdly, we show that language, that is, oral or textualized communicative and behavioral instructions which mobilize idealized and morally marked figures of personhood, serves as a guiding principle for individuals to exert control over their own and other's bodies and minds and to guide them in their attempts to meet the demands of employers as well as of those individuals and actors managing benefits and distributing resources. Finally, we claim that it is through language, that is, through one's communicative ability to enact a specific subjectivity, that one gets to be recognized as a desirable worker. In sum, we will show that language is both object and medium of governmentality and is therefore at the core of a biopolitical practice that creates compliance for professional precarity, poverty and unemployment through the management of young people's bodies, including their emotions and minds.

This chapter is structured as follows: firstly, we will present *Connections* and its training program and discuss the rationales that underpin the provided training activities. Secondly, we will analyze the techniques and forms of expertise mobilized by instructors and coaches to guide young people in their management of their selves. We also present the tensions and conflicts that these training activities cause, and the strategies mobilized by coaches to prevent participating individuals from questioning the ability of this employment program to help them access jobs.

Governing unemployment

Connections was funded in the 1970s and since then has worked with different groups of people understood to be affected by poverty and homelessness in the borough of Newham, which is categorized as one of the most economically deprived and racially diverse areas of the United Kingdom. The charity provides services in the domains of "Advice", "Health" and "Youth and "Employment" and has as its main goal to "support people in coming together, overcoming barriers, building purpose and making the most of the place they live in". The employment program in which we conducted research is part of the organizational section "Youth and Employment". The program lasts for ten weeks (six hours, three times a week) and is run three times a year in order to be financially profitable. Indeed, this training program is sponsored by an American investment bank and is emblematic of the current transformations of the management of unemployment and poverty in the city of London. The public-private co-operations between Jobcentres and other organizations previously mentioned do not simply involve processes of outsourcing of vocational training activities to organizations such as *Connections*. Employability programmes provided by charities such as *Connections* are frequently sponsored by corporate investors who benefit from these cooperations in terms of tax breaks and positive publicity. These partnerships are not only of financial nature. Often, such as in the case of the investigated employability program, the corporate actors who fund, or co-fund, these programs are involved in the formulation of the training objectives, and are also in charge of providing specific training activities to the enrolled participants.

The specific employability program in which we were able to conduct fieldwork is meant to contribute to disrupting poverty in East London and to create opportunities for the local unemployed youth. As noted by the charity's management, what all the training participants have in common is that they live in situations of social and economic precarity: some are homeless or have a criminal record; many of them were enrolled by the Jobcentre located in Newham; others were recruited in the community centers of East London; and others still were recruited in prisons or institutions dealing with juvenile crime. Most of the participants were born in London, are "native speakers" of English, and are "second generation immigrants" with parents from Nigeria, Bangladesh, Guinea, Somalia, Sudan, and Turkish Cyprus. In spite of their differences, in terms of linguistic background and educational and professional trajectory, all participants are categorized as NEETs. "NEET" is a category used by the British authorities (and other Western countries) to refer to young people between 16 and 24 that are "not in employment, education or training". The employment program provided by *Connections* is then seen as a means to subject these young people to specific techniques (group activities as well as one-to-one advisory sessions) that are meant to keep them off the streets, and eventually facilitate their integration into the labor market. The programs' themes and topics cover the following domains:

> Qualities and Skills
> Dreams and Goals
> Facing Barriers
> Leadership and Teamwork
> Workplace Ethics and Valuing Diversity
> CV Skills
> Interview Training
> Presentation Skills

This list of topics reflects *Connections*' focus on practices of self-management and emotional styling. Communication and literacy, self-presentation, resilience and motivation, emotions and personal traits, as well as multiculturalism, empathy, respect and values are at the core of each training activity. Less attention is dedicated to the acquisition and development of specific work skills required for specific professions. This focus on the management of participants' attitude and affective status is emblematic of a shift in the ways professional education is nowadays designed and conducted (see Allan, 2013 or Bell, 2017 for an analysis of the ways these processes occur in other contexts). While vocational schools continue to provide workers with professional knowledge and technical skills, the list of topics characterizing the curriculum of the training program provided by *Connections* represents a type of professional training scheme that responds to the labor market's need for flexibility (Del Percio & Van Hoof, 2017; Flubacher, Coray & Duchêne, 2017). Since professional knowledge and practice can be learned on the job and that under current configurations of labor, workers can no longer assume that they will be employed in the same profession throughout their professional lives, what professional education needs to focus on is the development of the workers' capacity to adapt themselves (physically and mentally) to different professional situations and to the unpredictability of the labor market. This also involves the socialization of workers into a professional habitus that subjects the self to a practice of constant self-monitoring and self-improvement (see Boutet, 2001; or Dlaske, 2016 for similar lines of arguments).

In the case of the employability program documented at *Connections*, the necessity to produce flexible workers for a changing labor market intersects with the need to manage the supposed mental vulnerability of East London's impoverished population addressed by this program. The young individuals targeted by the *Connections* training program are seen by public authorities as an "at-risk" group. The fact that these young people live in areas assumed to be problematic, have no occupation, nor involved in any productive activity is said to negatively affect their mental health, which in the long term, leads to situations of delinquency. This employability training was then meant to provide them with the entire package of life skills necessary to be successful in a flexibilized and precarious labor market and, at the same time, help them develop resilience and mental strength.

Indeed, when we were first shown the locations in which the training activities would take place, we quickly noted the motivational slogans and phrases with which the walls of the room in the second floor of *Connections* main building were adorned: "Do something today that your future self will thank you for" or "You can have results or excuses. Not both" or "If you don't find the time, if you don't do the work, you don't get the results" or "Old ways won't open new doors". Natasha, the employability coach providing the training, explained to us that these slogans are meant to encourage participants to work on themselves. These individuals, she argues, are often passive, depressed and demotivated. They suffer from mental illness, have low self-esteem and lack self-confidence. In many cases, she continued, they feel betrayed by society and public institutions and tend to victimize themselves. This employability training wants them to take responsibility for their own lives and futures. We need to reset their minds and souls, she explained.

It was not the first time that program participants were presented to us as vulnerable and mentally unstable. A couple of weeks before the start of the training activities, Alfonso had met the management of *Connections* and the team of professional coaches responsible for providing employability trainings to young people. Alfonso had only recently taken over his position as a lecturer in London after different jobs in other European countries. He was not accustomed with the local discourses on youth unemployment. He kept using the word "unemployed" when talking about training participants and their training participants: What is the social and professional background of the unemployed registered in the program? How do you usually recruit these unemployed young people? What do these unemployed individuals expect from the training program? What are the possibilities of these unemployed youngsters being integrated in the job market? After the end of the meeting, one of the managers of the program noted that it would be wise to avoid the term "unemployed" when addressing training participants, especially when they are present. Many of them feel frustrated and are depressed, he explained. Some are on medication. The term "unemployed" has negative connotations, which could negatively affect their minds and motivation, and its use could present an obstacle and thus be counterproductive. Use positive terms, the manager advised, such as "professionals" or just "participants". Call them by their own name so that they feel personally addressed.

These concerns about the young people's emotional vulnerability that manifest themselves in both Natasha's and the manager's discourse about the training participants are interdiscursively related to a longer history of knowledge linking poverty and social marginality to emotional deviance and mental instability (Foucault, 1988, 2003), which is mobilized in the sphere of employability programs through powerful expert reports and briefings on youth unemployment (Smith, 1990). More particularly, the communicative practices documented at *Connections* are interlinked with a body of expertise produced both in academic and policy-making circles that argues that the only way of challenging the systemic causes of poverty and unemployment is by fostering resilient selves, i.e. producing minds that are able to cope with, adapt themselves to, and navigate flexible labor regimes (Siraj et al., 2014; Powell, 2018). We will demonstrate in the next sections that these forms of expertise about the self do not directly act upon the unemployed subjects, but rather they are mediated by a whole set of disciplining techniques that target people's minds and their understanding of their selves. We will document how these techniques operated on the ground. We will investigate the effects of these techniques and reflect on how, why and with what consequences these techniques were sometimes endorsed, or sometimes challenged by participants themselves.

Disciplining subjects

In one of the first training sessions documented, Natasha asked participants to prepare a list of their personal qualities and to hierarchize these qualities according to their value on the labor market. She explained that participants should also think about their weaknesses and those personal traits that might be an obstacle for their professional integration. Ursula, a 23-year-old homeless women who was sitting next to Alfonso wrote down in her notebook the following list of qualities: "organized", "honest", "reliable", "adaptable", "enthusiastic", "team player", "resilient" and "good at communication". For personal weakness she noted: "punctuality", "education", "work experience" and "race". She underlined with her pen the word "race", looked at Alfonso and whispered in his ear that while public authorities like to highlight the fact that London is such a multicultural city, race continues to be a feature complicating people's access to employment. Ursula was not new to this type of exercise. She had already attended several of these programs since her access to unemployment benefits was dependent upon her attendance. Each training session, Ursula explained to us, is based on the same type of activities, the same expectations. After a while you become good at anticipating instructors' questions and at giving the expected answers.

Ursula's way of responding to the expectations of instructors and counselors is a coping strategy shared by many unemployed people who we have met during our fieldwork and who have learned that being able to benefit from the British benefits system depends on their ability to enact what Bonnie Urciuoli calls a skills discourse (2008), that is, a mode of speaking that aligns people's subjectivities with principles of quality, competitiveness, flexibility and entrepreneurialism. It would be wrong, however, to assume that job seekers such as Ursula naively buy into this skills discourse. As we will show in the next paragraphs and sections, we would rather consider this discourse as an unequally distributed communicative resource (or a register) that some of the individuals we met have acquired in the many training session attended and which they have learned to strategically mobilize in order to be seen as particularly motivated and therefore deserving state support.

Now, given Ursula's ability to enact this skills discourse, we were not surprised when during the following discussion that participants had with Natasha (the instructor) about what employers would look for when interviewing candidates, Ursula correctly suggested that being "reliable", "flexible" and "enthusiastic" is often more important than having a good education and lot of work experience. Natasha confirmed that studies had shown that recruiters consider candidates' education and professional experience as less important than their moral integrity and passion at work. Therefore, everybody could get a job, she said, if only people would learn to know who they are, recognize their own qualities, highlight their weaknesses, and convincingly sell their strengths during job interviews.

This idea – that everyone can manage and control their life in accordance to their needs and desires – is emblematic of the (neo)liberal rationales informing these training programs. According to Dardot and Laval (2013), it is this assumption that makes people work on themselves, invest in training and lifelong learning, speculate about their futures, calculate their gains and losses and accept the precarization of their lives and working bodies. We will come back to this point later. For the moment, let us just mention that, while this rhetoric of hope visibly seemed to give some relief to the tense faces of the participants in the room, we remember Ursula starting to laugh nervously. We noted that she would react with this laugh every time she did not seem to agree with someone's reflections. In a later conversation, Ursula explained to us that this way of speaking by the instructors is a means to create a positive climate. Instructors usually tend to downplay the hopeless situations which people like her are in and make participants believe that their future is dependent on their willingness to work hard. Ursula noted that in her case, working hard had not helped and that after months of employability trainings, she still slept in one of the city's hostels for homeless women.

Ursula was not the only one contesting this rhetoric. Other participants, who had initially been registered in this training, stopped attending the program after the first couple of sessions. Along with Ursula, in their feedback to the charity justifying their dropping-out of the program, they claimed that this type of optimistic rhetoric and the proposed activities (especially the self-management practices) were not what they had expected. Rather, what they needed was concrete, hands-on support in terms of CV writing, interview training and guidance about navigating London's labor market and the complex network of offices, organizations and agencies that support job seekers in their attempts to find employment. What distinguished Ursula from these other participants who had left the program before its termination (this is at least how Ursula herself rationalized it), was that Ursula had learned to take the program for what is was: a space giving her access to free lunch for ten weeks and the chance to build an important network with other individuals in her same life situation; an opportunity to show that she was ready to work on herself; and, ultimately, an obligation imposed by the officer at the local job center.

The invitation for participants to work on themselves was a leitmotif running through all of the training activities. In a further training activity, participants were asked to define specific goals in terms of personal development. Natasha reminded us that "hard work", "discipline" and "perseverance" were the precondition for professional success. Personal guidance and development methods from management and business could help us in this process, she noted. The goals that we defined for ourselves needed to be constantly monitored in order to progress in our development, Natasha added. SMART, she explained, is one of these models. It helps us make sure that our personal goals do not end up alongside our New Year's resolutions. Natasha projected a slide on the board with a table and explained that SMART was an acronym giving specific criteria to guide us in the setting of our goals: "S" stands for "Specific", she clarified and noted "what exactly do I want to achieve and why?" "M", Natasha added, "means measurable, how can I measure my progress and how can I know when I have achieved my goals?" Further, "A" stands for "achievable", are my goals realistic? "R", she continued, "is relevant, is this a worthwhile goal at the stage I am at?" And finally, "T" means, "time-bound", "when am I going to work on this goal? And how long will I give myself to achieve it?" She then noted that later developments of the model had added two steps to the guide transforming "SMART" into "SMARTER": the "E" standing for "evaluation", stressing the need for the achievement of objectives to be constantly checked and revaluated. Finally, "R" she continued, is "Review" and stands for "Reflection about the goals achieved and eventual adjustments of the goals that one has set".

Natasha explained to the participants that the SMART model had been developed by an American consultant, George Doran, who, already back in the early 1980s, had realized that failures in project management, employee performance management and personal development are caused by unrealistic expectations and insufficient monitoring of decisions, personnel and work processes. Natasha further noted that success, both organizational and personal, depends on peoples' capacity to be rational, to subdivide larger objectives and aims into smaller, more achievable ones and to constantly monitor progress. Therefore, Natasha argued, the best way to keep track of one's progress is to write it down, to clearly define the specificity of one's goals, to explain how one would measure its progress, to describe the criteria one would use to assess whether an objective would have been achieved, to explicitly label the relevance of this, and to state the timeframe within which a specific goal must be achieved. In other words, managing oneself is, according to Natasha, an essentially communicative process, it is linked to specific textual practices that allow individuals to reflect on themselves and to monitor or adjust their life projects and ambitions.

This identification of people's minds as a site of regulation echoes with contemporary changes in the theories of human resources management and the psychology of work. To be sure, as Gramsci (1977) and Foucault (1975) argue, the body of the worker as well as her/his morality has always been subjected to forms of strict control and rationalization in order to maximize its productivity. However, historians of work show that the current reconceptualization of "employees" as "human resources' and "organizational assets" have radically affected the ways managers think, plan and control workers and work processes (Cameron, 2000; Taylor, 2011). Indeed, considering the worker as a "resource" increasingly implies the recognition and consequent exploitation not just of the physical, but also of the creative, emotional, and interpersonal component. As a consequence, scholars note (see, e.g., Nankervis et al., 2011) that the regulatory emphasis is on the "intellectual capital" of the worker, on her and his "emotional intelligence" and "personal commitment" as well as on his or her intrinsic will to contribute to the success of the company they are working for (Tubey et al., 2015).

During our fieldwork at *Connections*, we were able to document how these theories of human management gradually penetrate the everyday work routines of charity workers such as Natasha. When talking to her about the preparation of her classes and the training activities, Natasha noted that she was trained in social work and had no expertise in managing unemployed young people. When appointed by *Connections*, she was meant to work with the young children of the neighborhoods' community center, but she had had to replace the colleague originally in charge of this employ-ability training who had left. As she explained, there is not much time for her to rationalize what exactly she is doing: it is not her job to develop sophisticated market theories and models for the activation of unemployed young people. Her job, she adds, is to apply these theories and models that, as she explains, she usually finds in textbooks and on the internet and that give her a useful perspective from which she can understand the situation of her training participants.

In spite of the apparent improvised nature of her training activities, a look at the literature on the making of neoliberal subjects allows us to say that the activities, knowledge and techniques that Natasha mobilizes during her program are similar to what is going on in other training and business contexts (see, e.g., Urciuoli's chapter in this volume). Scholars (see, e.g., Aubrey, 2000) have shown that models similar to SMART are used in business meetings, team building or personal development sessions involving managers and individuals in leading positions managing projects and per-sonnel. However, while these skills could be seen as realistic and useful in a context where people have to learn how to manage processes and people, in this specific case, the activities with which participants are asked to engage are completely decontextualized from the potential work practices and workplaces. At this stage of their professional career, the individuals Natasha is working with will more likely apply for manual, so-called non- or low-skilled jobs and occupy subordinated positions within their work settings. They will not manage processes, projects or personnel. So, we can argue, the disciplining techniques that they are asked to engage with are exclusively directed to their own selves and serve the inculcation of principles of quality and self-discipline that become an ethics encompassing not only participants professional lives, but their entire personae and domains of living.

Along with Natasha's instructions and her request that participants apply the SMART model to their own personae and life projects, participants diligently started to verbalize their goals and objectives. Even Ursula, who usually had a skeptical attitude towards the suggestions made by Natasha, seemed to appreciate the utility of this guide. She quickly identified a goal that, as she explained, was part of her larger attempt to find employment. She called it "learning to listen". She explained to us that her job advisors had often told her that she had to learn to listen to instructions. "Listening",

Ursula explained, was therefore relevant for getting, and especially keeping, a job. She thought that this objective was specific enough and achievable; she would give herself until the end of the training program to achieve this goal. She was, however, unsure about how to measure her progress in "listening" and decided that as a linguist, it would be Alfonso's job to come up with ideas about how to define whether or not she was making any progress. Alfonso could not come up with any meaningful way of measuring her progression in listening and following instructions, but promised her that he would ask one of his colleagues who measures listening skills.

Now, the list of qualities presented, as well as the business model of change, were all part of a larger set of training activities which submit participants to an auditing practice that, through language, that is, communicatively mediated practices of introspection and reflexivity as well as self-analysis, self-surveillance and self-management, enables them to keep control of their projects and ambitions as if they were a business. While more established models of societal governmentality assume that power and control are exercised by a bureaucratic system that governmentalizes bodies and minds as well as peoples' emotions and dreams, that is, that subjects individuals to a coercive regime of knowledge and discipline, these trainings give us access to an alternative, perhaps more subtle, but not less efficient practice of neoliberal governmentality that posits the unemployed self as agent of his or her own disciplining and regulation and capitalizes on an individual's wish to be free, both socially and economically. In spite of these differences, what these modes of societal control have in common is a practice of rationalization of, and reasoning about, the self and society. Indeed, both modes of governmentality are informed and mediated by a body of knowledge that both theorizes the self and, at the same time, serves its surveillance and disciplining. This knowledge then acts as a mediating principle for how instructors get to construct and understand unemployed young people, as well for how these young people understand and regulate themselves.

Along with what we have already argued in this section, in what follows we will demonstrate that the presented mode of societal control does not always, or not only, target people's minds and rationality, but also operates through techniques that affect people through their souls, aspirations and dreams, that is, forms of affect that create the condition for people's acceptance of the disciplining of their subjectivity. In particular, we produce an account of the circumstances under which *hope* becomes a key resource for making sure that, in spite of the difficulties they encounter on the job market, these individuals keep believing that a better life is possible.

Fostering hope

At the end of the program, after ten weeks of training activities in *Connections* locations, the American investment bank that sponsored this employability program had invited the training participants for a round of mock interviews at their headquarters in London's financial center. On the morning of the interviews, when we arrived at the underground station where Natasha had asked us to meet, a small group had already been waiting. They were nervously rehearsing the answers that they had prepared as if before an important exam. Indeed, in the training sessions preceding the mock interviews Natasha provided each participant with some questions that, according to her, could be asked by the interviewer. What are your strengths? What is your biggest achievement? List some of your skills and qualities. Where do you see yourself in five years' time? Tell me a time when you dealt with a difficult person, how did you handle the situation? What does "equality and diversity" mean to you? Describe yourself in one word.

The questions were a way for participants to learn to do what Natasha called "selling yourself", that is, to enact a type of persona considered to be particularly desirable by potential employers. Scholars (e.g. Gershon, 2017) have recently argued that that this marketing rhetoric used by job counselors, coaches and human resource managers is emblematic for a type of capitalism that interpellates individuals as brands, i.e. as sets of signs pointing to specific feelings and desires, that need to be managed and monitored in order to attain, maintain and, if possible, improve value on specific markets. According to this logic, Natasha asks her interlocutors to learn to think about and see themselves as valuable labor power that, in order to become tradable, needs to be packaged in specific ways (Del Percio, 2017; Lorente, 2017). In this specific case, the young participants are asked to see themselves through the lens of a set of questions that point to a type of worker that is considered to be particularly desirable. As we have seen in the previous section, this worker is a highly reflexive one, one that understand him or herself through principles of quality and self-development, one that is self-conscious and can rationalize his/her strengths and weaknesses, one that can manage emotions and challenges and one that has life projects and is able to project him or herself into a future. At the same time, for Natasha, this set of questions is, again, a powerful discursive resource enabling participants to anticipate the type of conversation they will be exposed to, to know the register they are expected to enact and to make sure that they meet the communicative demands of this specific speech event. So, if these questions do exert control over the type of person participants are expected to be and point to modern ideologies of personhood sustaining gender, class and racial differences (Heller & McElhinny, 2018), these questions are also seen as way to provide young people with the necessary communicative resources to do well during the interview and to emancipate themselves from their position of subalternity occupied in London's society (also see Roberts, 2013 for a similar line of reasoning).

All participants had been asked to select a real job offer for which they wanted to be interviewed. Some participants had chosen to apply for the type of position occupied by their parents: plumbers, bricklayers, mechanics, carpenters. Others "applied" for apprenticeships available in the neighborhood in which they were living in either security services or in retail. Others still just took the first advert they had found on one of the many online job boards. Natasha then sent the job offers and candidates' CVs to Jannette, a marketing officer who was responsible for the management of the program at the bank. Jannette in turn allocated every candidate to a volunteer from the bank who had agreed to conduct the interview.

Of course, this interview at the investment bank was just an exercise, a simulation of an actual job opportunity. At the same time, the lines between fantasy and reality were intentionally kept blurred. Participants were real job seekers, being interviewed for real positions, in real offices, by professionals in suits asking real questions. Candidates were also requested to dress formally as if it were a real job interview. Many of them had to borrow clothes from friends or parents. Others asked the social services to provide funds so that they could buy a shirt or a jacket, still others found some trousers in a local charity shop. Becoming a real job candidate was not just about learning to speak and behave in a way that their instructor considered to be professional; they also had to *look* like professionals. The fantasy was also kept alive because, just once, the simulation had turned into a reality; a candidate in a previous cohort had succeeded to convince the interviewer about her qualities and managed to secure a real position in administration. This could happen again, Natasha, kept repeating. If you work hard, you will succeed. This was another leitmotif running through the entire training program. Along with larger discourses on employability and professional integration produced by policy makers, employers and educators (see, e.g., Yeung & Flubacher, 2016), Natasha's discourse was underpinned by an idea that professional inclusion and socioeconomic independence is a choice, which depends on participants' willingness to work on themselves and adapt their behavior to the expectation of their employers.

Aamiina, one of the young women attending the training, had started to believe in this promise. She had chosen to apply for an apprenticeship as an accountant. Her parents came to London from Somalia and had always dreamt of a better life for their daughter; this is perhaps why she was the only one who really believed in social mobility. Aamiina had not dared to talk openly about her hopes, but told Vivian in confidence that given her good grades at school and since, as she said, a bank needs accountants, this could be her chance. Along with what she had learned during the training program, she had prepared the interview in detail: she carefully read the advert, analyzed the job offer, selected the relevant information, studied the companies' website as well as its mission and values, identified the qualities and skills expected of an accountant, adapted her CV to the expectations of the job offer and tried to anticipate the questions that the interviewer might ask.

We arrived at the headquarters of the investment bank around 9:30, one and half-hours after we had left the station in the outskirts of London. The building of the investment bank was one of the fancy new buildings hosting the city's international banking industry. After having received a visitor's badge, a security officer accompanied us to the second floor where we were asked to take seats in luxurious leather armchairs. While waiting for Jannette, we were able to observe the division of work within this particular work place. Security officers and porters were all black men. The cleaners were women and spoke Spanish. Receptionists and secretaries were white women in short skirts, most of them in their late twenties or early thirties. Some of them seemed a bit older and based on the exchanges we could overhear from our seats, we assumed that they probably occupied positions of authority within the secretarial team. For the rest, there were a lot of white men in suits, and some Asians with British accents. The bank and its organization of work seemed to us to perfectly mirror the hierarchies and differences structuring London's society. While observing these professionals from our leather seats we wondered what the training participants waiting for Jannette would think about the hierarchies and differences in this workspace.

"Can we touch this?" Fadouma, one of the participants, asked Alfonso as she pointed to an art catalogue placed on one of the side tables. The sculptures, pictures and art installations in the corridors made everyone feel more uncomfortable than we had expected. "Shh, don't speak so loudly", cautioned Mary. Amir had made a comment on another participant's blazer; it was too large. It was by observing this group of young people that Alfonso was prompted to think about Pierre Bourdieu's concept of the habitus (Bourdieu, 1977). This entire employability program was an attempt to promote these young people's socialization into a professional habitus that, once internalized, is imagined to give these people access to employment. The work they were asked to do on their selves, the clothes they had to buy, the scripting of their answers, all this was done in order to enable them to be recognized by potential employers as good, morally integral middle-class people. However, as Bourdieu (1991; also see Park, 2017) explains, their sense of insecurity and corresponding high level of self-surveillance and censorship, were an indication of the fact that the habitus is not just about the way one speaks, nor about peoples' tastes and behaviors, but also about the sense of ones' place in society. You could see from these young peoples' behavior that this was not a place where they felt they belonged.

Jannette greeted us and explained that the interviews would begin. The ritual was the same for all participants: one after the other, the candidates were received by an employee of the bank (all white, smiling and good-looking) and, after a formal introduction, participants were escorted into the offices where the interviews took place. Aamiina was called last. She had been waiting in her armchair and nervously read the job offer again and again; she had printed it out for the occasion. The first candidates had already come back from their interviews. "Yes, he was amazing, so self-confident, he is perfect for this position", concluded one interviewer before leaving. Another: "She was so well-prepared, really no negatives, I would have taken her." Yet another: "He really knows what he wants. So determined. Wow! Of course he would get the job."

Aamiina was interviewed by one of the senior managers of the bank. We were told that he had worked as a journalist before for an American broad-caster and that after some studies in financial law he had started a career in this investment bank. Aamiina wore an elegant, dark suit with a blouse. She had borrowed her clothes from her cousin who worked for a fashion retailer on Oxford Street in London. Twenty-three minutes later we saw her come out of the interview office with the senior manager. We tried to guess from her look whether or not he had made her an offer. "Welcome to the firm" he smiled, while referencing a famous film of the 1990s. The fantasy again. No real offer. Aamiina was quiet. "Yes, it went well", her look revealed that she had expected more.

For a moment we had all believed that the fantasy could become true. What we had forgotten, or just suppressed in a moment of over enthu-siasm, is that being able to capitalize on a professional habitus acquired, for example, through a training program such as the one we had documented, is not dependent on how good someone is at enacting that specific habitus, but rather on the interlocutors' ability and willingness to exchange a successful performance with some form of reward, material or symbolic (Bourdieu, 1977). What was very clear was that for the bank officers the interviews were an exercise, there was no job waiting for any of these young people, despite the high expectation within the group of participants. For the bank this event was a means to demonstrate to stakeholders and partners that it is committed to social change in London and that it collaborates with local charities on projects and activities that are meant to empower the local impoverished population. Therefore, Aamiina's performance could not be rewarded in any form, even though we were sure that she had done a great job at communicating her professional qualities.

Now, what became clear for us when discussing our observations at the bank with Natasha and other managers at *Connections* was that, even if the dream of getting employed by a bank in central London remained a fantasy for all participants, this event at the bank was important in order to to continue fostering feelings of hope within the group of participants. As we mentioned previously (also see for this Dardot & Laval, 2013 as well as Martín-Rojo, in this volume), hope and desire (for success and self-improvement) are at the core of every project of self-discipline, and create the condition for the perpetuation of the belief in the principles of quality, self-management and constant self-development that individuals are asked to orient to as key in achieving self-fulfillment, freedom and happiness.

Indeed, the objective of these mock interviews, Natasha clarified, had never been to offer anybody a job, even if some of them had believed that this could happen. Her insistence on the opportunity that this event could represent for the participants was for her a way to motivate them, to make them clear that even for someone living in East London, working in one of the glamorous banks in the city center could become a possibility. Loosing hope for a better future, Natasha explained, would mean *Connections* losing these individuals and risking that their lack of guidance would lead them to search for help on the streets and in the informal job market. What needs to be added to this is that losing these participants would also mean losing funding from the investment bank who had linked their financial support (and thus the jobs at the charity that were made possible through this funding) to a predetermined number of participants attending the trainings. In other words, while this mock interview was a means for training participants to expose themselves to a realistic interview situation and to receive useful feedback on their CVs, these interviews were also anchored in a larger attempt to control their minds and lives through the management of their affect (McElhinny, 2010), that is, through an institutional practice exerting power through the disciplining of individuals' feelings and by making sure that individuals keep believing in the emancipating potential of employability programs and in the neoliberal project of equality and inclusion that these programs stand for.

Complex governmentalities

The intention of this chapter was to produce an ethnographic account of the ways in which poverty and unemployment are managed in London, UK. We have taken the concept of neoliberal governmentality as a starting point to make sense of the multiple activities and processes through which different types of actors exert control over a group of young people who are categorized as socially and emotionally vulnerable and as representing a risk factor for themselves, as well as for society at large. We have, in particular, analyzed the ways in which these young individuals are encouraged to engage in a set of disciplining practices that ask them to bring their minds and souls into alignment with principles of quality and self-development and that require them to buy into the promise that social and economic mobility is solely dependent on their willingness to engage in a constant process of self-improvement and self-control.

We have argued that the techniques mobilized by coaches in employability trainings are powerful because they are anchored in a whole set of authoritative assumptions about the self, society and the (labor) market that naturalize the type of disciplining work that individuals are asked to do on their selves and that, at the same time, erase the structures of power and inequality that these processes of self-disciplining and self-regulation contribute to sustaining. We have also suggested that these trainings are persuasive because not only do they interpellate individuals as rational subjects, but they also invest in hope and in individuals' capacity to be affected and dream about a better future. Indeed, we have explained that individuals' hope, aspirations and desires for socioeconomic independence and professional inclusion is strategically used to create consent for the disciplining of peoples' subjectivities and the request of a life-long self-development and self-improvement process with which these young people are confronted. Finally, we have noted that this mode of doing governmentality is powerful since it bears the traces of older, but not less persuasive, discourses of progress, inclusion, equality, emancipation and change that for many decades have framed the material support provided by local charities such as *Connections* to the local population and that are now being used to convince young people that social and economic inclusion can be fostered through reflexivity, self-management and resilience.

There are clear continuities between the disciplining practices documented in this employability program and the trainings and classes for transnational workers that have developed on the base of the sociolinguistic work done in the United Kingdom in the 1980s and 1990s by scholars such as, for example, John Gumperz (1982; Gumperz, Jupp & Roberts, 1979; Gumperz & Roberts, 1991), Celia Roberts (1975; 2011, 2013; Roberts & Campbell, 2007) and Srikant Saranghi (Saranghi & Roberts, 1999). These scholars showed that, in order to facilitate migrants' access to resources such as social benefits and jobs, individuals needed to be socialized into specific registers that enable them to meet the institutionalized communicative scripts of gatekeeping organizations. Along with what happened in the counseling and interview situations documented in the groundbreaking work of these researchers, the young people we were able to follow were asked to present and understand themselves through institutionally scripted modes of speech. They were asked to conform to the cultural, professional and institutional expectations of their interlocutors and use a highly marked language that allows them to be recognized as professional personae.

What was different, however, was the training program's obsession with people's conduct and with their relationship with their own selves. What our ethnography showed is that being a good job candidate is no longer (or not only) about being able to speak like a professional. What these individuals are required to do is to comply with a neoliberal ethic that turns their selves into an enterprise that needs to be constantly managed and governed according to principles of quality and competitiveness. Language then represents only *one* aspect of a multifaceted and complex total persona that needs be monitored and subjected to a practice of constant development and improvement for the benefit of both the individual and for society at large.

Now, while scholars in language and neoliberalism have stressed the inevitability and all-encompassing nature of neoliberalism, in this paper we have tried to demonstrate that, as every other activity, neoliberal governmentality is never totalizing, but is rather invested, resisted, challenged (with more or less success) by different people with different positions and with different interests. In this respect, we have pointed to the fact that the British State invests in a neoliberal rationality to manage poverty and unemployment, but this is a historically contingent process that is subject to change and transformation. We have presented the story of Natasha who, on the one hand, draws on neoliberal models and theories as guiding principles for her work, but who, at the same time, is not fully convinced of the effectiveness of these models and thus does not fully commit to these principles as binding life ethics. Finally, we have pointed to young people's (unequal) capacity to enact specific neoliberal subjectivities in order to navigate benefit systems and to the moralized demands of employers, social services officers and coaches. We have shown how, at the same time, some of these young individuals are able to question this neoliberal rationality since it does not hold its promise of empowerment, freedom and emancipation. Indeed, one year after the end of the program, none of the participants were able to capitalize on the skills acquired during this training and secure formal employment.

The next step for us now is to get a better sense of how individuals such as Ursula, one of the young women presented in this study, are able to navigate these complex systems of control and inclusion/exclusion (see Vigouroux, 2013 for similar questions in the South African context), to challenge the histories of subalternization that position them at the margins of London's society, and to start imagining alternative futures for themselves and their families. This will require an alternative type of ethnographic inquiry, one that shifts its attention to the ways individuals invest in process of self-organization, solidarity and resistance (Greber, 2004; Narotzky & Besnier, 2014) as well as an analysis of the discourses, relations of power and terrain of subjectivities in which subordinated actors are enmeshed, make sense of their lives and enact processes of resistance and subversion (Urla & Helepololei, 2014).

References

Allan, K. (2013). Skilling the self: The communicability of immigrants as flexible labor. In A. Duchêne, M. Moyer and C. Roberts (eds.), *Language, migration and social inequalities* (pp. 56–80). Bristol: Multilingual Matters.

Aubrey, B. (2000). *L'Entreprise de soi*. Paris: Flammarion.

Bell, L. (2017). Soft skills, hard rocks: Making diamonds ethical in Canada's Northwest territories. FOCAAL 2017(79): 74–88.

Bourdieu, P. (1991). *Language and symbolic power*. Cambridge: Polity Press.

Bourdieu, P. (1977). The economics of linguistic exchanges. *Social Science Information* 16(6): 645–668.

Boutet, J. (2001). Le travail devient-il intellectuel? *Travailler* 6: 55–70.

Bristow, G. (2014). *A brief history of the job centre*. London: Mute.

Cameron, D. (2000). *Good to talk*. London: Sage.

Dardot, P., & Laval, C. (2013). *The new way of the world*. New York: Verso.

Del Percio, A. 2017. Engineering commodifiable workers: Language, migration and the governmentality of the self. *Language Policy* 17(2): 239–259.

Del Percio, A., & Van Hoof, S. (2017). Enterprizing migrants: Language, education and the politics of activation. In M. Flubacher and A. Del Percio (eds.), *Language, education, and neoliberalism* (pp. 140–162). Bristol: Multilingual Matters.

Dlaske, K., Barakos, E., Motobayashi, K., & McLaughlin, M. (eds.) (2016) Languaging the worker. *Multilingua* 35(4): 345–359.

Duchêne, A., & P. Humbert. (2017). Surveying speakers and the politics of census. *International Journal of the Sociology of Language* 252(4): 1–20.

Flubacher, M., Coray, R., & Duchêne, A. (2017). *Language investment and employability.* London: Palgrave Pivot.

Foucault, M. (1975). *Surveiller et punir.* Paris: Gallimar.

Foucault, M. (1988a). Technologies of the self. In L. Martin, H. Gutman, and P. Hutton, (Eds), *Technologies of the self: A seminar with Michel Foucault* (pp. 16–49). Amherst: University of Massachusetts Press.

Foucault, M. (1988b). *Madness and civilisation.* London: Vintage.

Foucault, M. (1991). Governmentality. In G. Burchel, C. Gordon, and P. Miller (eds.), *The Foucault effect* (pp. 87–104). Chicago: University of Chicago Press.

Foucault, M. (2003). *Abnormal.* London: Verso.

Fraser, N. (2003). From discipline to flexibilization? Rereading Foucault in the shadow of globalization. *Constellations* 10(2): 160–171.

Gee, J., Hull, G., & Lankshear, C. (1996). *The new work order.* Boulder, CO: Westview.

Gershon, I. (2017). *Down and out in the new economy.* Chicago: University of Chicago Press.

Gramsci, A. (1977). *Selections from political writings.* New York: International Publishers.

Greber, D. (2004). *Fragments of an anarchist anthropology.* New York: Verso.

Gumperz, J. (1982). *Discourse strategies.* Cambridge: Cambridge University Press.

Gumperz, J., Jupp, T., & Roberts, C. (1979). *Crosstalk: A study of cross-cultural communication.* Southall: National Centre for Industrial Language Training in association with the B.B.C. Continuing Education Department.

Gumperz, J., & Roberts, C. (1991). *Understanding in intercultural encounters.* Benjamins.

Harris, B. (2004). *The origins of the British welfare state.* London: Palgrave.

Heller, M., & McElhinny, B. (2018). *Language, capitalism and colonialism.* Toronto: Toronto University Press.

Kidd, L. (1999). State, society and the *poor.* London: Palgrave.

Lorente, B. (2017). *Scripts of servitude.* Bristol: Multilingual Matters.

Martin-Rojo, L. (2018). Neoliberalism and linguistic governmentality. In J. W. Tollefson and M. Pérez-Milans (Eds.), *Oxford handbook of language policy and planning.* Oxford: Oxford University Press.

McElhinny, B. (2010). The audacity of affect: Gender, race and history in linguistic accounts of legitimacy and belonging. *Annual Review of Anthropology* 39: 309–328.

Nankervis, A., et al. (2011) *Human resource management: Strategy and practice,* 7th ed. Melbourne, Australia: Cengage Learning.

Narotzky, S., & Besnier, N. (2014). Crises, value and hope. *Current Anthropology* 55(9): S4–S16.

Park, J. (2017). English as medium of instruction in Korean higher education: Language and subjectivity as critical perspective on neoliberalism. In M. Flubacher & A. Del Percio (Eds.), *Language, education and neoliberalism* (pp. 82–100). Bristol: Multilingual Matters.

Powell, A. (2018). *NEET: Young people Not in Education, Employment or Training.* Briefing Paper Number SN 06705. London: House of Commons Library.

Roberts, C. (1975). Industrial English language training for overseas workers. *Journal of Ethnic and Migration Studies* 4(3): 337–341.

Roberts, C. (2011). Taking ownership: Language and ethnicity in the job interview. In K. Pelsmaekers, C. Rollo, T. Van Hout, & P. Heynderickx (Eds.), *Displaying competence in organizations* (pp. 3–15). London: Palgrave.

Roberts, C. (2013). The gatekeeping of Babel. In A. Duchêne, M. Moyer, & C. Roberts (Eds.), *Language, migration and social inequalities: A critical sociolinguistic perspective on institutions and work* (pp. 56–78). Bristol: Multilingual Matters.

Rose, N. (1999). *Governing the soul: The shaping of the private self*. London: Free Associations Books.

Rose, N., & Miller, P. (1990). Governing economic life. *Economy and Society* 19(1): 1–31.

Saranghi, S., & Roberts, C. (1999). *Talk, work and institutional order*: New York: De Gruyter.

Siraj, I., et al. (2014). *Report on students who are Not in Education, Employment or Training (NEET)*. London: Institute of Education and Department for Education.

Smith, D. (1999). *Texts, facts, and femininity. Exploring the relations of ruling*. London: Routledge.

Spicker, P. (2018). *Social policy*. Bristol: Policy Press.

Taylor, S. (2011) *Contemporary issues in human resource management*. London: CIPD.

Tubey, R., et al. (2015). History, evolution and development of human resource management: A contemporary perspective. *European Journal of History and Management* 7: 139–148.

Urciuoli, B. (2008) Skills and selves in the new work place. *American Ethnologist* 35(2): 211–228.

Urla, J. (2012). Total quality language revival. In A. Duchêne & M. Heller (Eds.), Language in late capitalism. London: Routledge.

Urla, J., & Helepololei, J. 2014. The ethnography of resistance then and now: On thickness and activist engagement in the twenty-first century. *History and Anthropology* 25: 431–451.

Vigouroux, C. (2013). Informal economy and language: Practice in the context of migrations. In M. Moyer, C. Roberts, & A. Duchêne (Eds.), *Language, migration and social inequalities* (pp. 225–247). London: Multilingual Matter.

Vigouroux, C. (2017). Rethinking (un)skilled migrants: Whose skills, what skills, for what and for whom? In S. Canagarajah (Ed.), *The Routledge handbook on language and migration* (pp. 312–329). New York: Routledge.

Yeung, S., & Flubacher, M. (2016). Discourses of integration: Language, skills, and the politics of difference. *Multilingua* 35(6): 599–616.

Towards an ethnography of linguistic governmentalities

Jacqueline Urla

Part of what it means to live in contemporary capitalism is to feel that the whole world has seemingly become overtaken by market logics. Choice, competition, continuous improvement, best practices, audit, strategic planning, value-added, innovation; these and other signature values and managerial technologies of entrepreneurial capitalism, once more restricted to the corporate boardroom or workplace, are now pervasive in many more sectors of our lives, in how we talk and rationalize our decisions, as well as in the operations of the institutions with which we engage. It is precisely this relentless spread, or some might say the colonization, of market-like discourse and logics that many authors have in mind when they talk about "neoliberalization". Neoliberalism, they argue entails much more than a free market economic model based on deregulation, austerity, and the roll-back of state's welfare mandate; it has brought with it something on the order of a whole-scale cultural shift for organizing not only economic but social life more broadly.

While this observation is no longer new, much remains to be done to achieve a deeper critical understanding of how this process unfolds and its consequences. Martín Rojo and Del Percio's collection of essays pushes this project forward while adding an additional analytical element to the analysis of neoliberalization: governmentality. Their introduction argues, and the chapters demonstrate, that under neoliberalism the processes and cultural values of commodification and competition expand to become a template for organizing many other dimensions of social life – including language learning. In Bonnie Urciuoli's words, neoliberalization is in evidence when "Forms of knowledge and social practices … are imagined as a valued part of oneself as human capital because they maximize one's own market potential or give one's organization a market edge" (see Urciuoli, this volume). In this volume, however, the editors want us to see neoliberalization as more than a kind of unbridled commodification, more than the triumphant reign of an ideology of the free market. It often also brings with it technologies for governing conduct and particular ways of understanding the self.

A pause. Governmentality, the term Foucault gave to a political rationality oriented towards managing the health, productivity, and security of the population, precedes neoliberalism. This rationality and the various forms of expertise and technologies of knowledge it mobilizes, most notably social statistics, are traced by Foucault as taking shape under liberalism of the modern nation-state and industrial capitalism. It is archetypically represented in programs for social insurance, urban hygiene, public health, and social welfare programs. Understood as a modality of power and subjectification, this mode of governance depends on a certain amount of freedom, acting not through force, but on subjects' "hopes, desires, circumstances or environment" (Inda 2005: 1). As Foucault recognized, and later scholars such as Nikolas Rose (1999) and Nancy Fraser (2003), among others, went on to further explain, the tactics, tools and discourse of governmentality shift under neoliberalism with the move towards post-Fordist capitalist production, managerialism, entrepreneurialism, and "flexibilized" market logics. The focus on the welfare of the population as a totality begins to recede as workers, citizens, students, the unemployed are invited (or pressured) to demonstrate an entrepreneurial agency, that is, not only to see their lives and choices as projects of value maximization, but to see themselves as responsible for that value maximization. Neoliberalism normalizes a regime of governance through which responsibility for one's conduct and one's life circumstances are placed upon the individual and their will to improve. This constellation of economic logics and technologies of the self are referred to as "neoliberal governmentality". And, as more than one of the case studies in this volume makes clear, it is an entrepreneurial worldview in which structural inequalities and white supremacy are placed under erasure.

How the value and nature of language or communication is conceptualized and how language skills figure in neoliberal, globalized, and/or late capitalist economies has been the subject of growing interest (e.g. Block, Gray, and Holborow 2012; Duchêne and Heller 2012; Flubacher and del Percio 2017). If the relationship of language and neoliberalism (or late capitalism) are receiving growing attention, until recently, governmentality has not gained quite the same amount of traction in sociolinguistics. Nor have scholars of neoliberal governmentality more broadly engaged very significantly if at all with language either as an object of governance or as a medium for the practices of governance. By framing this as a collection on "neoliberalism, language and governmentality", the editors signal their intention to be attentive simultaneously to how language and linguistic conduct are commodified and exploited, as well as to how a particular kind of agency and subjectivity are implicated in the self-governance and self-capitalization characteristic of late capitalism.

The agenda is to bring under one roof close studies of how neoliberal logics, values, and subjectivity with regard to language and language learning are taken up (or not), and expressed (or not) in a range of domains: from the training programs of unemployment counseling centers in the United Kingdom, to language policies for construction worksites in Norway; from bilingual education laws and debates in the United States, to the way language skills are promoted in international baccalaureate and bilingual schools in the Spanish state. Educational contexts and formal language learning figure prominently in this collection as sites for studying the presence of neoliberal stances toward language learning. Building in some ways on Deborah Cameron's much earlier work, *Good to Talk* (Cameron 2000), Bonnie Urciuoli's study of the marketing of "leadership communication skills" is a window onto the ideological salience that "communication" has in figurations of the successful student that U.S. universities and colleges market to stakeholders. In keeping with the interest in subjectification, there is much attention across the papers not only to language ideologies, but also to the personal narrated experiences that social actors – many of them students- have about where language fits into their life trajectories. How and to what extent do we see an entrepreneurial subjectivity expressed in the ways speakers have of understanding their own "speakerhood", their ways of narrativizing their trajectories and choices in language learning, as well as in their linguistic practices? How does class or social status figure into the likelihood of actors to embrace this kind of agency and way of looking at their lives?

My comments here will focus on two issues relevant to this project. One is the issue of "uptake". What do these chapters teach us about how neoliberal economic rationality, both values and techniques, are adopted with regard to linguistic practices and conceptualizations of language and language learning? How is that uptake manifest? And of course, what do the authors think about its significance for how social actors think about the place of language in their lives? The second issue is more methodological. I want also to reflect on what these chapters have to teach us about the value of ethnographic approaches to the study of neoliberalism and linguistic governmentality.

Neoliberalism's uptake

This issue can be broken down into two parts: the question of how neoliberal market logics, values, and personhood spread and become translated into new sectors and then the issue of their uptake or adoption. And in both dimensions, I want to underscore the important reminder made by del Percio and Wong that governmentality is not just an ideology, but a set of practices, often seen as mundane or technical. Thus, we want to be attentive both to the appearance of specific terminology and logics or reasoning, but also various kinds of *practices* which accompany and materialize the values and worldview of that are being adopted. This is a topic to which I will return.

Cris Shore and Susan Wright's essay "Coercive Accountability" (2000), was an early and helpful reflection on this process as it was reconfiguring higher education in the United Kingdom in the 1990s. Shore and Wright note that an early sign of neoliberalization is the adoption of what they call keywords and "semantic clusters" into new sectors. They draw an analogy with what anthropologist Marilyn Strathern (1992) called the "domaining" effect "whereby the conceptual logic of an idea associated with one domain is transposed into another, often with unanticipated outcomes" (Shore and Wright 2000: 60). Tracking such terminology is *diagnostic* of the spread of neoliberal logics and values. Martín Rojo and del Percio concur, noting how particular words and slogans from the new managerialism such as "quality", "leadership", "value added", "human capital", "skill set", as well as phrases (e.g. "the need to compete") are becoming adopted and normalized in an ever wider set of contexts. Seemingly innocuous terminological shifts, like the substitution of the term "job seekers" for "the unemployed" that del Percio and Wong note in their study of job centers, can flag epistemological shifts in how workers are expected to understand themselves and how self-responsibilization is conveyed.

Language is thus an important vehicle by which neoliberal values are spread, conveyed, and normalized. Using the tools of interactional and discourse analysis, scholars in these chapters are attentive to the discursive features and what we might call the lexicon of neoliberalism as a means by which neoliberal values are communicated in the websites and promotional literature, for example, of schools and social service agencies. In keeping with the interest in subjectivity, papers attend both to idealized constructions of subjectivity, such as those that schools or social services promote, but also to how the students and the users of social services narrate their experiences. Martín Rojo, for example, set about gathering a vast amount of interview data on how an economic view of language and language learning has become so seemingly normalized for many university students in Madrid. This provides her with basis for identifying the emergence of a distinctly neoliberal form of speakerhood that she aptly calls "the self-made speaker".

It is on the terrain of language – the terminology used, but also the shape in which arguments are made and life choices are explained – that we can observe the spread and deployment of neoliberal values and ideals at different scales. While Martín Rojo and Pujolar show this in examining individual narratives, Flores shows deploys a critical discourse analysis of proposed legislation of bilingual education in the United States. The assembled texts make clear that sociolinguists have tools to offer the documentation and uptake of economistic and neoliberal thinking, for unpacking semiosis and communicative practices that can give a textured understanding of how governance is exercised. This is a point that Ben Rampton (2016) made clear in his review of the gatekeeping and conversational analysis work of John Gumperz. Kamila Kraft's close analysis of safety manuals and trainings, along with interactions between supervisors and workers shows the discursive mechanism by which the responsibility for accidents are placed onto workers' presumed inadequate linguistic capabilities.

Sociolinguistic tools can take us beyond the analysis of the semantic or ideological load of key words and phrases, that has been common in studies of governmentality, to explore in closer detail not only policy discourse and promotional materials but also taken-for-granted communication routines like the intake interview, or coaching sessions, through which particular self-understandings are inculcated and required. This is shown in greatest detail and brilliantly in the chapter by del Percio and Wong. The specificity with which they theorize the various ways linguistic practices are both medium and object of governance merits extended citation.

> (…) language plays a key role for the everyday *doing* of the type of neo-liberal governmentality documented in this paper. We will demonstrate that *language* is the medium through which a neoliberal rationality is circulated by different sorts of individuals and actors, gets to penetrate and colonialize every sphere of social life and interpellates individuals as neoliberal subjects. Second, we will explain that it is through language, i.e. practices of reflexivity and introspection mediated through writing, speaking and thinking about oneself, that individuals come to under-stand themselves as specific self-projects that need to be constantly monitored, analyzed and managed. Third, we show that language, i.e. oral or textualized communicative and behavioral instructions vehiculating idealized, and morally marked figures of personhood, serves as a guiding principle for individuals to exert control over their own and other's bodies and minds and to guide them in their attempts to meet the demands of employers as well as of those individuals and actors managing benefits and distributing resources. And finally, we claim that it is through language, i.e. through one's communicative ability to enact a specific subjectivity, that one gets to be recognized as a desirable worker. In sum, we will show that *language is both object and medium of governmentality* and is therefore at the core of a biopolitical practice that creates compliance for professional precarity, poverty and unemployment through the management of young people's bodies, including their emotions and minds. (italicization added)

As we consider the imbrication of language in this mode of power, there is also a warning here for us not to limit our focus to the referential dimension of language when considering its governing effects. Bonnie Urciuoli's essay in this volume on "communication skills", in leadership training, like her earlier work on (Urciuoli 2008) skills discourse, suggests that the meaning of some keywords like "quality", "leadership", or "innovation" are often highly ambiguous, functioning like empty signifiers the function of which is to perform an alignment between the speaker (or in this case, the college) and corporate enterprise culture. Leadership communication skills are heavily promoted, but there appears to be little evidence that students either internalize neoliberal values nor learn any identifiably distinct communica-tion techniques. Combining ethnographic observation, semiotic, and astute materialist analysis of the shifting orientation of higher education under neoliberalism she is able to show how the growth of the highly profitable skills workshop industry – all the rage in universities and colleges – ties into and feeds off higher education's increasing orientation to capturing a larger share of the student market.

Urciuoli's argument points to the fact that any analysis of the spread of neoliberal terminology, values, personhood, and practices needs to be situated in the broader political economic context that enables these forms and values to find traction. The chapters looking at education in Spain (Hidalgo McCabe and Fernandez-Gonzalez working on Spanish-English bilingual schooling, and Sunyol and Codó looking at International Baccalaureate Diploma schools) as well as Martín Rojo's work with University students in Madrid do this very well. Martín Rojo, prefaces her inquiry into the linkages students make between language learning and capital accumulation with a discussion of what has been happening to higher education in Spain: the public funding cuts, the rise to power of the conservative government and its affinity for neoliberal reforms, and the more specific context of Spain's long period of political isolation under the Franco regime. All of this fuels some of the observed passion for internationalization and language training as well as the necessity for schools to be more competitive for students. This kind of political economic analysis is a critical part of preparing the fertile grounds on which concept of the self-made speaker grows. Similarly, del Percio and Wong's analysis of the discursive shifts in job center practice begins with a longer view of the decline of state provisions for the unemployed and the poor in the United Kingdom and the increasing delegation of services to private charities. Kraft also provides a solid understanding of the history of policies that enabled the shift towards "flexible" or "leasing" labor contracts. While we want to resist falling into a simple kind of economic determinism, this context has to be a part of the equation. I would critique some work on governmentality, including my own, for not elaborating more explicitly on the political economic context, pressures, and outcomes that governance strategies have for structural inequality. I think in some of these chapters we find good models of how to integrate these analytical goals.

Along with this political economic grounding, I want to underscore, as noted earlier, the importance of approaching governmentality (liberal or neoliberal) not just as a mode of reasoning, not just as an ideological project, or a mentality. Though it is that, governmentality is also, as del Percio and Wong note, a set of practices, activities and configuration of spaces. One must examine not just discourse, not just what people are saying but also what they are *doing, or required to do*: the documentation, auditing, ranking, inspections, evaluations, and self-presentations they must produce. Showing that these seemingly mundane, often technical instruments are in and of themselves structuring conduct, implementing norms, and agents in the creation of new kinds of self-managing subjectivity is one of the more valuable theoretical contributions of governmentality studies. Technologies of knowledge, routines, protocols, and practical instruments of discipline and regulation are agentive elements of the apparatus of governance. While it is our habit in academia to focus on grand theories and theorists, for Foucault, Rose, and other scholars of governmentality it has always been important to attend to the middling forms of experts and expertise (e.g. in human relations, organizational management, risk management), and grey literature reports and policy papers that inform the practical apparatus of governance. As scholars, it is important for us to inquire into the genealogies of these practices and the expertise that validate them. Where do they come from? Where do they draw their "theories" about work, human nature, productivity? And how do they circulate and become marketed in various kinds of (sometimes lucrative) training regimes? How are they mobilized in policies (Shore and Wright 1997; Shore, Wright, and Però 2011)? Del Percio and Wong provide a good model of this approach in the analysis of the "SMART" program routines of goal setting and reflection through which trainers sought to discipline the job seekers into becoming a resilient and continuously improving self. As they make their way from their points of origin in management studies, these practices become decontextualized into generic skills for a successful life and delivered to people not likely to ever find themselves in managerial roles.

As neoliberal rationality, values, expertise, and practices are appropriated into new contexts, we cannot assume that their uptake is automatic. Some of the chapters in this volume explore precisely this point: not everyone "buys in" and sometimes it appears that buying in may not even be the point. As noted, Urciuoli found that students who participated in the leadership workshops seemed neither to have internalized any particular skills nor their attendant neoliberal subjectivity. However, Urciuoli does not see this as failure. Rather, the fact that the workshops continue prompts her to see that the critical function leadership programs play is actually more outward facing: a performance for stakeholders and parents of the student "product" they are marketing.

The data one has is determining of the ability with which we can answer questions about uptake, agency and internalization. Del Percio and Wong's rich ethnography allow them to explore this question with sophistication. At the job centers where they observed over a long period of time they came to see that the "neoliberal rationale is rather mobilized, rationalized and dialectically engaged with on the ground by (some of) the unemployed subjects who problematize and challenge the program and contest its inability to promote their access to jobs and socioeconomic inclusion". Their chapter brings attention to the agency and skill of the presumptive "governed" some of whom have learned to negotiate the system, knowing when and how to strategically display the requisite dispositions and habitus the state requires from them in order to be considered deserving of state support.

Joan Pujolar's subtle analysis of the life histories he collected from adult Catalan learners opens up an additional insight on the relationship that class may have vis a vis adoption of what Ilana Gershon has called "neoliberal agency" (Gershon 2011). At the core of neoliberal modes of governmentality is a notion of the individual who manages herself and life choices in terms of maximizing their value and resources. Was this kind of self-understanding visible in the life narratives he collected? Did the subjects in his study strategize about language learning as an investment, asset accumulation and self-improvement? He identifies a more active vision of one's life trajectory versus a more passive one. And he argues that these stances seem to be connected with one's social standing. Classed experiences lead some actors to be much more likely to see their life as a "project" that they can shape through their strategic decisions. People who are structurally marginalized are more likely to view life as something that happens "to" them. The ability to imagine having an "agenda" or a life project is, thus, a subjectivity shaped by material conditions. One finds echoes of the still very relevant insights sociologist Paul Willis (1977) made with regard to working class boys toward schooling and the ideology of a meritocracy that promises upward mobility through hard effort. It could be that embracing a kind of linguistic entrepreneurialism is premised on mobilizing a certain faith or hope that rewards for efforts will come. Yet the neoliberal subject is fraught with uncertainty and indeed as Sunyol and Codó argue, incentives to self-capitalize thrive precisely on risk and uncertainty. What Pujolar's data seems to suggest, and del Percio and Wong as well, is that this affective structure of both hope and fear is less motivating for people who inhabit the margins of the socio-economic order and experience first-hand the consequences of race, class and gender inequalities.

By way of conclusion, I want to identify some of the ways these chapters are contributing to understandings of neoliberal forms of governance.

1. They explore the contours of a distinctly neoliberal understanding of speakerhood, language learning and language education. Martín Rojo's conceptualization of "the self-made speaker" has given name to a subjectivity that will be fruitful for us to consider in many contexts. At the same time, the chapters advance a deeper understanding of the role of communicative routines and interactions in the practices of governance, taking us well beyond the ideological analysis of the neoliberal lexicon.
2. They bring attention to the place of affect as elements in technologies of the neoliberal self. They point to the reliance and cultivation of hope and desire for success, the fear or uncertainty of the future, as intrinsic to the projects of self-management and continuous improvement. How exactly these sentiments are generated, expressed and for whom they are more or less motivating are all aspects to continue to explore.
3. They invite more exploration of the uneven uptake of neoliberal speakerhood and agency. How does class, race, or gender (not taken up in these papers, but potentially relevant) figure in the degree or form in that neoliberal values are taken up? The chapters show that neoliberal governance is not uniformly adopted and some seek to engage issues

of class and race as it relates to the experience and exercise of govern-ance. What kind of material pressures demand the performance of the terms of the responsible and motivated self? For whom is desire, hope and consent the primary modalities of their engagement in regimes of self-governance and self-improvement, and for whom is this engage-ment driven by coercive mechanisms? Resistance to the entrepreneurial self is possible, but the stakes can be quite different. What questions or forms of knowledge that disenfranchised people have are foreclosed in neoliberal understandings of success and self-management? These are important questions to bring to bear as we seek to integrate the analysis of structure inequality with governmentality.

Along these lines, Flores's astute analysis of the shift in the framing of dual language programs and multilingualism as an "engine of social mobility", pays particular attention to the erasures of racialized capitalism's structural inequality endemic in neoliberal discourses that assume everyone is on a level playing field. His essay, adds an important component in identifying the centrality of racialization in the discursive operations of both liberal and neoliberal governmentality. It will hope-fully help to bring raciolinguistic ideology more in conversation with the analysis of linguistic governmentality than it has tended to be.

4.   As an anthropologist I think we can also see the value that qualitative research and especially ethnographic approaches, based on more immer-sive observation, can bring to the study of linguistic governmentality. Interviewing and life histories can give us insights in the "uptake" of neoliberal values and subjectivity. Discourse analysis of these narratives, written and oral, can show how these conceptions are mobilized. Sustained ethnographic observation of training activities, communica-tive routines and other interactional means by which conduct is directed help us to achieve a fuller understanding of the apparatus of governance and how it works. It also has the potential to provide a more textured understanding of the ambivalences, compromises and strategies of actors caught up in governance in various roles, whether as recipients or as service providers.

One of the attractions of the analytics of governmentality, write Rose, O'Malley and Valverde "has been its capacity to render neoliberalism vis-ible in new ways" (2006: 99). But they say, there has been a tendency to overgeneralize how governance works, to collapse many diverse activities and regulations under the singular label of governmentality, and to ignore the more contingent and variable nature of their assemblage of programs, strategies and technologies. They argue, and I would agree, that we might do better to talk in terms of social rationalities of government so as to avoid implying there is a singular and homogenous entity "governmentality". A second criticism levied against work on governmentality has been the tendency to focus on its *logics* more than on its implementation, ignoring "the role of agency, experience, and resistance, thereby producing an image of government as a juggernaut that is somehow willing itself into existence, implementing itself into reality by mysterious means (Frankel 1997; O'Malley et al 1997)" (2006: 99). It is my sense that the focus on identifying the logics and *saviors* of governance may have led to this impression and that ethnography, with its thick description of context, practices and local meanings is a critical method in correcting this. Whether the critics are correct or not, Rose et al. clarify that the orientation of governmentality work is not or should not be "ideal typification, but an empirical mapping of governmental rationalities and techniques ... there is no assumption that the mere existence of a diagram of government implies either its generalized acceptance or implementation" (ibid.). The chapters in this volume take us in this promising direction, providing us with a variety of contextually and empirically rich studies that expand our understanding of how neoliberalism and governance meet on the terrain of language.

References

Block, D., Gray, J., & Holborow, M. (2012). *Neoliberalism and Applied Linguistics*. London: Routledge.

Cameron, D. (2000). *Good to Talk: Living and Working in a Communication Culture*. London: Sage.

Duchêne, A., & Heller, M. (eds.) (2012). *Language in Late Capitalism: Pride and Profit*. London: Routledge.

Flubacher, M. Ch., & Del Percio, A. (eds.) (2017). *Language, Education, and Neoliberalism*. Bristol: Multilingual Matters.

Frankel, B. (1997). Confronting neoliberal regimes: The post-Marxist embrace of populism and realpolitik. *New Left Review* 226: 57–59.

Fraser, N. (2003). From discipline to flexibilization? Rereading Foucault in the shadow of globalization. *Constellations* 10 (2): 160–71.

Gershon, I. (2011). Neoliberal agency. *Current Anthropology* 52 (4): 537–55.

Inda, J. X. (ed.) (2005). *Anthropologies of Modernity: Foucault, Governmentality and Life Politics*. Malden, MA: Blackwell.

O'Malley P., Weir, L., & Shearing, C. (1997). Governmentality, criticism, politics. *Economy and Society* 26: 501–17.

Rampton, B. (2016). Foucault, Gumperz, and governmentality: Interaction, power and subjectivity in the twenty-first century. In N. Coupland (ed.), *Sociolinguistics: Theoretical Debates* (pp. 303–30). Cambridge: Cambridge University Press.

Rose, N. (1999). *Powers of Freedom: Reframing Political Thought*. Cambridge: Cambridge University Press.

Rose, N., O'Malley, P., & Valverde, M. (2006). Governmentality. *Annual Review of Law and Social Science* 2: 83–104.

Shore, C., & Wright, S. (2000). Coercive accountability: The rise of audit culture in higher education. In M. Strathern (ed.), *Audit Cultures: Anthropological Studies in Accountability, Ethics and the Academy* (pp. 57–89). London: Routledge.

Shore, C., & Wright, S. (eds.) 1997. *Anthropology of Policy: Critical Perspectives on Governance and Power*. London: Routledge.

Shore, C., Wright, S., & Però, D. (eds.) (2011). *Policy Worlds: Anthropology and the Analysis of Contemporary Power*. New York; Oxford: Berghahn Books.

Strathern, M. (1992). *After Nature: English Kinship in the Late Twentieth Century*. Cambridge: Cambridge University Press.

Urciuoli, B. (2008). Skills and selves in the new workplace. *American Ethnologist* 35 (2): 211–28.

Willis, P. (1977). *Learning to Labor: How Working Class Kids Get Working Class Jobs*. New York: Columbia University Press.

Neoliberalism as a regime of truth: Studies in hegemony

Monica Heller

This volume asks us to understand neoliberalism through the Foucauldian lens of governmentality. In that sense, it suggests that neoliberalism is a regime of truth, in two ways. The first is simply the workings of relations of power, that is, control over the production, distribution and consumption of material and symbolic resources, and over the value and meaning they have. The second related form is derived from the value and the meaning: it is the way of understanding the world which privileges some interests over others, and which legitimates, normalizes and masks that privileging. A regime of truth allows for the production and reproduction of a specific set of political economic conditions, which work out better for some than for others, and better in some ways than others for individuals.

The sociolinguistic and applied linguistic literature has tended to approach neoliberalism more from the second dimension than the first. It has asked, notably, as the editors point out, how a regime of truth gets discursively constructed. This has required examining texts which can be argued to be either exemplary or key building blocks, texts which lay out how we should think neoliberally, which instruct us in neoliberal discursive framing, which provide us with keys to what the truth is that contemporary sources of power wish to establish. It seems to me that the focus here has been on texts which are part of shifts in state activity away from welfare assumptions and practices, and towards that which we have decided to call "neoliberal". The state has been at the centre of this analysis: how it explains why it is no longer funding, say daycare, but instead funding development of small enterprises; or why it no longer is interested in petitions for political rights, but rather wants to hear about economic growth potential. How do you make it make sense to shift focus in this way?

The answer has largely been: you appeal to the central discourses of capitalism and democracy. You talk about the generation of wealth; you talk about placing it in the hands (or bank accounts) of individuals, not some faceless collection of bureaucrats who might not use it responsibly and ethically; you talk about transparency. You evoke these tropes, and you engage in concomitant communicative practice: if you want to get my attention, you need to do it in this way. This was abundantly apparent twenty years ago in my own fieldwork, when community collectives used to petitioning the welfare state for funds for community "vitality" through claims to political rights on the terrain of language, culture and identity were told that that would no longer work: funds would be available only for economic development. The result was that some people learned how to talk the new talk (fill out the new forms, provide the new kinds of evidence); others had to withdraw from, or were forced out of, the discursive space.

Our approaches have also asked the next question: so what kind of public are we imagining? If the hallmark of the nation-state was, as Benedict Anderson (1983) put it, "imagined community", are we still investing our energy in constructing such a collective form of citizenship? Instead we see the abandonment of what Anderson called "print capitalism": collective, institutional and highly mediated modes of interaction; the state goes straight for the individual. Indeed, the interlocutor is now imagined more as the individual on social media (see Trump on Twitter, or, allegedly, Bolsanaro and WhatsApp) or accessible by cell phone (the preferred mode of communication employed by the Conservative Premier of the Canadian province of Ontario: here's my cellphone number! Just call me! Don't demonstrate in front of the legislature, we can fix this).

But of course it is not enough to speak to people in certain ways, or to try to socialize (or force?) people into participating in certain kinds of discursive or communicative arrangements, although this is part of the set of unavoidable constraints or conditions that facilitate specific kinds of interpellation. Somewhere there needs to be the connection to the actual social actor, the imagined neoliberal citizen, if you like. One way to address this question has focussed on zones of socialization, on the spaces where social activity concentrates on making the personae a neoliberal regime of truth prefers. This has drawn attention especially to education and training (although an argument could be made that we could learn a lot from other spaces of socialization, like the family or the peer group). The literature on that subject points over and over to a particular persona: the flexible entrepreneur of the self. The Company Man of the 1950s and 1960s (the loyal, if alienated, salaried worker) is replaced by the individual (gender irrelevant); if the first saw their individuality subsumed by the corporation, the second fuses them into one. This is a different kind of communicative subject from the rational, freely choosing, consenting, member of a national body.

One effect in sociolinguistics/linguistic anthropology or applied linguistics has also been to turn attention to the workplace. Work, as a social activity, barring a few exceptions, has not been a central space for sociolinguistic investigation; attention has focussed on institutions of the welfare state (especially education, health care, the media), on social identity-based movements, or on something called "community", imagined as a bounded (if fuzzily) collective of people who have something communicative in common, and who can be located in time and space in a here and in a now. Sometimes that communicative connectivity is understood as shared communicative form, sometimes as shared practice, sometimes as shared norms; but, despite arguments long-established in ethnomethodology and social anthropology, we have looked less at boundary processes than at putatively substantive common meaning. Work fit uneasily in that frame, as a space where it is difficult to argue for identitarian community, and where instead relations of power centred on economic resources are central. But for an entrepreneur of the self, arguably, everything is work, and it is no longer so easy to sidestep that field.

It is no doubt for that reason that attention to class is resurfacing; once quite confined in sociolinguistics to British and French enquiries into language and industrial capitalism, or reduced to a structural-functionalist variable in Labovian variationist sociolinguistics in the United States and the United Kingdom – and then almost lost from view altogether – class is re-emerging as an analytic in an attempt to investigate the extent to which a neoliberal preference for individual action is actually empirically observable as a mode of social organization, or is better understood as a new legitimating discourse for perduring forms of socially unequal processes and structures of economic production.

This leads to a final set of questions related to this aspect of an orientation to neoliberalism as a regime of truth: if we are trying to produce flexible entrepreneurs of the self, what kinds of subjectivity does this entail? Can we see such forms of subjectivity in action, that is, is there an observable set of practices which indicate flexible entrepreneurial selves as a form of social organization? Have people (all people? some people? which people?) internalized – consented to – this regime of truth? Does it in fact frame our understandings of how the world works, and guide our social action, if not as a determining overrider of anything resembling individual agency, at least as a set of constraints that we accept as legitimate, or even, possibly as so obvious as to become invisible? Or do we see disconnects, gaps, contradictions which might point us toward a different kind of analysis, one which foregrounds possibilities for and attempts at resistance, at alternative imaginings, or perhaps simply traces of ways of being better suited for an earlier regime?

This is both a theoretical and a methodological problem. By putting neoliberalism and governmentality in the same frame, this book is asking us, I think, to approach neoliberalism as a terrain for observing the workings of hegemony. This is not, then, simply a question of what some powerful actors would like us to do, or be, or believe, but more profoundly one of the conditions under which we act in those ways, and develop those subjectivities. Things might have dimensions of coercion, if only as "we are cutting these programs, so you can't do this any more unless you find other resources for it". But as we know, hegemony works much better with consent. Consent, in turn, raises the question of consciousness, of reason and affect, and of agency, whether individual or collective. What are the moral values and structures of feeling (Williams 1983) which organize our experience of the world, and through which we make sense of things? Why those? And why do they stick – or not? If those are the questions we ought to be asking if we want to understand neoliberalism, where might we go to find evidence? What does a neoliberal subject look like, sound like, act like? And how do we empirically make the chain among discursive spaces and from observable practice to sedimented, structured distribution of resources across them? If I ask these questions, it is because they are not only long-standing ones in the field, but are also gaining in acuteness in the face of such phenomena as growing wealth gaps and contradictions between cosmopolitanism and reinforced national borders.

And now I want to shift our gaze slightly. A thread which runs through our work on neoliberalism, through this book, and definitely through my discussion above, is the thread of history. There is an assumption in our work that we must take the "neo" in "neoliberalism" seriously; it is not an empirically unfounded one, since we have all experienced and documented changes in educational programmes, in interactions with the state, in what we use to interact with each other or find out what is going on in the world, in how we (try to) put food on our plates and a roof over our heads, or any number of other ways of being and doing. But the question remains of what exactly is new here, and why it emerged in the form that it did. Here my concern is to raise questions about what information we need to have in order to go beyond description, and towards explanation.

The book invites us to see our historical moment as one of transition between regimes of truth. This may be because we require new ways of legitimizing existing relations of power, or perhaps instead new relations of power themselves construct new regimes of truth. Here I will argue that it is more because of the former than the latter, and that indeed an increasing transparency of relations between state and capital not only produces new constraints on citizenship, but also, necessarily, on what it means to work.

I think that we can usefully build on Eric Hobsbawm's (1987, 1990) account of the link between the formation of the nation-state and the emergence of the bourgeoisie and its interests in industrial capitalism out of the metropolitan European accumulation of wealth through the workings of empire and mercantile capitalism (and here I am drawing heavily on Heller and McElhinny 2017). To oversimplify, Hobsbawm argues, more or less, that for the European bourgeoisie, markets of about the size of what emerged as nation-states in the nineteenth century were understood as optimal ways of organizing industrial production (as connected to colonial relations for raw materials and consumption of manufactured goods), trade, and, most importantly, the removal of political control from aristocracy and the Church. This required making states, and legitimizing them as nations (hence the Andersonian making of community through the discursive space affordance of print technology, and later radio and television; hence the construction of narratives of historically and geographically rooted community and the invention of tradition; Hobsbawm and Ranger 1983). It also required making citizens: hence obligatory education, standard languages, military service (Weber 1976; Grillo 1989), and producing citizen-subjects with their particular structures of feeling, their subjectivities, their aims and their obstacles. And as a fundamentally capitalist undertaking, it also required reflection on just how widely wealth was to be distributed, with competition and exclusion legitimized on the terrain of differential citizenship (Bauman and Briggs 2003). Racialization, feminization, sexualization, infantilization, all could be bought to bear on the legitimation of exclusions, marginalizations or demotions from the category of "citizen", exploitations of the thereby hierarchized, or removal of their potential for competition or contestation. In this regime of truth, the state is the central actor, but, as Hobsbawm insists, it is the state as main facilitator of industrial capitalism.

But capitalism is competition. What happens when a market is saturated? You need new markets, bigger markets, niche markets, cheaper sources of labour and raw materials, symbolic added value (Heller and Duchêne 2012). The optimal-size state (and into which colonies were eventually made to fit) is no longer optimal size, and the modes of regulation inadequate to purpose. So if anything has changed, if we follow Hobsbawm, it is not the nature of the relationship between state and capital; rather, while in the past this relationship was masked through the concept of the nation and differential citizenship, it became necessary to let the private sector take the lead in continued expansion and intensified competition on globalized terrains that are no longer so readily regimentable via metropole-colony or nation-state techniques. A relationship that was always there is now perhaps simply made more transparent. (Here the question must be what that transparency affords.)

If this is the "neo" in "neoliberalism", then it is important to ask why our gaze has remained locked on the state and on the agencies it relied on: media, education, health care, political border control. Certainly, these are spaces where we saw emerging before our very eyes and ears different ways of being. And it has been crucial to understand their challenges, their often uncomfortable transitions and transformations. It has been crucial to understand the state, what it is doing, what it thinks it is doing, how it explains itself to itself and to its populations. And if, as I mentioned above, we are only now turning to the world of work as a key site, surely this is in recognition of the ways in which it has come out of the shadows, or from behind the curtain, as a terrain of legitimacy better suited to expanding and intensifying capital. But perhaps we can learn even more by re-examining our assumptions about what the key discursive spaces of neoliberalism are, that is, by asking anew where we might find the activities that are most consequential in terms of the regulation and legitimation of resources, of their distribution and their value. This requires understanding neoliberalism as one element in a set of relations among institutionalized actors (including those of capital, like the corporation, or the financial market), the things they care about, and the ways they try to make things work, both practically and discursively (if we can even make that distinction). And so perhaps what is at issue here is less "neoliberalism" as the central keyword, and more a particular moment in the history of capitalism. This history of capitalism is also a history of modernity, or, perhaps, to stay with Foucault, a genealogy of ideas about social change, time, and the role of the social actor – and that includes us.

Because of course we are not outside the processes we are trying to understand, and the material conditions of our work have been directly affected by neoliberal policies. The democratic expansion of post-secondary education connected to the post–World War II welfare state allowed many of us involved in the knowledge-production enterprise to feel that our mission was only indirectly connected to capitalism, and that we could build a peer-run collective. Work on language and interaction could build on long-standing efforts to extract language as a technical object from society, or, as most of us contributing to this volume might have done, to connect language to the promises of the welfare state.

Neoliberalism has stabilized those conditions materially, introducing the university to flexible entrepreneurship through the replacement of tenure-stream jobs with temporary contracts, research funding tied to state priorities, and rigorous audit of production, among the many practices many of us have been inducted into in the last 15 or 20 years or so. In the field of anthropology alone, in the United States, the percentage of MA and PhD graduates employed in the public sector, private sector and NGOs has shot up. We are of necessity both distributed in a wider variety of workplaces than before, and more transparently connected to the economic conditions of our work. No wonder then, that some of the attention to neoliberal governmentality in our field has turned on our own workplaces.

The question is how to use that reflexivity. With Bonnie McElhinny (Heller and McElhinny 2017), I have suggested that it is helpful; it can help us understand why we ask the questions we ask, and get a handle on what each of us, as socially situated actors, may be best or least well-placed to undertake. It can help us move away from the arrogance of the canon, identify what we do not – and maybe can never, or should never – know, and re-value listening and watching as forms of producing knowledge. It can also help us evaluate what it means to commodify knowledge. And, finally, it can help us understand what resources we need, and where they are going to come from. This is in many ways a kind of flexible entrepreneurship, but maybe one of the collective. And the thing about entrepreneurship is, it lets you imagine all kinds of worlds.

References

Anderson, B. (1983). *Imagined Communities*. London: Verso.

Bauman, R., & Briggs, C. (2003). *Voices of Modernity: Language Ideologies and the Politics of Inequality*. Cambridge: Cambridge University Press.

Grillo, R. (1989). *Dominant Languages*. Cambridge: Cambridge University Press.

Heller, M., & Duchêne, A. (eds.) (2012). *Language in Late Capitalism: Pride and Profit*. London: Routledge.

Heller, M., & McElhinny, B. (2017). *Language, Capitalism, Colonialism: Toward a Critical History*. Toronto: University of Toronto Press.

Hobsbawm, E. (1987). *The Age of Empire 1875–1914*. London: Abacus.

Hobsbawm, E. (1990). *Nations and Nationalism since 1760*. Cambridge: Cambridge University Press.

Hobsbawm, E., & Ranger, T. (eds.) (1983). *The Invention of Tradition*. Cambridge: Cambridge University Press.

Weber, E. (1976). *Peasants into Frenchmen*. Stanford: Stanford University Press.

Williams, R. (1983/1976). *Keywords: A Vocabulary of Culture and Society*. Oxford: Oxford University Press.

Index